FUZZY MANAGEMENT

Fuzzy Management

*Contemporary Ideas and Practices
at Work*

KEITH GRINT

OXFORD UNIVERSITY PRESS
1997

Oxford University Press, Great Clarendon Street, Oxford OX2 6DP
Oxford New York
Athens Auckland Bangkok Bogota Bombay
Buenos Aires Calcutta Cape Town Dar es Salaam
Delhi Florence Hong Kong Istanbul Karachi
Kuala Lumpur Madras Madrid Melbourne
Mexico City Nairobi Paris Singapore
Taipei Tokyo Toronto Warsaw
and associated companies in
Berlin Ibadan

Oxford is a trade mark of Oxford University Press

Published in the United States by
Oxford University Press Inc., New York

British Library Cataloguing in Publication Data
Data available

Library of Congress Cataloging in Publication Data

Grint, Keith.
Fuzzy management: contemporary ideas and practices at work /
Keith Grint.
p. cm.
Includes bibliographical references (p.).
ISBN 0-19-877500-8 (hardcover).—ISBN 0-19-877499-0 (pbk.)
1. Management. 2. Decision making—Data processing. 3. Fuzzy
logic. 4. Chaotic behavior in systems. I. Title.
HD30.19.G748 1997
658'.001'511322—dc21 97-23316
CIP

ISBN 0-19-877500-8
ISBN 0-19-877499-0 (Pbk)

Typeset by Best-set Typesetter Ltd., Hong Kong
Printed in Great Britain on acid-free paper by Bookcraft (Bath) Ltd., Midsomer
Norton, Somerset.

For Kris, Beki, Katy & Sand

Acknowledgements

I would like to thank David Musson and Leonie Hayler at Oxford University Press for their advice and encouragement with this project, Val Martin at Templeton College for all the advice she gives me but which I consistently fail to take, and my students and colleagues at Oxford for persistent application of the 'so what' question. Much of the material for the final chapter is based on fifteen years of teaching negotiating skills, first with John Gillies at Oxford University and Peter Seglow at Brunel University, and subsequently with Eddy Finn of Feedback and Peter Wilson of Swansway Associates. I am especially grateful to Stephen Ackroyd, Sarah Dancy, and Mihaela Kelemen, who all read the whole manuscript, for their advice and suggestions—though the resulting work is wholly my responsibility, warts and all. As ever, my deepest thanks go to Kris, Beki, Katy, and Sand for making it all worthwhile.

Contents

List of Figures   xi

Introduction: 'So What?'   1

1. Fuzzy Logic: *Managing in an Occluded World*   9

2. Managing Fashions: *A Eulogy for Flared Trousers*   31

3. Chaos, Culture, and Evolution: *The Configuration
   of Organization*   59

4. Managing Change Through Commitment:
   Autistic, New Model, or Pandorian Organization?   85

5. Deep Leadership: *In Theory*   115

6. Mismanaging Risk: *The Madness of Cows*   147

7. Negotiating: *Groundhog Ground Rules*   177

References   207

Index   219

List of Figures

1.1 Dead or Alive?   16

1.2 Alive or Dead?   17

2.1 Management Fads, 1986–95   33

2.2 Fad Modelling   35

2.3 Structuring Change   49

3.1 Metaphors of Change   73

3.2 Chaos and Strategy   82

4.1 The Sweep-it-Under-the-Carpet School of Management   87

4.2 The Learning Organization   88

4.3 Top Ten Critical Change Issues   94

4.4 Forms of Acceptance   100

4.5 Attitudes to Work   101

4.6 Trust in Organizations   102

4.7 Loyalty to the Organization   104

4.8 Commitment to a Club   105

6.1 Cattle with Confirmed BSE and Cattle Slaughtered, 1988–95   156

Introduction: *'So What?'*

Theory is where you know everything and nothing
   works;
Practice is where everything works but nobody knows
   why;
Here we combine theory with practice:
Nothing works and nobody knows why.

THIS book has its origins in five related areas. The first is the
email message quoted above that came my way via one of my
doctoral students (Robert Padulo). In the message the theory
and the practice are both derailed by the absent other. In this
book my intention is to demonstrate how theory, in particular
some forms of contemporary theory, have practical consequences for managers who use them.

The second and related origin lies in a paradox at the heart of
many management schools but is more overt at bridging institutions like Templeton College, where students can be under-
graduates or postgraduates of Oxford University in the
morning and senior executives from multinational companies
in the afternoon. The paradox embodies the familiar academic
notion of 'distance'—trying to ensure that academics remain as
objective as possible about the nature of knowledge; and 'utility'—trying to remain relevant to the concerns of the different
groups of students. Traditional university students normally
have a different definition of utility from post-experience students: both groups may be interested in knowledge for its own
sake, but the former have one eye on examinations and the
latter have one eye on the practical benefits of knowledge.
While students need to understand so that they can reconstitute the work on the Monday's examination paper, executives
need to understand so that they can re-examine the constitution of work on Monday. Although almost all my previous
written work has been oriented towards the traditional

university student, this book is intended to mirror the situation that Templeton sustains: a bridging work between the two worlds of university and employment.

The third origin—which has clearly parallel traces to the previous two—concerns my growing discomfort with a world contained by binary opposites. The entire world of electronics may be digitalizing before our eyes, but most of the rest of the world is not good or evil, right or wrong, true or false, but pretty good, probably right, and possibly true. This retreat from certainty, often associated with postmodernism, has usually been associated with the collapse of all kinds of things: morality, religion, and justice, to name just three. In management faculties the division between the modernist side (the (really) useful academics) and the postmodernist side (the (useless) really academics) is played out *ad nauseam*, with usually little attempt by either side to see whether there might be something of practical consequence in some elements of postmodernist theory. This book makes such an attempt.

This brings me to the fourth source of this book. Much of what is taught in management or business schools, or written about in business or management books, often appears as a banal paradox. It is banal in that it appears to regurgitate what everyone already takes for granted and knows to be true. It is a paradox because, despite being full of common sense, it doesn't seem to work. If management was as easy as many of the more popular 'how to' books would have us believe, then why do we (and I include myself in this) find management so difficult? Why, if leadership is simply about (successful) risk-taking, don't we take more risks? Why, if customer satisfaction is so critical—and so obvious—do I spend so much time in shops waiting to be served, while the assistants gossip to each other and find the words 'please' and 'thank you' so difficult to say? Why, when everyone knows how important a strategy is, do so many workers appear completely ignorant of where their organization is going? Why, if our computers and databases are so sophisticated, are we unable to predict what will happen next? And finally, why, if we know so much about change management, do most organizations most of the time appear so inept at managing change? These kinds of questions have puzzled me for a long time and the uncertainties that they induce are not at all pleasant to contemplate as a practitioner of management. A traditional reaction to uncertainty is to revert to whatever or whoever offers a clear, simple and persuasive solution to the problem. One might call this approach to problem-solving the 'deterrent' approach. It is a deterrent in so far as once enacted it fails in its primary purpose. For example, if the President of the USA was ever to push the nuclear trigger in retaliation against an attack from another power, then it would have failed in its primary purpose of deterring attack. The 'deterrent' solution in management terms only works as long as the manager merely buys the book or pays for the consultancy: if that manager was ever to implement the 'solutions' entailed in the book or consultant's suggestions, the result would be failure. The failure of the deterrent solution to many managerial problems seems to me to be premised upon a naïve view of the world. *If* the world is as simple and straightforward and predictable as the deterrent solutions imply, the solutions may indeed work—if workers just need to be 'empowered', and this just means telling them to get on with their jobs without any supervision, then everything should fall into place. But if three-quarters of all change programmes—of any description—seem to fail in their own terms, perhaps the world is rather more complicated—more fuzzy—than we first thought. This book is an attempt to establish why so much taken-for-granted knowledge is not firmly embedded in the rock of truth, but precariously balanced on the sands of uncertainty—and why this shifting foundation means there may be other ways to approach management that would prove more useful. Of course, to reiterate a previous point, if managers find that the only mystery to managing is why other people find it so difficult, then perhaps such paragons of managerial virtue have no need to consider an alternative perspective. But if you are not one of these—read on, Macduff!

Finally, the fifth source is my own previous work—which has tended to be analytic rather than prescriptive, critical rather than apologetic, and I have been more interested in ideas than practice. As with many other academic writers, my work is usually intended to be read by my peers, not by practising managers or MBA students, nor indeed (if my students' complaints are valid), by any kind of student. But this has posed an increasing irritation to the people who suffer from my lectures and presentations, which can be summarized in a response that more than one person has articulated: 'very interesting, but so what?' This is my 'so what' book. It is a book intended to take a selection of what I regard as the most significant elements of contemporary social theory and explore how they imply particular practical consequences for managers. It is not an attempt to mark out the most important theories, but to illustrate why theory matters. If theory does not have any practical consequences, then it is not only practising managers who can safely ignore it; we all can. But I do not think this is valid for one moment: how we think about the world appears to me to have significant consequences for what we do and how we interpret what the consequences of our actions are. To take a simple example, if I believe in a theory of fate I may be unconcerned about my driving practices because I know that when my time is up there is nothing I can do about it, but until that time I can do anything I like. This is not an idle speculation because many of the world's most influential leaders seem to have scrambled to the top on the basis of an unshakeable faith in destiny. At a more mundane level, belief in fate can allow people to rationalize any experience: 'Ah well, I know having that accident with the toilet door was terrible but thank God only my head came off, I was obviously not meant to meet the rim creeper yet.'

If, then, theory is inescapably tied to practice, what are the consequences of some of the current ideas in organizational and management theory? Since this is not a theoretical excursion, I do not intend to generate any new insights in that direction and have already suggested what these might be elsewhere (Grint, 1995b; Grint and Woolgar, 1997). Instead, this book is designed for those people who have found the current management orthodoxies inadequate, who are interested in alternative ideas and how they might be applied to management practice, but are not enthralled by the esoteric world of theoretical books about theory.

It begins, in chapter 1 'Fuzzy Logic: Managing in an Occluded World', with a review of the traditional approach to knowledge, rooted in Aristotelian binary logic (right/wrong, black/white), and progresses through an analysis of fuzzy logic, in which the issue is no longer one of black or white, but various shades of grey. At first, this seems eminently suited to the world of philosophy and fine art, but not management. However, I suggest that by taking a notoriously 'hard' case (medicine) we can begin to see how such fuzzy logic may have a role to play in how we manage. It may be that we are continuously tempted to impose a pattern of stability upon the world by reducing it to black and white, but we should not forget that it is we who are doing the patterning here, and this has important consequences for how we manage practically in the world.

Chapter 2, 'Managing Fashions: A Eulogy for Flared Trousers', takes what is probably the only permanent thing in management—change—and seeks to explore it through an array of theoretical approaches. Underlying a lot of change is a strong sense that much of it consists merely of fads and fashions, hyped up by 'gurus' and promoted by consultants for their own reasons. Taking the motif of flared trousers, I suggest that there is probably more to this than meets the eye and that theory may help us not just explore the dynamic world of change, but consider whether we really do need to engage in change ourselves. After all, if we change our clothing just to fit in with the rest of the population this suggests that we waste a considerable amount of money: if only I'd kept those flared trousers just a little longer I wouldn't have to buy another pair. If personal expenditure is driven by the need to comply with normative pressures, why should we believe that organizational expenditure is any more rational or normatively resilient? And if it isn't, should we be rather more careful in expending huge sums on change programmes that last only as long as it takes a guru to dream up the next fashion?

If the warnings on the costs of discarding one's flared trousers or adopting particular theories of change do not dissuade our manager from engaging in change, then, in chapter 3 'Chaos, Culture, and Evolution: The Configuration of Organization', I take a different approach to the issue by focusing upon two radical innovations that have only just begun, towards the end of the twentieth century, to make a major impact upon organizations: chaos theory and evolutionary theory. By linking the two together, I explore the significance they have for organizations seeking to change their culture and their strategy. Again, this is not to become prescriptive and to assert that an organization must follow my advice, but to illustrate how adopting particular theories leads to particular consequences.

The popularity of culture change amongst organizations seems to be indicative of a radical overhaul of our approach to, and interest in, commitment. In chapter 4, 'Managing Change Through Commitment: Autistic, New Model, or Pandorian Organization?', I consider the extent to which failure to change is rooted in an avoidance of risk-taking and in an inadequate concern for the commitment of the organizational members. Using an episode from the English Civil War, I outline how important commitment may be, but then suggest that recent evidence bodes ill for organizations seeking this route. Moreover, one of the issues about commitment is that it has a habit of biting the hand that pretended to feed it. In other words, if managers develop a rhetoric of commitment but do not really believe it is necessary, shop- and office-floor workers may nevertheless adopt the rhetoric and pose a radical dilemma for those who speak 'commitment' but practice 'tnemtimmoc'. Finally, I consider the weakness of the commitment approach by adopting actor-network theory and illustrating its potential advantages over voluntarist approaches to change.

If change has been something of a perennial plant in the management garden since the 1970s, then leadership, especially of change, looks distinctly like a hardy weed—it is everywhere, it seems always to have been there, and no one knows how important it is, nor how to improve it, nor how to get rid of it if we suspect it doesn't do much good. In chapter 5, 'Deep Leadership: In Theory', I examine the significance attached to leadership in the environment of organizations by assessing ideas about individual appraisal, and then assess the significance attached to leaders in organizational environments through four current (1990s) theories: structural contingency theory, population ecology theory, institutional theory, and constructivist theory. I conclude that we may have to rethink our appraisal systems to take account of our fuzzy perspectives, and that we may have overestimated the importance of hierarchical leaders and underestimated the importance of non-hierarchical leaders—deep leadership—that is, people who 'lead' others without formal positions of authority to support them.

The uncertainty of the world surrounding managers leaves many people with a deep sense of unease, and chapter 6, 'Mismanaging Risk: The Madness of Cows', pushes this uncertainty towards its logical conclusion in a case study of BSE, in which disquiet about risk should, in theory, have been transformed by increased dependence on the certainty of scientific knowledge. Many managers and organizations are faced with uncertainty and risk every day, and we have come to believe that risk is best managed by the application of rational procedures and a rigorous approach to the facts. However, the BSE case illustrates an alarming tendency to attribute to science the ability to distinguish truth from falsehood which it may not be able to sustain. Indeed, I suggest that the issue is not one of risk but of trust, of politics not science, and suggest that managers heed the organizational lessons of the mad cow fiasco if they do not want to end up in the cow muck.

Finally, in chapter 7, 'Negotiating: Groundhog Ground Rules', I run back through the lessons of the book, not by providing a list of bullet points but by developing a model of a practice that sits at the heart of virtually all forms and levels of management: negotiating. Modelling the idea on the scene re-run in *Groundhog Day*, this concluding piece introduces elements of negotiating theory and supports them with references back to the theoretical ideas developed in the prior parts of the book. In a fuzzy world there is little as fuzzy as negotiating, but the particular theory of negotiating we carry round in our heads usually has remarkable consequences for the way negotiations in particular, and the fuzzy art of managing in general, are played out.

1

Fuzzy Logic: *Managing in an Occluded World*

Do not read this sentence.

INTRODUCTION

IMAGINE a world in which the predictive power of computers was so limited that economists could not predict the level of inflation or unemployment any better than refuse collectors; where you could not tell whether someone was dead or alive; where you never knew—with absolute certainty—that the person you were about to commit to prison was actually guilty of the crime; where you could not be sure that your car would get you home; where your promotion prospects depended solely on the subjective whim of the creature you laughingly refer to as 'the boss'; and where the success of your local sports team rested as much on chance and the referee's sight as on the skill that your team deploys. In theory, none of these things should happen; in practice they all do. Managerial theory may not be composed entirely of 'pragmatic paradoxes' like the one quoted above, but, like many other forms of thought, it does tend to rationalize away the paradoxes, chance, luck, errors, subjectivities, accidents, and sheer indeterminacy of life through a prism of apparent control and rationality. If, for one moment, we actually thought that our worlds could come tumbling down round our ears in the next ten minutes, we might be a little more wary. But instead we tend to imagine away this fuzzy world and displace its occluded nature with a clarity of vision and control that becalms us. This book is concerned with ways of using some of the most recent developments in social science theory to illustrate what many would regard as an oxymoron: practical theory.

Now imagine not something that should happen but doesn't, but rather something that can happen but shouldn't: a toaster which does not burn the toast, but which has no manual settings to adjust for the thickness or type of the bread. We are not talking about 'white' or 'brown' differences here, nor 'thick' or 'thin', but 'whitish, with a few whole grains of wheat and quite thick'.

Traditional Western approaches to the world of management tend to be rooted in Aristotelian binary logic, where the world is divided into good and bad, right and wrong, truth and lies, black and white, life and death, 0 and 1, and so on. This principle has not only become encapsulated in digital computer developments, but has encouraged us to perceive our world, and our place in it, as one where clarity of decision-making is premised upon the clarity of our perspective. In short, effective management depends upon taking the *right* as opposed to the *wrong* decision, having analysed the data *correctly* rather than *incorrectly*, after considering *both sides* of the argument. Good management is really concerned with good *boundary* management: decide which side of the boundary something should fit into, and the rest is easy. Such 'formal' logic underlies most of contemporary mathematics.

Note how powerful these dualisms are: many modern democracies are themselves founded upon government and opposition; news media attempt to get the truth by weighing up *both* sides of the argument; courts decide whether the defendant or the prosecutor is telling the truth; and industrial relations stem from the resolution of conflict emanating from the *two* sides at work. There are powerful arguments from semiotics (the science of signs) and from linguistics which suggest that these binary approaches are a significant aspect of the way we construe the world—such that we can only understand the meaning of 'bad' if we understand its opposite, 'good'. And, following this approach, there are powerful arguments from structuralist anthropology which imply that the meaning of social phenomena can only be determined by their relationship to other phenomena, not in and of themselves. For example, that the significance of a seating plan for a wedding does not lie in the seat you occupy, but in the position that the seat occupies in relation to others in the status hierarchy (how far away are you from the bride and bridegroom?).

But doesn't it seem strange that arguments only have two sides, that we must choose which side we are on, that we are either 'one of them' or 'one of us', that grass is either green or it isn't, and that if one side is telling the truth the other side is lying? It may appear that we constitute our world through a series of dualisms, or binary opposites that reduce complexity to an unequivocal pair of opposites, but our language is not limited to binary opposites and is quite capable of taking continua as basic to description. Thus, we do not just have black and white, but we have grey, and beyond this dark grey and light grey, and so on. So is there a price to pay for this reduction of analogue to digital? Indeed, is it that we are reducing the world to dualisms because the world is otherwise too complicated to cope with, or is the world actually split into dualisms and all we have to do is recognize where the divisions lie? Put another way, where do the patterns that we perceive in the world come from—are they really out there, or do we impose a pattern on the enormous mass of data that floats into our sense organs from every angle?

It is most certainly easier to cope with complexity by constructing a mechanism for dividing the data into a Manichaean split between white and black, but it is actually dubious as to whether such divisions are appropriate, let alone helpful. For instance, only people who have never been employed might assume that the *only* important division at work lies between workers and managers. For those who have, even the managers' world appears to be carved into a myriad of fragments: marketing versus sales versus production versus accounts versus human resources; careerists versus free-riders versus clock-watchers; directors versus managers versus Chief Executive Officers (CEOs) versus chairs; outsiders versus insiders versus ex-insiders and neo-outsiders; men versus women versus blacks versus whites versus Asians versus Japanese, and so on *ad infinitum*. Of course, there are also overlapping loyalties that unite and redivide this amalgam, and these alliances are permanently shifting. Within and across these divisions any debate concerning any business leads to a far more complex argument, not limited to both sides but potentially embroiling hundreds of sides. Even if we reduce the hundreds down to two could it not be that both sides in a dispute are telling the truth as they see it, and that there is no way of establishing what the 'real' truth is? For instance, when we want to appoint the next CEO, do we pick the 'best' person for the job or do we pick the person who is 'probably' better, at least better than the rest in terms of organizing their CV, claiming the credit for turning round companies that were already turning, avoiding blame for good companies which crashed under their guidance, and who, moreover, turns out to have gone to the same school and university as the outgoing CEO and is married to a member of the government, something that could prove extremely useful to us in the future? In effect, isn't the selection choice extremely fuzzy rather than clear-cut?

Even though the dividing line between terms like good and bad, or between numbers like 1 and 2, appears to be clear, it nevertheless depends upon the relationship of one to the other for meaning. For instance, making a 'good' profit depends upon the context: a £1 million profit from a company employing 1 million people and with £100 million capital is poor compared to a company making the same profit from employing 10 people and with £1 million capital. Similarly, and perhaps ironically, such an unclear and poorly demarcated—or fuzzy—concept as 'a few' embodies relational properties too, such that, following Hormann, quoted by Treadwell (1995), 'a few' jumbo jets tend conventionally to be assessed as being a smaller number than 'a few' grains of salt; and 'a few' flowers in a flower shop tend to be more than 'a few' flowers in the desert. For all the controversy over fuzzy theory it is self-evident that human speech is deeply rooted into the practical benefits of imprecision. When I ask my children how much sugar they would like on their cornflakes in the morning I do not expect them to say '467 grains please', but 'just a bit' or 'not much' or 'loads'. So even though we pride ourselves on accuracy, and certainty, we often operate across boundaries rather than within them: when I engage in speech, either in a lecture or a discussion, I frequently omit entire words or use the wrong syntax—inded mi listners and reders kapacty four reconstrtin my ntentions stownds me! The capacity for not obeying rules is a consistent and significant aspect of human behaviour. As Zadeh argues:

The exploitation of the tolerance for imprecision and uncertainty underlies the remarkable human ability to understand distorted speech, decipher sloppy handwriting, comprehend nuances of natural language, summarize text, recognize and classify images, drive a vehicle in dense traffic and, more generally, make rational decisions in an environment of uncertainty and imprecision. (1994: 7)

Fuzzy thinking, first established by Lotfi Zadeh's work on fuzzy sets, but based on the multivalue logic of Jan Lukasiewicz in the 1920s, suggests that Aristotelian binary thought may be a way of simplifying an inordinately complex world, but that simplification is precisely that—a distorting simplification of reality. In Zadeh's words: 'As the complexity of a system increases, our ability to make precise and significant statements about its behaviour diminishes until a threshold is reached beyond which precision and significance become mutually exclusive characteristics' (quoted in Kosko, 1994: 148). Or, in Kosko's own rather more direct words, 'Bivalence trades accuracy for simplicity' (ibid.: 21). A fuzzy world is premised upon approximate reasoning, where the vegetation is neither 'green' nor 'not green', but where it is various shades of colours which move through thousands of colorations that involve virtually every colour; where managers are not just good or bad, but relatively good or bad on a 'granulated' scale that involves all the managers of the organization or all those of which the measurers have experience. In this world, firms are not profitable or unprofitable, but they have levels of profitability that are critically dependent upon how that profitability is measured—and that can be in any one of hundreds of ways at the hands of creative accountants.

The only major exception to this fuzzy world is mathematics—but this escapes the occluded world of fuzzy logic only because it is constructed around a set of artificial rules that are designed to operate as tautologies: $1 + 1 = 2$. Or is it? Realist or absolutist approaches would suggest that mathematics is discovered not constructed, and that it remains absolutely true at all times. Those of a more relativist or fallibilist approach might suggest that mathematics, while not an arena in which $1 + 1 =$

whatever you like, may be a place where the answer can never be absolutely true under all conditions—even though it may be held to be true under 'normal' conditions. The difference, then, is not between necessity and arbitrariness, but between necessity and contingency. In short, under particular conditions it may be that mathematical truths alter. Ernest (1994, 1996), for example, suggests that under Boolean algebra $1 + 1 = 1$, while under Base 2 modular arithmetic $1 + 1 = 0$. Now, since I am not a mathematician, I am not in a position to confirm or deny these propositions, and I simply have to trust him or not as the case may be—and this exactly mirrors parallel relationships to other experts. When your doctor tells you have some horrendous-sounding disease, which requires a period of complete inactivity and multifarious drugs, you either trust him or her and do what he or she says, or you don't; but very few of us are able to offer an expert opinion of the expert opinion—otherwise we would be experts too. In effect, much of what we take to be scientific—that is, objective—knowledge, we take on trust rather than verify ourselves, and I shall consider the consequences of this in chapter 6.

The practical implications of this fuzzy logic—and note that the logic is not fuzzy but the phenomena it deals with appear to be—are being deployed in the 1990s across a range of areas: washing machines, for instance, are being designed with fuzzy logic chips which do not provide the usual binary logic that requires us to state whether we want a hot or cold wash, with or without a long rinse, but which assesses the size of the load, the kind of material and the quantity of dirt, and then adjusts the wash according to how much light manages to get across the water inside the tub: the less light that does, the dirtier the clothes and the longer the wash. Indeed, Matsushita's *Aisaigo Day* ('beloved wife's machine' is one literal translation) is just the latest of Japan's investment in fuzzy logic technology that had already reached $2 billion by 1992 (*Success*, October 1994: 39). It also boasts anti-lock brakes, lift systems, automatic transmission systems, auto-focus cameras, and auto-stabilizing video cameras, self-adjusting helicopters, and the Sendai (a city in Honshu, Japan) subway system—which claims that trains stop within 7 cm of the designated spot, and whose passengers are alleged not to use the 'hanging straps' when standing up.

There is even a Yamaichi Fuzzy Fund for handling financial trading systems that went into commercial operation in 1988 (a year after a dry run had recommended selling stock eighteen days before Black Monday in 1987), and many more products beside—including the 'beloved breakfast machine': the toaster (Munakata and Jani, 1994). Many of these products were developed in the Laboratory for International Fuzzy Engineering (LIFE), which began in 1989 and is now supported by all the leading Japanese corporations (McNeill and Freiberger, 1994). The USA has made something of a start in the field: in 1995 the Saturn division of General Motors patented a fuzzy automatic transmission system, which mirrors humans' decisions for changing gears rather than following the designed automatic systems that currently engage gears when the arbitrarily fixed r.p.m. limit is reached. Relatedly, in the same year Whirlpool won a $30 million prize for designing the most energy-efficient and environmentally friendly refrigerator, using a compressor design incorporating a fuzzy logic chip. Developments in the 1990s have led to a fuzzy logic-based scanner which can scan damaged bar-codes (Rogers, 1996) and a fuzzy logic cooker-top controller that can sense when something is about to boil over and take corrective action (*Appliance Manufacturer*, 1996: vol. 44, no. 2, pp. 86).

So, does this list of technical advances and hard currency accumulation simply mean that fuzzy logic enhances rather than challenges the growth of rational science? Perhaps. Later, I will be examining the practical implications of this for managers, but let us consider first a hard case: a science that has long been premised very precisely on the pursuit of one side of a binary division, life, doing its utmost to push back the other side, death: medicine.

MEDICINE AS A FUZZY PHENOMENON

Let us establish what a conventional binary method set allows us to do with the problem: it is very simple—you are either 'alive' or 'dead'—and the graphical representation of this would be as is shown in Figure 1.1.

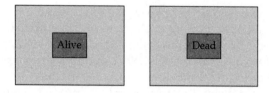

FIG. 1.1 Dead or Alive?

Medicine is supposed to be about preserving life and avoiding death and, we might assume, advances in science make this clear polarization of consequences even clearer: as knowledge and technology advance, so death retreats and Aristotle's division between 'is' or 'is not', 'alive' or 'not alive', becomes ever more transparent. Yet the development of medical science, paradoxically, seems to generate a fuzzier, not a clearer, picture of the division between life and death. We might, for example, want to argue that what counts as death is a social and cultural construct. For some Australian Aborigines death can occur when an individual is expelled from the tribe. For some religions there is no death, there is just a transmutation from one bodily form to another. But let us forget all this cultural stuff—a dead body is a dead body isn't it? Well, that depends; certainly, the fear of premature burial in the late nineteenth century was significant enough for the development of 'dead houses', where those defined as dead by doctors would be laid out—just in case they were not. In Mark Twain's (1883) graphic description of one such establishment in Munich:

Around a finger of each of these fifty still forms, both great and small, was a ring; and from the ring a wire led to the ceiling, and thence to a bell in a watch room yonder, where, day and night, a watchman sits always alert and ready to spring to the aid of any of that pallid company who, waking out of death, shall make a movement—for any, even the slightest movement will twitch the wire and ring that fearful bell. (quoted in Kastenbaum, 1991: 30)

In Nelson's day, 'dead' sailors, when being prepared for burial at sea, were sewn into their hammocks—the last stitch went through their nose: if no tears resulted, the sailor was slipped over the side. But surely we have now surpassed these crude 'division bells' between life and death. Death is no longer defined by the failure to move, but by medical science (see Grint and Woolgar, 1997, for an extended discussion of this problem). Does death, then, mean the absence of pulse, or fixed dilated pupils, or the absence of brain activity, or something else? Even if we narrow the definition down to 'brain death' (itself a relative newcomer deriving from 1959) we are still left with three different versions of this: 'whole brain death', 'cerebral death' and 'neocortical death'; the precise nature of each is not as important as the point that there is still disagreement as to which definition is the most acceptable (Kastenbaum, 1991).

Nor are such disputes confined to medical journals or irrelevant because of their 'academic' nature. For example, research by Kemp and Sibert in 1991 on child drownings suggests that we should take great care in describing a person as dead. Between 1988 and 1989 330 children 'drowned' in England and Wales. Of these, 33 were taken from the water with fixed dilated pupils (usually taken as a sign of death), of whom 10 recovered fully, 13 died and 10 survived with brain damage. One of those who survived had been under water for 60 minutes and had a body temperature of 23 °C. Kemp and Sibert argue that under certain conditions (e.g., hypothermia) the

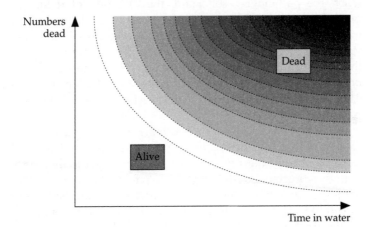

FIG. 1.2   Alive or Dead?

requirement for oxygen is much reduced, and thus 'dead' children can be brought back to 'life'.The result is a very different representation of the situation, as shown in Figure 1.2. The critical point here is that the division between life and death is neither bipolar nor unilinear—there are cases where it is not clear whether the individual is alive or dead.

Even when we leave the macro-level of collective statistics and descend to the micro-level of individual cases, it is not clear that disagreements about the cause of death decline with increased medical experience to the extent that we know whether condition A or condition B was responsible for death. Cameron and McGoogan's research (cited in Open University, 1992) compared correlations between diagnoses of death in 1,000 hospital autopsies that had previously been diagnosed by clinicians of various kinds, and found that 39 per cent of the clinicians' diagnoses of cause of death were disputed by the pathologists' autopsies, while 66 per cent of patients had discrepancies between clinicians' diagnoses and pathologists' autopsies. Now one might want to argue that discrepancies can be so minor as to be irrelevant to the argument about the cause of death being essentially fuzzy. However, Cameron and McGoogan suggest that in half the cases the discrepancies would have affected the treatment. One might also want to argue that, by definition, only difficult cases reach the pathologist, so, again, the difficulty of diagnosis pre-exists the correlation between clinician's diagnosis and pathologist's autopsy. Yet in the case of myocardial infarction (one form of heart attack) 198 patients were diagnosed with this by both clinician and pathologist, in 58 cases the clinician's positive diagnosis was not confirmed by the pathologist, and in 51 cases the clinician's negative diagnosis was disputed by the pathologist.

Of course, we might still want to argue that the clinician is seldom in the best position to diagnose the cause of death and thus we would expect the pathologist to be closer to the 'truth' than the clinician. But, first, the discrepancies between the two are large enough to suggest that clinicians are not the kind of people one should go to if one was feeling ill. Second, this implies that pathologists agree on the evidence—but do they? If the 'truth' is automatically reflected in the tissues of the body one might wonder how there can be a dispute over the cause of Robert Maxwell's death, or whether Rudolf Hess really killed himself. How can pathologists disagree unless the evidence is in a perpetually fuzzy state?

The upshot of this is that people can be deemed to be 'dead' or kept 'alive' through a whole panoply of technologies that hitherto would not have existed, but whether they are kept 'alive' seems not to be premised upon clear-cut, object decisions. Ultimately, the point of 'death' is being shifted away from any apparently obvious or natural criteria (like inability to breath or inactive heart) to a much fuzzier world where someone has to take a decision to stop the equipment working. But when that decision should be taken and who should make the decision is another can of veritable worms (if that isn't an inappropriate metaphor in the context). So perhaps advances in science and knowledge make our world more not less occluded, they make it more not less apparent that we have to impose meanings on an amorphous mass of data. As a further example, in September 1996 American doctors experimented with a system for reducing the temperature of crash victims with head injuries below that ordinarily considered safe whilst they attempted to repair brain damage—what was once 'truly' irreparable brain damage is no longer (*QED*, BBC2, 11 September 1996).

Does this approach have implications for those of us who are not on the borders of life and death, but are, nevertheless, in serious situations? If we assume that the legal system is premised upon very serious questions of guilt and innocence, criminality, justice, and punishment, then the answer must be yes. So how might this fuzzy principal operate here? Essentially, this fuzzy principle is *already* the crux of the legal system, because the jury is frequently given two very different versions of the truth and asked to decide which one is most believable. In effect, the judicial system is premised upon conflicting truth claims. Do we ever really know precisely what happened in any particular trial to the extent that the accused is definitively guilty or innocent, or do we simply have to side with the defence or the prosecution and assume that one account is the more likely—the most persuasive construction of the truth? That several people have recently been released from

prison in the UK, and had their convictions quashed, suggests
that even persuasive constructions of the truth are contingently
fuzzy.

FUZZY MANAGEMENT

If fuzzy principles appear to prevail in two particularly 'hard'
cases like medicine and the law, then what does it imply for
management? I want to consider in this book in general, and in
this chapter in particular, what the implications are for managing in a world that either *is* fuzzy or is a world about which
we can only ever establish *fuzzy pictures*. In fact, it doesn't
really matter which of these two is the more appropriate, since
the result is the same—we live in an uncertain world where
predictions are only ever fortuitously right, where the environment is constantly changing, and in ways that are themselves
subject to change, and where the only thing that is certain is
that nothing is certain.

Despite, or perhaps because of this endemic uncertainty
about the way we understand the world, and how this affects
the way we try to interact with it, theory in management books,
perhaps more than almost any other context, arrives at the
manager's door laden with moral and political baggage:
theory, according to some anti-theoretical accounts, is apparently irrelevant to the 'real world' of management where decisions are taken on the basis of facts, or rationality, or
whatever happens to be the anti-theoretician's particular dislike. This often becomes manifest in contrasts that are held to
exist between the 'real' world and whatever is being depre-
cated, usually the 'unreal' world of academia. The criteria for
constructing the boundary of reality have always escaped me.
At the same time, debates *within* the world constructed by
management theorists are often just as acrimonious as those
that occur between management theorists and 'practitioners'.
Perhaps the latter is an exaggeration, since, by and large, practitioners of management very often do not engage in debate
with management theoreticians—they just ignore each other.
In practice, the whole circus appears vaguely ludicrous: those

who argue that theory is irrelevant to the real world adopt a *theoretical* position in their anti-theoretical ardour which assumes that (theoretically) facts stand for themselves; that is, that the world of reality is self-evident and open to a non-theoretical investigative approach which will reveal the world in its transparently obvious truth. This, presumably, is why everyone agrees about everything all the time—because everything is so blatantly obvious. On the other hand, if there are occasions where we disagree about the meaning of something, about whether something is true, about whether one thing caused another to happen, about the meaning of life—to name just a few problems—then perhaps we should consider what it is that the theories imply.

The assumption that the world is both certain and knowable encourages us to look for—that is *discover*—facts that exist, rather than to consider the extent to which we do not so much discover as *create* the world through our efforts. Such ideas currently fill the social science journals, but here I want to engage in a rather different pursuit, which does not intend to extend the boundaries of theoretical knowledge, nor to join forces on one side or another in the battle for the intellectual high ground; rather, it concerns the *deployment* of theories. In short, the book revolves around the familiar hypothetical conundrum: what difference would it make if some of the contemporary post-war theories from social science were used by managers? Or, in a rather more pithy form beloved of sceptics of theory: 'so what?'

Let us begin with a familiar example that has in the 1990s taken management by storm: customer focus. In this approach to management, most visibly embodied in Total Quality Management (TQM) and Business Process Reengineering (BPR), the key to successful business is to get as close as possible to the customer: to 'discover' what the customer 'really' wants and to redesign businesses around those wants. There is no sophisticated theory involved in this—all that is necessary is to ask the customer what he or she wants, accumulate the data, and embody the demands in the product or service. To assume that the customer does not know what he or she wants is, of course, the kind of arrogant assumption that leads businesses into the red. Or is it?

There are several problematic elements of such a discovery-oriented approach to the customer and fuzzy logic might perhaps provide a theoretical explanation for what appears to happen. Let us take a couple of examples to establish whether customer sovereignty is necessarily the best way forward. First, the television. It is probably self-evident to most people with children that life without a television is no longer possible. And it may also be self-evident that television manufacturers who ignore what consumers want are likely to be edged out of the market. But did the television begin life through the demands of the consumer? Did parent-consumer groups up and down the lands of the world compile petitions requiring the development of technology to keep their children amused prior to its appearance? I don't think so. Did Roman soldiers stuck on Hadrian's Wall in the coldest and wettest part of what is now England complain to their commanding officers that: *Barbari! In hoc curru nulla arca sonorum adsit!* ('What no radio!' is a (very) rough translation, following Beard, 1995). I don't think so. The point, then, is that consumers, under some circumstances, do not necessarily know what they want until they are persuaded that the fuzzy gap on their floor really does need to be filled by the latest gizmo that they had always wanted, without ever realizing it.

But, second, let us now assume that a particular product already exists; we no longer require customers to imagine non-existing goods, but to select what it is they require from a range of existing products. Again, the Aristotelian approach is to assume that customers either want a product with x facilities, or they don't: either they do want a decent pen, or they don't. Under these criteria we sell a particular pen for £5 or $8, and if we want to know how to sell more we get closer to the customer: we survey their opinion and ask whether they want more expensive nibs, or pens that can pierce drink cans and still write, or more colourful barrels, or a longer guarantee, or a cheaper price, and so on. In this scenario the producer is entirely subservient to the customer and can only survive by *discovering* what it is that the customer really wants. But what happens when we muddy the Aristotelian waters a little and add some fuzziness?

Simonson and Tversky's (1992) evidence, although not premised upon fuzzy logic, suggests that the introduction of fuzziness may prove a positive step for business in its attempt to channel customers. For example, when people were offered the choice between $6 cash and an 'elegant' pen, 36 per cent chose the pen. When a second, cheaper, alternative pen was introduced, the proportion choosing the 'elegant' pen rose to 46 per cent. Similar experiments reproduce similar results—introducing cheaper alternatives increases the proportion of people choosing the more expensive option. Or, contrarily, introducing more expensive alternatives increases the proportion of people choosing the moderately priced option. By and large, consumers seem wary of both cheap and expensive extremes and, other things being equal, plump for the middle. In other words, by introducing fuzziness to the choice available, producers may be able to persuade customers to choose a particular product.

We can consider the significance and problems of the Aristotelian approach in other ways. Levin and Gaeth (1988) asked respondents to evaluate minced beef on the basis of alternative labels: 25 per cent fat or 75 per cent lean. As expected, the majority expressed greater satisfaction with that beef labelled 75 per cent lean. Here is a nice example of fuzzy properties, because, of course, the beef is both 75 per cent lean and 25 per cent fat. The Aristotelian binary division between 'is' or 'is not' is displaced by the fuzziness of 'is' *and* 'is not'. But the significant issue is not that there is an interesting theory moving around in here, but that the theory has concrete ramifications for managerial practice: in this case marketing practice. Moreover, since it does not take a genius to recognize that both descriptions of the beef imply the same product, this is not a case where consumer ignorance explains their apparently irrational behaviour. If this level of manipulated choice can exist where knowledge levels are high, we would expect even higher levels of manipulation where ignorance is higher. What now of the assumption that we should stay close to the consumer? This does not suggest that companies can simply ignore their customers and do whatever they like, but it does imply that companies can configure their customers in certain ways (see Woolgar, 1991, on this configuration process in a different setting). Where Aristotelian methods of objectivity and truth are pursued, the producer merely asks what the customer wants, but if the customer does not know what she or he wants then the principles of fuzzy logic seem to offer an alternative approach.

Fuzzy logic also has implications for those who are interested in buttressing consumer choice and power, rather than just getting close to the customer. For example, as Aldridge (1994) has so clearly demonstrated, when *Which?*, the consumer magazine, assessed jeans, the analysis consisted of subjecting various jeans to tests to evaluate the strengths of the materials. Sure enough, on the 'objective' strength test some survived better than others, and we can conclude in Aristotelian manner that some jeans are 'strong' and some 'not strong'. But this can only be an appropriate test for strength, not for what consumers necessarily want from jeans. Undoubtedly there are some wearers of jeans who do want the strongest pair available, but it is just as likely that the majority are more concerned by the 'image' that the jeans embody rather than whether they will still be wearing them twenty years from the date of purchase. Since image, style, and the degree of fashionability of any item are notoriously difficult to assess—that is, fuzzy and subjective—the utility of the 'rational' approach persuades the examiners to examine that which can be evaluated 'rationally'—even if this approach is almost completely irrelevant. The lesson of this tale is surely that managers—here of a clothing company—would be well advised to heed the health warning that ought to be on the side of the rational approach: 'Beware, this may not be what you want.'

FUZZY MEASUREMENT

Another consequence of our desire for certainty in the face of the opposite is that managerial appraisals tend to be limited to whatever can be secured with certainty. I will consider in chapter 5 the significance of uncertainty for personal appraisals and suggest that a 360° approach may be a specific way of using the theory constructively. Here, I want to consider the more general issue of measuring performance.

It is often mooted that only those things that get measured get done, and that, since only certain things can be measured, it is hardly a surprise when managers are assessed on short-term criteria like achieving production targets or adding x to the department's bottom line. The consequence of not being able to measure things like 'good interpersonal skills', or 'competencies in mentoring', or even 'leadership', mean that we are forced back to measuring dollars, pounds, yen, production figures, and the like. Because we can, allegedly, only measure these, they become the only important criteria for evaluation. There is clearly a large question mark hanging over the consequences of this conclusion, but in what sense is the bottom line a concrete and 'true' phenomenon anyway? I am not concerned here with the difficulty of tracing the effects of any individual's contribution to the total achievements of an organization, but with establishing the sacrosanct aura that pervades 'the bottom line'. In what sense is the bottom line a true reflection of profits? As Hines explains:

[T]he financial accounts of an organization do not merely describe, or communicate, information about an organization, but how they also play a part in the construction of the organization, by defining its boundaries. An organization is not a concrete thing but a set of inter-relationships, and if it is to exist, then it must somehow be bounded or defined. Financial accounting controversies are controversies about how to define the organization. For example, what should 'assets' and 'liabilities' include/exclude: at what point does an asset/liability become so intangible/uncertain/unenforceable/unidentifiable/non-severable, etc., that it ceases to be considered a part of the organization? The answers to questions such as these, define the 'size', 'health', 'structure', and 'performance', in other words, the reality of an organization. (1988: 258)

If 'creative accounting' suggests that there are numerous ways to represent an organization's activities, then the rigid focus on it for the assessment of managers is doubly problematic. First, because the figures themselves are fuzzy. In 1996 one of the more remarkable examples of fuzzy accounting occurred when Rover, the British subsidiary of BMW, announced that its £91 million profits for 1995 had become a loss of £158 million under the different valuation criteria applied by BMW (*Observer*, 14 April 1996). Second, because the consequence of focusing upon the figures is to drive out of sight all the other elements of organizational success which, allegedly, cannot be measured. Of course it is not necessarily the case that managers are mortified by the tunnel vision employed. On the contrary, many managers are probably less than enthusiastic about the prospect of expanding the measures of performance from ostensibly objective product or profit numbers—however manipulated they may have been—to clearly subjective areas like interpersonal skills, leadership, morale, and so on. Yet, as Blenkhorn and Gaber (1995) have argued, in areas where the bottom line is not always critical or measurable, such as not-for-profit organizations, some measures other than the bottom line have been used for many years to assess managerial performance. For example, if you wanted to measure the performance of managers with regard to the morale of their subordinates, you could institute some kind of employee survey. If you wanted to assess a manager's 'customer-service', you could survey his or her customers. And if you wanted to measure their innovativeness, you could ask them for specific examples and compare these with the innovations devised by others. Many managers may be uncomfortable with this—but if managerial discomfort was a reason to avoid anything, then we would probably not be looking at a very effective organization. Naturally, managers may complain about the subjectivities of the performance system, but on one thing we can be almost certain: once managers have been measured and rewarded on a particular phenomenon it soon becomes an important part of their performance. And, equally naturally, this may have dire consequences: if managers' primary bonus scheme is rooted in a measure of employee morale, that morale may well rise in direct proportion to a collapse in other areas—like productivity.

The consequences are threefold: first, fuzzy logic suggests that many previously unmeasurable areas can be measured to some degree—we do not need to know that a manager has a leadership score of 5.73 on some speciously objective 'Richter Scale of Leadership' to know that most of the subordinates regard the manager as a 'good' or 'poor' leader. Whether we choose to measure managers on such criteria is, of course, an entirely different question, but the point is that anything can indeed be measured, and that the measurement is overtly fuzzy and not covertly objective.

Second, if we do decide to extend the arena of performance measurement we had better be very clear about the Pandora's box we are about to open. Balanced scorecards may be the thin edge of a Taylorian renaissance in Western business, as organizations scramble to measure everything in sight. There may even be an association between those companies that measure performance widely and those that achieve a translation of strategy into results (Kaplan and Norton, 1992, 1996; Lingle and Schiemann, 1996; Ruddle, 1996). But the crucial issue remains the same as it was before performance measurement expanded beyond the achievement of bottom-line results: what effect does the measurement system have on the behaviour of the individuals measured? Hence, while the balanced scorecard sees a shift from a single concern for financial results, and/or production figures, to include a customer perspective, a learning and growth perspective, and an internal business process perspective, it is always possible that a critical area has been missed or something else overemphasized. Even if the measures are precisely the ones you want, it has still to be determined what the relative balance of the measures are and how managerial performance will be rewarded or punished in the light of the results. In other words, the balance of the balanced scorecard is a contingent and not a permanently resolved issue.

Despite the assumption that it is the measurement itself that stimulates a change in activity and success, it may still be that it is not the substance of the system that invigorates organizations, but the process through which they go to get to the system. In other words, it is perhaps not that managers respond to mechanical stimuli in a Pavlovian way (10 per cent increase in employee morale = higher salary, ergo be nice to the workers), but rather that to get to the agreement that higher morale is an essential element of the organization's objectives—and therefore the performance review—requires people to negotiate over what exactly the organization is trying to achieve and why? Once the agreement has been reached it should then be clearer to all what the objectives are, and managers should begin to pull in roughly the same direction. This 'reflexive' explanation for the success of balanced scorecards is paralleled by arguments that performance related pay, where it does appear to 'work', does so because it coerces managers to reflect upon their subordinates far more than they would otherwise do (see Kessler and Purcell, 1992).

Third, we should now be clear about the relationship between measurement and reality. The traditional approach suggests that we measure what exists, usually to bring it under greater control. For instance, we measure managerial innovation to get a better grip on the current situation and, subsequently, to encourage further innovation. But does this measure gauge what exists, or create it? Isn't it the case that not only does the measurement alter reality by changing managers' behaviour so that they suddenly become 'innovative'— and participate in the innovation bonus scheme—but that the measurement scheme creates the phenomenon we now label innovation? This does not mean that we begin to imagine innovations that do not exist, but that the way we define what counts as an 'innovation' generates subsequent innovation. For instance, if we define it as 'a change made in anything established' (*The Pocket Oxford Dictionary*, 1942) then we can look forward to hundreds of innovations, as I put forward my bonus claim based on holding my teacup with my left hand and saying 'good evening' as I arrive in the morning. If, however, having used up the annual bonus budget in the first ten minutes, we reconstruct 'innovation' to mean 'a change made to an established practice that your boss considers to be worthy of the term', then we have created another form of phenomenon—and I spend a lot of my time wining and dining my boss to discuss business matters.

The point should be clear: we can measure anything we like, but we should not confuse ourselves about what it is that we are measuring. If my accountant decides the company is on the rocks and displays the accounts in a particular light, my shareholders will run for cover and the company will collapse. If my accountant displays the figures in a different light, nobody panics and the short-term deficit (necessary to finance my long-term expansion plans, of course) has no effect. In short, organizations are fuzzy phenomena and it is we who define them into, or out of, existence.

CONCLUSION

I began this chapter by asking you to consider a world where instability and uncertainty prevailed. A conventional response to uncertainty is to impose certainty upon it, to make the complexity more malleable by sieving the data into categories that make the world easier to understand: good or bad managers, profitable or unprofitable organizations, dead or living people. I have argued that the imposition of such boundaries may be inevitable, but we should not confuse the model for the world, nor should we try and establish a true picture of the world. As I look out of my window, I can see an expanse of grass surrounded by an array of trees—but is this a true picture? Should I mention the flowers that I have just noticed? Or should I describe the ornamental grass that wafts in the autumnal breeze? How many elements of the grass plant should I reproduce? The point of the representational problem is just that— I cannot represent the entire picture, I have to be selective. If I am a tree specialist I would probably be able to differentiate the kinds of trees, but I cannot—so they are just 'trees'. Were I to try and generate a system of measuring this picture, so that the forester would know what I wanted to keep, I could use binary systems: trees and not-trees—just attend to the former; or conifers and not-conifers—just trim the latter. If I used a fuzzy logic approach I could say: 'just trim the trees that look to you in need of trimming'. The action of the forester will depend upon the system I use for differentiating one thing from another. The world is fuzzy and what we might consider are ways of making this fuzziness more understandable, more malleable, and less threatening. The next chapter begins this process by considering what often seems to be the least understood and the most threatening of all events: change.

2

Managing Fashions: *A Eulogy for Flared Trousers*

[The Cranford ladies'] dress is very independent of fashion; as they observe, 'What does it signify how we dress here at Cranford, where everybody knows us?' And if they go from home, their reason is equally cogent: 'What does it signify how we dress here, where nobody knows us?'.

Mrs Gaskell, *Cranford*

THERE is little doubt that the late twentieth-century world of business and organizations appears to be one where 'all that is solid melts'. Nothing seems to be stable and the degree of dynamic movement appears to be increasing exponentially. If one searches through the *Harvard Business Review* published in the 1950s there are, unfortunately, very similar arguments—which suggests either that we have very short memories, or that movement is a relative thing (though the perception of turbulence after the chaos of the Second World War would, on the face of it, need to be considerable to make an impact), or that pundits of change were wrong in the 1950s. Which ever way we explain the conundrum it does seem that change is something inherent to the economic system at the turn of the century. Indeed, change—at least at the level of new business fads and fashions—sometimes seems to be modelled on the fashion industry itself: since it is now winter, we need a new management fashion. Of course, managers are not driven by the ephemeral whimsies of fashion designers; in fact, you would be hard-pressed to find a harder-nosed bunch of individuals. Unless the bottom line is directly affected by the new idea, and unless its supporters can demonstrate that such improvements are unequivocally achievable by solid empirical research, there is simply no way that managers can be persuaded to take on board a novel idea or approach to business simply because it is fashionable. That is why most managers of whom I am aware, indeed almost all of us, continue to wear the flared trousers we bought in the 1960s. Not for us the instincts of the herd, which drive people with very little money to squander what they have on fashion. Except, this clearly is not the case. There must be literally billions of pounds worth of clothes hanging in wardrobes across the globe, unused because they are unfashionable, and much of it probably hangs in the rather more spacious houses of management. If we were to run our businesses and organizations on the whims of the Directors for the Abolition of Flared Trousers (DAFT) principles we would presumably waste millions of pounds and thousands of hours introducing novel ideas just because it seemed the right thing to do, or because everyone else was doing it, or because we didn't want to be the only company not using it. Of course, not everything changes all the time: we may not wear flared trousers any more, but we still wear trousers; we may not manage in the old 'command and control' way, but we still experience manifestations of this approach. However, where uncertainty or a lack of conviction prevails it may be that we are more prone to conform to the dominant trends of fashion. For example, children and teenagers seem much more prone to 'groupthink' in their clothing style than adults, self-confident individuals seem better able to resist group pressure than those lacking in self-confidence, and it may be that managers who are confident about their strategy are less influenced by the latest fad than those who are becalmed by their uncertainty and prevarication.

Irrespective of the receptiveness of individuals and organizations to change, there is little doubt that change has become an endemic feature of the post-war business world. The following is a list of changes over the last forty years based on Pascale's (1990) reconstruction: Decision Trees; Managerial Grid; Satisfiers/Dissatisfiers; Theory X and Theory Y; Brainstorming; T-group Training; Theory Z; Conglomeration; Management by Objectives; Decentralization; Diversification; Experience Curve; Strategic Business Units; Zero Base Budgeting; Value Chain; Wellness; Quality Circles/TQM; Excellence; Restructuring/Delayering; Portfolio Management; Management By Walking About; Matrix Management; Just-in-Time/ Kanban; Intrapreneuring; Corporate Culture; One Minute Manager; Globalization; Cycle Time/Speed; Visioning; Workout; Empowerment; Continuous Improvement/Learning Organization; Business Process Reengineering. If we assume that there are probably a few missing from this list (Intuition, Leadership, Balanced Score Cards, etc.) then we get to an interesting figure: every year, on average, a new fashion emerges.

Figure 2.1 covers the years 1986–95 and implies a continuing infatuation with change—assuming, of course, that the number of publications coincides with the enactment of the fashion and not simply with, well, the number of publications! Indeed,

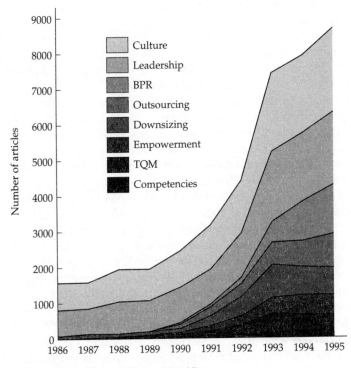

Fig. 2.1   Management Fads, 1986–95
Source: BPO (Business Periodicals On Disk)

the proportionate rise in publications with each year either implies that businesses annually ramp up the changes, or that the number of publications rises with the onslaught of new journals and new business academics. If we assume that some, at least, of the changes occur on the office or factory floor, there appears to be little connection between them,— although overlaps do exist, they are 'sold', that is marketed, as independent constructs. The result is that managers have to buy each change separately, because at each stage of the game the new approach is represented as 'the' solution to a multitude of problems. Even if you buy one and it does not seem to be the solution to the problem, you cannot take the chance that the next change is not the one that will resolve your problem. Hence, like any form of gambling, you are encouraged to buy because you couldn't live with yourself if you made the mistake of not buying a winning ticket; and, after all, someone must win.

Now the question is, do these changes generate significanct benefits? The answer is usually that it is very difficult to say because so many variables alter at the same time as the change is introduced that it is virtually impossible to know what difference any particular variable makes. There is a further question underlying this: given that we cannot say for certain that any particular change is worth the investment in time, money, and energy, do organizations normally have enough information to make a rational decision about introducing, or not introducing, a particular change programme? If a change occurs, on average, every year, then it is hard to see how this would be possible. Academic research on change programmes is, by convention, several years in the making, so this would not be an appropriate source for an organization to turn to looking for advice within a 12-month time frame. The alternative is to get consultants to provide advice on the very product they are about to sell, which may be a little tricky. Or, you might just see what everyone else is doing or reading or talking about—and do it. Of course, you might take a more radical step and ask the workforce what they think ought to be done—but what do people who produce the things you sell know about anything? No, far better to see what the rest are doing and do it. Unless, of course, they are wearing flared trousers.

In what follows I do not intend to explain any of the various change programmes mentioned above, since these can be secured by reading the books available at any major airport while you wait for your flight (to explain to the board what the organization should introduce this year). Rather, I want to spend the time considering—in rather more detail than above—why we seem to impale ourselves with a fetish for change. There is a very large number of change methods, programmes, and consultants, all of which are probably slightly different from each other. However, to bring a little order into this fuzzy world I will concentrate on five particular explanations of the fetish for change which cover most of the critical differences, with the fifth approach—institutional theory—encompassing elements of all the other four. This does not mean that the approaches are necessarily incompatible; rather, each approach may simply stress one element more than another. On the other hand, the degree to which this is plausible depends upon the approach.

If we divide the axes into four, as shown in Figure 2.2, in the first instance, then we can generate two pairs of alternatives based on, first, whether the main emphasis of the account lies with the logic of the approach or the emotional foundations and, second, whether the accounts are rooted in an internalist approach that focuses upon the importance of internal forces, either ideas or an individual, and an externalist approach that focuses upon the significance of exogenous or structural forces. The intersection of the two axes is also the location of a fifth

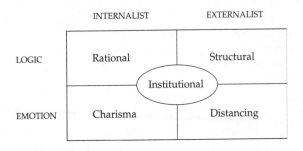

FIG. 2.2 Fad Modelling

form—the institutional approach—which presupposes that the critical influence upon the construction of management fashions is, in some way, fashion. That is to say, fashions change because that is the fashion, or, rather more clearly, fashions change because organizations mirror what is expected of them: if they consider that it is normal to change, they change; if they consider that doing nothing is normal, then they will do nothing. Hence, it sits at the fulcrum of the model, not because it is the most important approach, nor because it is the approach that contains all the other approaches, but because it operates as a mirror of the current fashion itself.

THE RATIONAL APPROACH

The first explanation is the simplest: we innovate all the time because innovation works. In other words, because in a dynamic market economy the only way to stay marginally ahead of your competitors (or customers/clients, etc.) is to generate some kind of competitive advantage through innovation. It is, then, the internal logic of the idea itself which ensures its success. For manufacturing companies this may mean innovative products, for service organizations this may mean innovative services. But here we are interested in rather more fundamental issues, such as the architecture and structure of the organization, or its punishment and reward mechanisms, and so on. So if we are looking to explain the success of 'management by walking about', for instance, we need to consider whether leading-edge firms are employing it, whether the business press is favourably inclined towards it, and whether the investment is likely to be more than compensated for by the ultimate pay-off. Since the world out there is a jungle, the law it invokes ensures that only the fittest survive—hence those management changes that work are the ones that survive.

There is a strong Darwinian flavour in here that we will meet again in chapter 5. On the one hand, population ecology theory suggests that the market does indeed select out the inefficient organizations, and there is little that managers can do to change the survival chances of their organizations because their degree of freedom to manœuvre is almost nil. On the other hand, if, by chance, organizations operate along strategies and structures that are appropriate for the particular niche they inhabit, they will prosper; but if they have inappropriate strategies and structures, they will fail. Structural contingency models provide for a greater influence on the part of managers, suggesting that they can take appropriate action to reconfigure an organization until it is suitably aligned to its organizational niche, but both approaches are functional. That is to say, both approaches suggest that we establish the efficiency of an organization by considering its health: sick organizations are inappropriate and will either die out or have to be radically changed. If you choose an inappropriate change model you are either finished or you will be very badly damaged by it. Such a perspective might then explain the huge number of business failures either by pointing to the mistakes of managers in choosing the wrong strategy and structure for the environment or by suggesting that the dynamism of the environment inevitably generates a massive annual cull of unfit organizations. In short, management fashions are not driven by greedy consultants cooking up solutions to problems that do not yet exist, but are a direct consequence of a turbulent environment in which not only is variety a crucial arbiter of survival, but only those ideas that are logically appropriate ensure survival.

Exactly what counts as 'logically appropriate' is, of course, subject to some debate, but, as Lyotard (1984) has argued, in the late twentieth century the issue is not whether the ideas are logical in the sense of being scientifically true (open to falsifiability), but whether they adopt the techniques and secure the results that are currently accounted legitimate—whether they 'perform' appropriately. In other words, whether they appear to be grounded in empirical evidence and whether the result of the idea is an increase in productivity, or efficiency, or profits. One might take this to its logical end-point: in so far as many of these models of change cannot be empirically examined, it is inevitable that a profusion of fashions will develop because there are no clear ways of distinguishing between those that are valid and those that are not.

THE CHARISMATIC APPROACH

A second explanation for the rise of management fashions focuses rather more upon the weaknesses of organizational leaders rather than the turbulence of the environment. In this approach, leaders are inadequate to the task (for whatever reason) of steering their organizations through troubled times. It may be that the background to this explanation is identical to the previous one: an unstable and increasingly competitive market where the level of information is either too large to handle or too small to make any difference. In the face of increased uncertainty, and where (literally) last year's organizational model proves increasingly inefficient, leaders are forced to look beyond themselves for salvation. Nor is it appropriate simply to examine the logic of any alternative strategy, because the leaders simply do not have the ability to analyse this—they are left to respond not logically but emotionally, and they tend to consider how an idea or individual may save them rather than examining what the external situation suggests they should do.

This may either come in the shape of a charismatic consultant on whom an enormous amount of faith is heaped, or it may come in a consultant who plays the role of the court jester. In this latter instance, consultants are employed not so much to solve the problems of the organization through their unique wisdom, but to force the CEO or equivalent figure to reflect upon their own actions. As most managers know, messengers bearing bad news are the first to get shot, yet if only good news is delivered when things are not going well the entire organization may descend into the mire. Hence, consultants are used who are relatively immune to the ire of the CEO when the former informs the latter that he or she is making a complete fool of himself or herself and simultaneously destroying the organization. Just as the jester of the Middle Ages poked fun at the King or Queen—and survived because of their protected position—so, too, consultants may operate and persuade CEOs to move one way or the other. And since the consultant is a disinterested party, at least in terms of political infighting, the degree of reliance placed upon consultant advice may far exceed that allotted to insiders' advice—even if the insiders are right and the consultant wrong.

The charismatic consultant does not have quite as long a historical record as the court jester, but there are clear similarities. As Clark and Salaman suggest, the persuasion of executives to take up a particular change programme is often reliant upon the actual *performance* of a notable guru:

[T]he task of the performer, in this case a management guru, is to bring the text to full realization by transforming the unfamiliar into the familiar so that the text has meaning for the audience to which their actions are addressed. The book or text is a distant inaccessible world which can only be made dazzlingly present and real and intelligible by the actions of the performer/management guru. (1996: 6)

One only has to witness the Tom Peters in action to see this. The content of the performance appears to be secondary to the performance itself, but the content is itself part of the performance. That is to say, Peters, and other management gurus like him, generate a high level of destabilization amongst the audience which effectively 'unfreezes' them, then the promise of salvation is offered if the participants agree to 'change', and finally the novelty of the new way is related back to the old ways so that participants may 'refreeze' the learning and the changes.

But the effective performer must also learn from Aristotle if he or she wishes to persuade the audience. As Huczynski (1993: 243–67) notes in his review of the public presentation of guru's ideas, the speaker's character and the emotional response of the audience are critical to persuasive performances. The significance allotted to the audience should remind us that consultants and/or gurus do not achieve their task in isolation. They may have a story to tell (see Jeffcutt, 1994), they may appear to embody a higher level of expertise and knowledge than anyone else, but they still have to recruit managers to their bandwagon, and they still have to be successful at what Gowler and Legge (1983) called, 'the management of meaning'. That is, they have to make the world seem more tractable, more understandable, more meaningful: in effect, gurus, consultants, and managers all trade in the same commodity—the manipulation, representation, and definition of symbols. The performance of the consultant or guru cannot, therefore, occur in isolation from his or her audience—it has to be worked at and achieved with the people he or she is trying to persuade (see Clarke and Salaman, 1996, for a review of this area).

In this respect, Jackson (1996) argues that we can adapt the work of Burke (1962) and Bormann (1985) to map out a particular route for the budding consultant/guru to take. Focusing upon Burke's rhetorical notions of 'identification' (a desire to identify with others), 'hierarchy' (a desire for more), and 'transcendence' (a desire to feel that their work is important), he suggests that the guru's performance (in Jackson's case Stephen Covey) is essentially a dramatic event, articulating the needs for identification, hierarchy, and transcendence from amongst the audience and providing them with a vocabulary to participate in the drama of the event. Relatedly, Bormann's 'fantasy-theme analysis' concentrates on the content of the message and reads it as the equivalent of any other drama, replete with action, characters, and the like. Within this drama, certain fantasy themes are developed which are configured to represent the future and explain the past to the newly constructed communities of believers. The whole approach is necessarily dramatic, for the fantasy is constructed by the converter but it must tap into the cultural mores of the converted if it is to be effective. For example, Churchill's visible and rhetorical embodiment of the British bulldog, unyielding in the face of a larger terror, might be seen as a fantasy theme that persuaded the British population to resist the forces of Germany. At the same time, it creates the pressure for greater identification amongst them, spurs them on to seek more than just survival, and imputes their actions with a mission of global import.

The other aspect of this which is worth highlighting relates to the location of the driver for change. *If* consultants are dependent for their influence upon their performance then we have to be clearer on the identity of those affected. For the most part, it is not going to be those middle managers who are responsible for implementing change who are going to be affected by consultants' performances, because they seldom see them. Instead, it is likely to be either the CEO or senior manager who attends and is persuaded; or it will be the colleagues and peers of these CEO and senior managers, to whom the

significance of the performance is passed on at a later date—
perhaps on the golf course, or at their club, and so on. If we
retain this knowledge, it explains what often appears to be a
perennial conundrum: why do organizations involve themselves in so much change when most of those involved in its
implementation often hold a rather jaundiced view about its
utility? Since the driver for change and the enactor of change
may well be different, the conundrum is, at least partially,
resolved.

Finally, one should note the significance of being regarded as
a fashion-setter rather than a fashion-taker. If part of the attrac-
tion of the charismatic consultant is that some of the charisma
may rub off on those who are first to use the latest technique,
then we might explain the desire of CEOs to throw themselves
on to the experimental altar. Moreover, there is something
exciting about being in at the sharp end, despite, or perhaps
because of, the inherent dangers there. As General Patton re-
minded his troops before the Normandy invasion:

There's one great thing that you men can say when it's all over and
you're home once more. You can thank God that twenty years from
now when you're sitting by the fireside with your grandson on your
knee, and he asks you what you did in the war, you won't have to shift
him to the other knee, cough and say, 'I shovelled crap in Louisiana'.
(quoted in MacArthur, 1992: 219)

Or, as Shakespeare's Henry V remarked in his attempt to woo
Princess Katharine after the battle of Agincourt and she had
refused to kiss him because it was not the custom: 'O Kate! nice
customs curtsy to great kings. Dear Kate, you and I cannot be
confined within the weak list of a country's fashion; we are the
makers of manners, Kate' (*Henry V*, v. ii). Just as monarchs
established what counted as good manners, so too gurus can
establish what counts as good management practice—if they
can persuade the CEOs—and this is often achieved by linking
the core of the new idea to a raft of existing ideas that have
already achieved a high degree of acceptance, such as customer
service, quality, and the like.

Finally, under this consultant-oriented rubric we might consider their role as sin-eaters, that is as scapegoats for the organization or for the CEO should things go wrong. Of course,

this is hardly a novel role, but it is an important one, allowing managers to distance themselves not simply from a failed change programme but also from responsibility for a successful one. Here we can consider the way consultants' reports become the repository of the guilt that may follow a restructuring, 'after all it was what the experts said needed to be done— we didn't want to go down the redundancy route but we had no option'.

THE DISTANCING APPROACH

Herbert Spencer, writing in 1874, would have had some sympathy with the notion of progress, but had a particular slant on it that leads into the next explanatory account. For Spencer, the whole of progress—of all varieties—could be accounted for by the process of differentiation: all phenomena progressed by moving from the homogeneous to the heterogeneous, from the simple to the complex. Thus, we would expect organizations to change permanently as they became progressively more complex, facilitated, no doubt, by increasingly heterogeneous consultants. Twenty-five years later, Thorstein Veblen's *Theory of the Leisure Class*, first published in 1899, took the notion of progress in a different direction by considering the way material progress facilitated a feature of social life that appeared anything but progressive: that is, the continuous retrenchment of status divisions. Veblen suggested that the increasing abundance of material goods in the USA generated the possibility of using the 'conspicuous consumption' of luxury goods as a means of distancing oneself from those with subordinate status. A similar process appears to occur without conspicuous consumption, but with conspicuous relabelling: thus the historical distinction in Britain between middle-class meal times ('dinner' in the evening) versus working-class meal times ('dinner' at midday and 'tea' in the evening) have altered through time to the point where the working class has 'dinner' in the evening but the middle class now has 'supper'. The point, therefore, need not be what form the social-distancing or the reproduction of social hierarchy takes, but that it happens at all, and that it is an emotional rather than a rational response to change.

In terms of clothing fashions this distancing phenomenon is tightly associated with identity construction: it is because your parents wear certain kinds of clothes that you do not, and vice versa. Furthermore, groups may consciously avoid mimicking their alleged social superiors (Simmel, 1957). For example, the lounge suit is still the uniform of most managers, while shop-floor workers wear overalls and office staff wear something in between. The significance of this can be established by the role uniforms play in some of the change programmes themselves. For instance, many vehicle or vehicle-part manufacturers in Britain have adopted 'workwear', which consciously decreases the social distance between managers and employees through the collective provision of a standard uniform for all members of the company, irrespective of their status (Rover is probably the most obvious example).

What change programmes may do is provide the worn-out manager with a new identity which is distanced from a previous one. Here, the distance secured is from something the manager once was, not someone the manager seeks to retain a degree of superiority over. We might turn to consultants because they offer us the prospect of something rather more exciting than that we were used to.

There was a time when management, at least in Britain, was about as exciting as waiting for a bus to arrive. It was neither an attractive occupation nor an enticing undergraduate degree. For most of British, and indeed just about every other nations', industrial history the last things the elite of the country wanted to get involved in was management of any variety, least of all industrial management. The more invisible and distant the income source, the higher the status was in general. Britain was probably the most affected by this cultural assumption and it was not until late in the twentieth century that the status of management, either as a career or a degree subject, rose to any significant extent (Grint, 1995b: 52–61). Being a rock singer, or a professional sports player, or a movie star was exciting; being a manager was about waiting for your pension. In the USA and Germany the status of engineers has historically been much higher than in Britain, where management has hardly been the first choice of those individuals seeking a dynamic or exciting life. The elite of nineteenth-century Britain could choose the excitement of the army, the security of the church, or the wealth of the city, but they would seldom choose to manage a factory in the North of England. For most of the twentieth century, at least until the 1970s, only those fascinated by machinery would probably have taken an industrial management position as the first choice from university. Indeed, it was not until 1980 that Oxford University began its first undergraduate degree with management as part of the curriculum. In the 1990s, however, things began to look rather different. Management and Business Studies started to attract the strongest not the weakest students, management education at all levels has continued apace, and the salary levels of top industrial managers rose high enough to provoke regular outrage from the media. Where once we might have suggested that individuals seeking the high life spent on the edge of chaos and stress should join the army, it became equally appropriate to suggest they join the ranks of management.

I want to take this analogy with the military a little further by considering the extent to which late twentieth-century developments in management, especially through the reengineering rhetoric, have reconstituted, or at least attempted to reconstitute, managers as the new 'corporate warriors'. As Champy asserts: 'Management has joined the ranks of the dangerous professions' (1995: 7). This sudden departure from safety and security to danger and insecurity is linked to the destruction of the staid and predictable environment that allegedly prevailed before the 'nasty nineties' arrived (though this is disputable, it is not an issue here; see Grint and Case, 1996).

For senior managers, therefore, we might suggest that change programmes offer the possibility of maintaining—or re-establishing, or even reducing—some distance between themselves and middle managers through an array of change programmes. Alternatively, it may be that inter-organizational not intra-organizational rivalry is the causal element, as rival organizations vie for the position of the 'leading edge' with each other (see Abrahamson, 1996). It is not, then, *which* change programme that is important, but that the idea of an innovative and powerful group of leaders exists who have the ability to change direction as and when they please (see also Anthony, 1977). If this hypothesis is accurate we would expect to see change programmes increase in velocity as status divisions between senior and middle managers decrease. In other words, if the emotive issue of status maintenance is as significant as it appears to be, then no amount of logical social engineering will obliterate the differentiations and, on the contrary, novel ways of maintaining the social distance between status groups will emerge as fast as change programmes seek to undermine them.

Similarly, the concept of change as fashion should also alert us to the point that different fashions mediate between the potentially overwhelming choices that are available—clothes, cars, ideologies, religions, and so forth (Blumer, 1969). Fashions are not anarchic and there do appear to be consistently demarcated patterns: the goth, the punk, the skinhead, the executive, the student and so on. We are faced, then, not with a million choices of what to be but with far fewer, which embody obligatory—but not mandatory—accoutrements. For example, academics tend to be liberal-minded and wear casual clothes. Fashion thus generates a series of normative boundaries that ease the difficulty of choice. For management fashions the same principle applies. Faced with an enormous amount of information and choice about what to do, managers' decisions are made significantly easier by adopting whatever the class leaders are adopting. These choices are not logical but emotional, and they are externally not internally oriented: we choose fashions because they appeal to our vanity and these fashions are not constructed by us as individuals but by collectives of others.

Nor should we limit the utility of distancing to individuals or organizations. It may be that whole nations become bound up in patriotic movements to slough off dependence on 'the other' and generate a new or renewed national self-confidence. For example, it does not seem coincidental that the BPR phenomenon arose in the late 1980s from a USA already battered by the inroads of Japanese companies. Where Japan appeared to have a clear advantage through TQM, Americans were faced with either copying their way back to predominance—a contradiction in terms—or developing a specifically American innovation that made use of American talents and cultural history. In the words of Wilf Corrigan from LSI Logic:

One of the great advantages of America is that Americans have no memory. The reason why I left Europe was because there's such a long memory that you can't initiate change. But Americans have no memory at all. I'm convinced an American workforce can come into work on Monday morning and find the whole production line has changed and by coffee break they're used to the new environment. (quoted by Davidow and Malone, 1993: 215)

This is especially critical in the face of competition that hails from outside the boundary line, from 'the other' (i.e. Japan) and where the 'solution' to the 'problem' is deemed to lie in a long discarded folk memory where the particular organization or nation was ostensibly stronger than it currently is. Thus, BPR's popularity is dependent upon developing a form of rhetoric that induces people to forget about responsibilities for and complexities of the present, and remember only the aspects that reflect or support the strategy for change.

Overall, it seems that the majority of change programmes of all variants fail. Both a cause and a consequence of this is the search for yet another change programme that will deliver the goods virtually overnight without organizations—or at least the senior managers—having to go through too much soul-searching or organizational sweat (Pascale, 1991).

In this context BPR appears rather like a veritable 'fire-and-forget' missile. Once a sufficient number of middle managers and development managers have taken the new programme on board, those at the top can forget about the problem—at least for a little while. The consequence of this is that change programmes change. In short, that change for the sake of change resembles the adoption of fashionable clothing—that, for example, BPR or TQM or MBO are accepted and regurgitated not because they may be evaluated as objectively 'good' ideas, but because they are fashionable ideas. As a result, managers only accept the changes in the same light that they accept changes in fashion—one does not buy a suit to last for ever, but until fashion dictates that we should not be seen wearing it in public, and our dedication to it, therefore, is temporary. In effect, BPR's popularity—itself measured by CSC Index's own

'Top 20' chart of managerialist buzzwords—seems to be as much to do with the organizational resonances that its supporters generate with contemporary developments elsewhere as with any 'inherent' rationality of the idea. That is, the way in which new approaches render an account of the problem and a solution that sets up sympathetic 'resonances' with related developments. BPR's popularity, according to this approach, also lies in the resonances it 'reveals' between old and new business systems that were previously right but are now inappropriate. Hence:

[It] isn't another imported idea from Japan . . . [it] capitalizes on the same characteristics that made Americans such great business innovators: individualism, self reliance, a willingness to accept risk and a propensity for change . . . unlike management philosophies that would have 'us' like 'them', [it] doesn't try to change the behaviour of American workers and managers. Instead, it takes advantage of American talents and unleashes American ingenuity. (Hammer and Champy, 1993: 1–3)

We can surmise that a major reason for the persistence of change programmes, from this perspective, has less to do with the performance of the consultant or the logical promise of radical business improvements and more to do with the emotional significance of internal status and identity construction in the face of increasing complexity.

THE STRUCTURAL APPROACH

The last of the distinct approaches, the structural approach, considers the extent to which the explanation for change lies completely outside the remit or control of individuals or groups and falls squarely within the requirements of the 'logical requirements of the situation'—which tend to be economic structures.

This approach also takes account of the incremental development of management fashions: that is, each fashion may not necessarily undermine the former, but may, rather, appear as a wave that builds upon its predecessor, retaining the progress made before, while discarding the weaknesses and extending the residual strengths (see Watson, 1986). The metaphorical wave may also embody an alternative 'tidal' concept, in which management fashions can, in part, be explained by management's need to alter its control strategies to suit the conditions. In Flander's original term (1965), when the economic cycle generates growth, and its attendant conditions favour the growth of workers' control over the production process, management must 'regain control by sharing it'. Thus, management fashions can be considered as directly responding to the economy, either enhancing or reducing direct control over labour as determined by the 'logic' of the situation. Naturally, if managers choose an inappropriate—that is, irrational and illogical approach to the problem of control—they will fail.

Management theory, especially American management theory, has generally been construed to represent this rational development towards a more effective system over time. One of the most popular models tends to divide management styles into three modes, shifting from coercive to economically and rationally utilitarian to normative, in line with work changes. (see, for example, Etzioni, 1961, and Edwards, 1979). A rather different approach taken by Barley and Kunda (1992) replaces the evolutionary pattern with a bipolar or pendulum pattern, as control shifts from normative to rational and back again across time. Thus, they consider the USA to have experienced five distinct patterns: industrial betterment (normative) from 1870 to 1900; scientific management (rational), from 1900 to 1923; human relations (normative), from 1923 to 1955; systems approaches (rational), from 1955 to 1980; and, finally, organized culture (normative), from 1980 to the(ir) present (1992). Very crudely reduced, we could say that the normative approach was rooted in securing the commitment of the employees, while the rational approach was rooted in securing control over employees.

Barley and Kunda offer two related explanations for this patterning. First, an account derived from structural anthropology, drawing on the ideas of Levi-Strauss (1966, 1969), in which cultures are said to revolve around a pair of oppositional elements that are essential to, but unresolved by, the cultures within which they exist. For example, life and death or the homogeneity–heterogeneity duality which

Spencer developed, or the community–individual opposites which both Durkheim and Weber wrestled with. In explaining organizational change, the approach suggests that the oppositional pairing of normative and rational offer incompatible accounts of the way organizations should be managed, and since the incompatibility cannot be resolved in favour of one or the other on a permanent basis, organizations are forced to swing from one to the other and back as they attempt to resolve the irresolvable. If this model is accurate, we would expect the emphasis on organizational culture, which marked the 1980s and has continued through the 1990s, to be replaced slowly by a shift back towards a rational approach. We might, for example, consider the increased interests of the late 1990s in psychometric developments and in balanced score cards to be an early indication of such a development. It should be noted, though, that the rational approach is the dominant partner for the most part; it is just that normative influences are sometimes more visible but they seldom dominate.

In fact, we could generate a further pair of alternative approaches here—Hobbesian and Rousseauean—as a means of differentiating between the normative and the rational. For instance, Taylorism and TQM approaches are both 'rational', rather than normative, but the former excludes subordinates from control, while the latter requires it. The result would be a 2 × 2 table, as represented in Figure 2.3. In this approach the limits are not just those of the rationality/morality binary, but

	RATIONALITY	MORALITY
AUTHORITARIAN *(Hobbes)*	Taylor/Ford BPR/psychometrics	Human relations Charismatic leadership
PARTICIPATIVE *(Rousseau)*	Belbin's teams TQM	Neo-human relations Culture/empowerment

FIG. 2.3 Structuring Change

also one derived from the work of Hobbes and Rousseau. Hobbes's work, especially *Leviathan* (published in 1651), often noted as marking the beginning of the modern age, asserted that political absolutism was the only long-term solution to the crisis and conflict of the times (the English Civil Wars). Without such a sovereign, people revert to their 'natural state': a war of all against all. Under the sovereign, the people surrender their rights to individual freedom in return for protection, and the sovereign is then free to do whatever is necessary to preserve the peace. In contemporary terms this implies a unitarist approach in which organizational leaders have total control over, and the unquestioned obedience of, the other organizational members; only in this way can an organization prosper. We can see this kind of thinking in Taylor's and Ford's late nineteenth- and early twentieth-century approach to production, in which shop-floor workers had virtually no right to question or resist their superordinates at work because it was considered rational to construct such an authoritarian structure. As the notion of scientific expertise was questioned, in the 1920s and 1930s, the alternative 'moral' form of authoritarianism can be seen operating under the managerially manipulated teams of the human relations approaches, or under the charismatic label, best reflected in the organizations led by gurus such as Jim Jones, Bhagwan Shree Rajneesh, and Shoko Asahara (Storr, 1996).

The participative alternative derives from the ideas of Rousseau's *Social Contract*. Here, the 'good society' cannot be rooted in the surrender of the population to an unconstrained sovereign because the people themselves are sovereign. In contrast to Hobbes, Rousseau argued (in 1762) that it is only because of the actions of sovereigns and equally authoritarian societies that people become like animals, for in the state of nature there is merely harmony and freedom. (Fans of McGregor's (1960) Theory X and Theory Y should note the similarity of his ideas to those of Hobbes and Rousseau here.) In effect, the population must perceive no division between their individual interests and those of the society as a whole, and must participate in the construction of such a state. In employment terms this can be translated through such developments as 'organizational culture' and empowerment—in which employees are supposed to be involved in the construction of, and are, hence, forthright supporters of, the 'new' organization. Similarly, as we shift from the 'moral' to the 'rational' side, we might consider TQM and Belbin's team roles as representing this approach, in which all individuals are crucial to the success of the organization, and their consent must be freely given, but in which science plays a strong role in determining the 'best' team make-up or the 'best' way of improving quality (see Belbin, 1981).

Why exactly the strategy changes from one form to the next is as disputable as the original division. It is possible that change occurs when the current strategy is deemed to be generating declining marginal rewards—as in the case of Ford, for example, and the change to the human relations approach between the world wars. Or it may be that the Rousseauean forms only develop when the fears that support a Hobbesian approach begin to wither. For example, when the Nazi threat was lifted in 1945 management could begin to experiment with systems beyond those developed to destroy the enemy of order. Subsequently, perhaps Rousseauean participative approaches are displaced by Hobbesian authoritarian styles when the 'golden age' promised by the former is shown to be unachievable. This may explain the shift from the early 1980s forms of empowerment and TQM to the early 1990s experiments with BPR (see Grint, 1994).

Barley and Kunda (1992: 387) suggest it is possible that moral or normative methods are employed during times of crisis, and rational methods during times of relative calm, but since this does not match the patterns of labour unrest it seems unlikely to explain the changes. Their own preference is for an explanation that links the normative–rational cycle through an alternating emphasis on the significance of managing labour (normative control) and capital (rational control), and this is locked into the long waves of economic and technological development first developed in the 1930s and 1940s by Schumpeter (1976) and Kondratieff (1935). Long waves, which last approximately fifty years, involve a period of rapid economic expansion spurred on by accumulated capital investment and particular technological developments, followed by a period of consolidation and contraction as declining returns set in. Thus, we have a first wave, which coincides with the beginnings of the industrial revolution and lasts until the mid-nineteenth century; a second wave, which continues until the last decade of the nineteenth century and which coincides with steam machinery, railroads, and the like; a third wave from the 1890s until the Second World War, dominated by electricity and the internal combustion engine; and a fourth wave, which brings us up to the present period (the 1990s), when electronics, air transport, and synthetic materials predominate. Barley and Kunda (1992: 391) suggest that these long waves are mirrored by the managerial ideology swings, as the expansion phase of each one is accompanied by a rational approach, and the contraction phase is linked to a normative emphasis. Of particular interest here is the way this argument attempts to meld two otherwise antagonistic explanations of change. Where most accounts are either idealistic—where change derives from the power of ideas—or materialist—where change derives from material forces—Barley and Kunda's approach combines the two together. What we should see in the future, then, is not just an increased adoption of rational ideologies within management, but the advance of novel technologies that facilitate the beginnings of the fifth long wave.

What are the implications of this account of change for our consultants or managers? At first it might seem that they (and we) are in the hands of structural forces that we may be able to understand but can do little about. Yet the central message is actually not as deterministic as it sounds. It may be that what is required is for managers to understand the structural forces that impinge upon them and alter their methods and ideologies so that they are symmetrical with, and aligned to, the current state of affairs. For example, if we assume that the model is accurate then we should soon start to see an increase in capital investment, technological advancement, and economic growth, along with a gradual switch from normative to rational ideologies. As I mentioned above, we may consider the rise in psychometric testing, balanced score cards, and the urge to measure whatever can be measured, as the beginnings of a new rational wave. Hence, those managers who adopt these approaches first, or who employ consultants offering such services first, are the ones most likely to secure an early competitive advantage. Conversely, those who continue to use old normative means—and old technologies—may well find themselves redundant in the not too distant future. In effect, management fashions change for different reasons: in the long term (cyclical periods of around fifty years), change occurs because of a combination of economic, technological, and ideological reasons; in the short term (cyclical periods of less than five years), it may be that each variation in managerial ideology merely extends the underlying leitmotiv. Put another way, it implies that short-term change is likely to have no more than a marginal effect upon performance, and that the leaps of performance are probably associated with the point at which the gradual downturn in economic activity changes to begin the new upturn. Coincidentally, this means that as we approach the end of the century, we are on the verge of a great leap forward—now where have I heard that before?

THE INSTITUTIONAL APPROACH

The possibility that change programmes are enacted because of a guru performance or a meeting of minds on the golf course may appear a little whimsical when we are discussing the significance of the issue at hand. However, institutional theory (Meyer and Rowan, 1977; Scott and Meyer, 1994), which sits at the intersection of the twin axes in Figure 2.2, suggests that organizational decision-makers, especially under conditions of uncertainty, are forced into taking action that resembles the lead taken by others in the field. For instance, if—after a substantial research programme—a leading car producer adopted self-organized teams, rather than a conventional assembly line, to build vehicles, then its competitors may well assume that teams are more efficient than assembly lines. If they were not, why would a respected company like this adopt such a production system?

Under this approach the normative influences upon individuals are too great for most to resist—not only does it seem rational to copy a field leader, but the possibility that the mimicry is undertaken for normative rather than rational reasons is itself denied. The result is that we would not be seen dead wearing flared trousers, not because they are old-fashioned but (we persuade ourselves) because they are such an irrational garment to wear. The power of normative influences is often difficult to establish for that very reason—they are normative. One might, for example, consider the conventional Western reaction to the wearing of the *chuddar* by women in some Islamic societies. This may appear to be a considerable infringement of their personal rights and a wholly irrational element of culture. Yet we in the West simultaneously generate our own normative controls that in and of themselves appear rational rather then normative. For instance, we do not expect to see adults completely naked whilst wandering around in public. Yet such behaviour is perfectly acceptable in other societies and acceptable in the West under certain circumstances. Normative influences, then, are primarily significant at a level that evades conscious analysis; they are, as they say, perfectly normal.

Given this, it would appear remarkable if managers were not subject to the same kind of normative pressures at work. Do we expect leaders to have visions? If not, can they be regarded as legitimate leaders? Assuming the answer to this latter question is no, then we might also expect organizations to follow one another into the whirlwind of change—because everyone else is doing it, therefore so should we. Naturally, some of the changes will not work properly, but the underlying philosophy of the West, at least since the Enlightenment, has been that progress is natural and therefore that change is usually for the better. Furthermore, since progress implies change, stasis implies a lack of progress. In short, once a change programme has been up and running for a year or two, then its potency as a manifestation of progress is 'progressively' eroded to the point when the very term becomes a cliché for old-fashioned.

This inherent tendency to decay naturally plays straight into the hands of those who have an interest in generating change: consultants and trend-setters. For these groups, change is rather like a game of problem-construction, in which the winner is the person who develops more solutions than anyone else. Now the real point of the game is not to produce solutions to problems that already exist, but to generate problems through the creation of solutions. For example, our inability to measure certain things—like customer satisfaction within a service environment—is not a problem until a method is devised to measure it. At this point, customer satisfaction that is not measured appears to be a problem that has always been with us—and the measuring method is marketed as a solution to it (see Grint, 1995a, for an example of this applied to computer problems).

Perhaps we should also consider the way each apparently novel approach renders an account of the problem and solution that sets up sympathetic 'resonances' with related developments. That is, the way it captures the *Zeitgeist*, or 'spirit of the times'. There are precedents for this in the popularity of previous managerial philosophies (see Rose, 1990). For example, Taylorism and Fordism can be understood in relation to the contemporary developments of social statistics: the early twentieth-century rise of the eugenics movement in the USA and its attempted legitimation through scientific measures of IQ (Kamin, 1977; Karier, 1976a, 1976b); the high point of pre-1914 beliefs in the efficacy of scientific rationality—soon to be radically disturbed by the events of 1914–18 (Pick, 1993); in light of the changes in disciplinary and temporal schemas adopted originally in armies and prisons (Foucault, 1979); and, of course, in the development of the assembly-line system, or rather disassembly-line system, in the Chicago slaughter houses, then 'processing' 200,000 hogs a day (Pick, 1993: 180). One might want to go further here and suggest that the kind of mechanical tactics adopted by the British Army, at the battle of the Somme in 1916, for example (Ellis, 1993), are precise replicas of the scientific management displaced from the factory to the killing fields of Flanders. Relatedly, the human relations reaction to Taylorism and Fordism can be read as a shift from the 'rational individual' approach to the 'irrational group' approach, as the development of Communism and Fascism appeared to be explicable only through an assumption about the fundamentally irrational needs of people to belong to groups and to construct their group identity through the destruction of 'the other'. The defeat of Fascism and the arrival of the cold war subsequently provided fertile ground for the reconstruction of neo-human relations in the form of democratic individualism; the 'evil empire' was neither of these, and, particularly in the UK (Donovan Commission, 1968), the informal group, so long propounded by the human relations school, appeared to be the cause of the problem of economic malaise, not the solution. This time the alternative was written in the language of Lewin's democratic leadership (Lewin et al., 1939), or McGregor's Theory Y version of responsible employees (1960), and Maslow's (1954) and Herzberg's (1966) quest for self-fulfilment through work. Finally, we can posit the arrival of the 'cultures of excellence' approach where the limits of modernism and Fordism are perceived as the stimulus to change. Reengineering, in this perspective, is the summation of this development, which has itself been tightly linked to the wider political movement towards the enterprise culture and the individual customer, and against collectivism and state control of any kind (see du Gay and Salaman, 1992; du Gay, 1996).

What are the consequences of this final approach for practising managers? Given the power of normative forces, it may be difficult to establish what a manager should do—but rather easier to predict what he or she will do. In other words, if fashion (un)consciousness is so influential, then perhaps managers should not be embarking upon change programmes all the time—because there is little evidence that they work as well as is claimed—and being fashionable is not necessarily a good reason to turn the organizational world upside down. On the other hand, if this is what is expected of organizations, then those that resist will be labelled as 'old-fashioned', as no longer at the 'cutting edge', and as unworthy of support. So the dilemma remains a powerful one. Perhaps managers should endeavour to secure the position achieved by Henry V after Agincourt and become not the follower of fashions, but the maker of them.

CONCLUSION

Where does all this leave our managers? Should we discard our flared trousers immediately on the grounds that they are no longer legitimate attire and we all want to look trendy and progressive (institutional approach); or because they do not align themselves with the long waves of managerial trousers—that is, they smack of touchy-feely hippies and we are now into a hard-nosed expansionary phase where only pin-stripes will do (structural account); or because the guru doesn't wear them (charismatic account); or because the supervisors are wearing them and we need to (re)demonstrate who is in charge (distancing account); or because, after all, you simply cannot iron them properly and they keep getting caught in the lift doors so they are completely irrational (rational account)? Or perhaps all five explanations seem equally viable.

If nothing else, we might want to reconsider the latest buzzword the next time it comes flying through the email. Do we really need to restructure everything again? Is there any empirical evidence that this new system will work? Dare I ask the CEO where he or she got this crazy idea from? Just because another nutty professor is attempting to make a career on the back of an idea does not mean we should implement it—does it? On the other hand, maybe it will work, maybe I can get a promotion out of this if I champion it now, maybe my career will suffer if I don't run with it—even if I know it will not work. Which of these scenarios do we fall into?

Let us just recall where we began: flared trousers. At what stage did it become patently obvious that we would never wear them again? Not at first, when those drain-pipe jeans looked ridiculous. But after a lot of looking at the drain-pipes, they began to look, well, normal; and the flares looked, well, bizarre. Perhaps we can run this example past ourselves again. At what point did decentralizing everything to profit centres and strategic business units look normal? Remember the good old days of hierarchy, when everyone knew who was in charge and what they had to do? One thing does appear to run through all the models of explanation: history does not repeat itself precisely, but there is this *déjà vu* thing which keeps coming back to me.

In the next chapter I want to take a closer look not at the explanations for the various changes, but at the arguments that follow from this: *if* you decide to change an organization, are there limits to what you can do, how far you can go, and the extent to which you can control the changes? Moreover, to what extent can contemporary theory help managers in the challenge of change?

3

Chaos, Culture, and Evolution:
The Configuration of Organization

Thus it happens that, as I have said, two men, working in
different ways, can achieve the same end; and of two men
working in the same way one gets what he wants and the
other does not.

Machiavelli, *The Prince* (1981 [1532]: 79)

INTRODUCTION

In the last chapter I considered the way in which organizational change has become an endemic feature of contemporary
management, but concluded that this need not leave managers
without useful techniques for developing a strategic response
to such fads and fashions, providing they develop an understanding of why change occurs. In this chapter I want to wade
a little deeper in the opaque world of theory to examine chaos
theory and evolutionary theory.

Conventional theory asserts that the world is predictable
and stable, and able to be explained by causal links that can be
measured and monitored. Once we know what works, and
what does not, we can use it to good effect. This explains why
Chancellors of the Exchequer in Britain consistently 'fine tune'
the economy—but it does not explain why they equally consistently fail on virtually every occasion (Dell, 1996). The
trouble is, as Machiavelli implies, it seems to be the case that
something intervenes to throw the machine off balance. For
Machiavelli, it was explained by fortune or luck, for us it can be
explained by chaos theory. Luck suggests that events are random, that anything can happen and usually does. Chaos theory

implies that in the short term anything can happen, but that in the long term patterns, or 'strange attractors', are discernible. Evolutionary theory also insists that there are limits to change and that one cannot 'start over' with the same organization.

If the world and, more importantly here, the world of organizations, is made up of machines composed of a multitude of pieces, then management's job is to control the machine by keeping the parts going; as long as the machine works we can predict what it will do and how it will do it. Thus, managers are really organizational maintenance engineers: wherever the machine breaks down, or organizational fires break out, managers attend and resolve the problem (see Grint, 1995b: 45–67). It is important here to note the bias towards reactive and restitutive behaviour: managers only go into action when things go wrong, and the priority is to return things to the previous equilibrium. In effect, the feedback system is almost wholly negative.

But what if organizations are more like gardens than machines? (see Stacey, 1992). Managers can certainly *affect* events in the garden, but much of what happens is beyond the gardener's control in a far more radical sense than that implied by the fires that break out in machines. Gardeners have virtually no control over the fortunes of the weather, which is a chaotic system whose prediction is difficult. In effect, we can discern the 'strange attractors' that impose an overall limit to climatic fluctuations, but within these boundaries the weather is rather chaotic. Yet just because it is chaotic does not mean that gardeners are impotent. On the contrary, it means they have to manage their gardens in a much more fluid way: they plant seeds only after certain conditions, like frosts, have *probably* disappeared; they thin out the plants only after they have grown—though exactly when this criterion is satisfied depends upon the gardener. Sometimes a late frost will be forecast—perhaps only a few hours before it happens—and the gardener must rush out and cover the plants if they are to be saved. But the frost *may not* come after all; or the covers *may* be knocked aside by a hungry rabbit. *If* organizations are more like gardens than machines, the style of management that has developed for hundreds of years may not be the most appropriate in the circumstances (see Trisoglio, 1995). The fact is that many social systems are anything but machine-like; we simply have the wrong metaphor, because social systems 'are iterative recursive systems that can exhibit discontinuous change over time' (Gregersen and Sailer, 1993: 792). Rather than worrying about putting the covers back up—returning the system to stability—perhaps managers should consider farming the hungry rabbits instead, and reinforcing the initial success of the switch by going into immediate partnership with a fast-food chain to produce millions of McRabbit sandwiches or Fluffybunny burgers. The point is that even this instantaneously successful shift may not last, and the company must start looking for new openings immediately (Vegebunnies, Horsefly Delight, etc.).

Note how important time is here, for a traditional 'snapshot' analysis of organizations may imply a level of control and order that is not manifest when the same organization is viewed across time. Indeed, the temporal element is especially critical because chaos theory does not imply that an organization is actually the antithesis of the machine-like order the text books would have us believe: it is not that organizations are anarchic in the pejorative sense of being completely out of control (though there are clear connections between some elements of anarchism and radical political theory and self-organization—see Brinton, 1975; Gombin, 1978; Woodcock, 1962). Rather, the suggestion is that what appears to be chaos at one level is actually rhythmic or patterned at a higher level (see Kiel's (1993) analysis of a US government agency, for example); and the best way to cope with the erratic developments at the lower level—on the shop or office floor—is to give those people closest to the action the authority to do whatever they consider necessary in the circumstances.

However, irrespective of the theoretical developments of chaos theory, it is nevertheless the case that there exists in the late 1990s a profound and pervasive assumption that the world is self-evidently more dynamic than it ever used to be. Whether there has been a radical gear change in terms of shifting from a world gone past that was composed of closed and stable systems to a contemporary world of open and dynamic systems is a moot point. Certainly, as I mentioned earlier, there are many *Harvard Business Review* articles from the 1950s replete with stories of the dynamic new markets, so it may be that it is our perceptions and assumptions about the world that have changed rather than the world itself. Perhaps the idea of an increasingly dynamic world is the equivalent of an increasingly violent one, or one where educational standards are constantly slipping from some hazy period in the 'golden past' that does not really stand up to rigorous research on the issue. On the other hand, perhaps there are links between the dynamic world and a theory necessary to explain it.

MODELLING CHAOS THEORY

Whatever the state of the world, as far as our requirements here are concerned, chaos theory implies six critical points:

1. organizational life is both predictable and unpredictable;
2. causal analysis is virtually impossible;
3. diversity rather than homogeneity is a more productive base;
4. self-organizing principles reduce the concern that anarchy may prevail over chaos;
5. individual action, in conjunction with the multiplier effect, concentrates responsibility at the lowest point: individuals;
6. scale-invariant properties and irreversibility are components of all chaotic organizations.

Let me now provide some detail for these claims.

1. Organizational life is both predictable and unpredictable

In complex systems it is impossible to predict the future position of any variable at a micro-level, even if there is a stability at the macro-level where 'strange attractors' exist to limit the extent of macro-change. The turbulent nature of events in complex systems, however, is not just unpredictable but has an alarming multiplier effect: in the most frequently quoted example, 'a butterfly stirring the air in Peking today can transform storm systems next month in New York' (Gleik, 1987: 8).

Ditto and Munakata (1995) reduce the 'dramatic' effect of a butterfly down to two days, which is a little unnerving. I had thought about chasing a dog sauntering past my window, but the thought of starting a hurricane in Tokyo on Thursday has worried me a lot.

However, despite the instability of weather systems, there are regular patterns underlying it. For instance, the weather has a consistency of temporal change which we know as the seasons. No single day's weather, at least in Britain, can be predicted because of the chaotic nature of the weather system, but we can be fairly certain that most days in January in London will be colder that most days in July in New York. This regularity underlying the irregular dynamic is referred to as a 'strange attractor'—it appears to set limits on the degree of chaos over time and appears to 'pull' the extremes back to the norm through time. In weather terms, we can expect storms to occur at certain periods of the year; although occasionally they will be both unusually ferocious and occur outside the normal stormy season, we would not expect them to get exponentially worse nor for all storms to disappear for ever. In other words, the system as a whole may be self-replicating, but the elements of the system are chaotic. At the level of humans this means that while the activities of any individual may appear to be random and chaotic, this does not mean that the activities of the group as a whole are consequently random and chaotic. On the contrary, to pick another example from nature, although the activities of each ant may appear random, the overall result is an extremely powerful social *organization* of ants. One implication of this is to assume that control systems need not be imposed from above but are, ultimately, self-constituted. I shall return to this later.

2. *Causal analysis is virtually impossible*

As a direct result of the above, analysing causal links within complex systems becomes virtually impossible because of the chaotic relationships that exist and the way that the initial conditions generate potentially large and unpredictable variations through time—we simply cannot trace the relationship between the butterfly's wings and the storm, and it is the relationships, not the things in themselves, that are critical.

One practical consequence of this lies in the critical role played by everyone in the chain of causality: unless each contribution is made in the direction and proportion required, the actual result will probably not match the required result. To effect the required result, therefore, means ensuring that each contribution has the motivation and capacity to act in the appropriate direction. The greater the symmetry between the requisite actions and ~~actual actions, the~~ more likely will it be ~~that the strategic intent is achieved. Since subordinates~~ and others usually have their own reasons for complying with the superodinate's requests (or not, as the case may be), the latter will have to provide local incentives to try and ensure some alignment between aim and result.

A second consequence is that strategy should not be about predicting the future—which is unpredictable by definition— but about devising methods and systems for handling the unexpected when it happens. In other words, about devolving power down to those who have to act immediately when the unexpected happens. As Stacey asserts: 'The new frame of reference exposes much of the received wisdom on strategic management to be a fantasy defence against anxiety, and points instead to the essential role of managers in creating the necessarily unstable conditions required for that effective learning and political interaction from which new strategic directions may or may not emerge' (1993: 11). This, of course, is similar to Mintzberg's and Waters's (1985) claim that strategies are necessarily emergent rather than deliberate, and implies that much of the work of managers, in planning the future, is merely a ruse designed to persuade others—and themselves— that they have control over something which is inherently uncontrollable (Thiétart and Forgues, 1995: 25).

3. Diversity rather than homogeneity is a more productive base

The chaotic nature of systems has implications for the way managers manage: those organizations that insist upon united cultures and the elimination of dissent are likely to make catastrophic errors in the long run, since they will be unable to react quickly enough to the inevitably chaotic changes in the system. Those organizations that have a shared goal, but not a unitary culture, are perhaps less likely to achieve short-term advances towards their goal, but are also less likely to make catastrophic errors by failing to respond to changed conditions. The practical ramifications of this are that programmes to instil strong corporate cultures are themselves problematic, and managers should, instead, be encouraging dissenting voices and counter-cultures (Pascale, 1990, 1994). 'Let a hundred flowers bloom' rather than 'bring on the clones' ought to be the password, because the emphasis shifts from top-down *control* to *self-organization*.

The connotation is that managers, who typically construct a multitude of rules to control complexity, should be generating a small number of interactive guidelines to facilitate complexity. For example, Caulkin (1995) recounts the story of Mike McMaster, Managing Director of Knowledge Based Development Ltd., who replaced the usual thick manual of rules concerning work with four short principles designed to support an increase in productivity at the construction site of an offshore oil platform.

This also shifts the concern from the problem of providing incentives for your (presumably unmotivated) subordinates to the problem of constructing organizations that facilitate the resolution of chaos by experimental self-organizing groups whose primary drive is linked to their *making a difference through personal contribution*. Of course, persuading people that they can make a difference through participating in self-organized units poses severe problems for those people who have developed work styles more suited to the execution of hierarchically inspired orders. But that is the point: it is relatively easy to rearrange the deck-chairs on the *Titanic*—but with what purpose?

4. *Self-organizing principles reduce the concern that anarchy may prevail over chaos*

There is an assumption in chaos theory that natural systems which are failing have to disintegrate before they can reintegrate into new formations. Conventional systems theory implies, first, that systems tend naturally to maintain a homeostasis, or dynamic equilibrium (Kast and Rosenzweig, 1970), and, second, that failing systems can be reinvigorated by incremental adjustments until the equilibrium is restored. However, it may be that an equilibrium is not what is required under the circumstances. That is, that the complex dynamics of the environment require an equally complex and dynamic organization if it is going to survive. It might, for example, be the case that an organization is trying to devolve responsibility and to empower subordinates to operate more independently. However, managers in this organization insist on retaining control. One strategy suggested by chaos theory would be to overload the recalcitrant manager to the point where it is physically impossible to retain control: perhaps by increasing the number of direct reports from a manageable 25 to an unmanageable 150. At some point the manager will simply be unable to remain in control and will have to allow the system to disintegrate so that it can readjust itself—self-organize—under the new conditions.

The chaotic reconstruction of organizations, therefore, implies experimental developments involving the entire organization, or, if this is practically impossible, representatives from all parts of the organization. Hence, we should not expect to see radical overhauls of organizations developed by the board of directors, nor by the senior managers, but by representatives from all groups: cleaners, secretarial staff, maintenance workers, sales representatives, shop-floor workers, managers, technicians, accounts staff, receptionists, telephonists, IT staff, and anybody else involved. If *all* these groups are represented, then not only will the generation of ideas be richer (though slower), but the ultimate agreement on where the organization is going is far more likely to be positively accepted than negatively acquiesced to, as it often is in most traditional organizations.

The consequences of relying on bottom-up developments need not be high risk. As Joynson and Forrester (1995) suggest, the solutions to most organizational problems are already known to the workers—but their bosses prevent them from implementing them. Nor need this imply that hierarchy should be stripped out of all organizations; since Weber's (see Grint,

1991: 108–11) original work, it has been clear that bureaucratic forms of organization are extremely effective and efficient in certain circumstances, in particular, under routine and stable conditions. The point is: should the entire organization be flattened, or should those elements that require flexibility to operate be freed from hierarchical subordination? One small example of this might be to consider the way that motivational systems (incentive pay and so on) are imposed from the top and assumed to be universally applicable. The assumption is that everyone is obviously motivated by the same thing (although this equally obviously varies with the particular scheme, to include money, time, promotion recognition, etc.), and therefore employees do not need to be asked what they are interested in, nor what motivates them; so who would dream of allowing employees to organize their own motivational scheme? The result is a patchwork of schemes across time and space that inevitably decay and are, at best, only marginally effective.

5. *Individual action, in conjunction with the multiplier effect, concentrates responsibility at the lowest point: individuals*

In the event, chaos is both ordered and disordered, depending upon which level you are concerned with. The achievement of any organizational objective only occurs through the activity of each and every organizational member. What they do may appear to be random at the individual level, but the ultimate result of the combination of activities may be the achievement of the organizational goal. Moreover, the significance of the butterfly effect should not be underestimated, since it suggests that even limited developments in one discrete area may, through the multiplier effect, result in major change. The achievement of goals is thus the result of the reconfiguration of networks of people, things, and ideas—the destruction of the old and the reconstruction of the new on a permanent basis. The challenge for managers, therefore, is to ensure that cultures and organizations do *not* ossify into homogeneous concrete, but remain sufficiently fluid for organizations to change. In effect, it may be that management's prime role is to compensate for the known tendency towards chaos by paying closer attention to individual discretion and/or by instituting systems that channel the organization towards greater stability through anti-chaotic procedures (see Gordon and Greenspan, 1994). Alternatively, one might want to consider the way a fortuitous initial inroad into a market may be multiplied to such an extent that other allegedly 'better' products are progressively driven out. For example, it can be argued that VHS is technologically inferior to Betamax, but that the former's initial—and initially marginal—superiority in the software market led to a ratchet-like increase in its sales over the latter. This positive 'swarming' behaviour is parallel to the kind of negative panic that sets in amongst armies which, for no clear reason, appear to be beaten by a similar sized and armed force, where an initial advantage of the latter instigates a catastrophic hysteria amongst the former—see Keegan's (1976) account of the rout of the French Imperial Guard at the battle of Waterloo. Another feature of this model is that the entry of a single competitor to the market may be sufficient to disturb the entire system. Levy (1994: 171), for example, suggests that Dell's mail-order computer strategy forced all the competitors into a major rethink. Dell, the computer manufacturer, forced all the competitors into a major rethink.

6. *Scale-invariant properties and irreversibility are components of all chaotic organizations*

Since, as the theory suggests, chaotic phenomena have scale-invariant properties of the kind best known as fractals, we should be able to see similar ordering properties at different levels of the same organization (Thiétart and Forgues, 1995: 21). Just as fractals look the same at whatever level one views them at, so we might suggest that the fluctuation in stock prices is similar whether we consider it on an hourly, daily, or yearly basis (Levy, 1994: 172). If the model holds good, then organizations should look remarkably familiar at all levels. However, it is also the case that even the minutest variation in conditions will generate differences across time, so it is unlikely that the organization will return to any prior state or condition. (This also has two major and hitherto unknown consequences: the chances of you repeating the same mistake twice are negligible, and the notion that we are doomed to repeat history if we do not know it is, as Henry Ford said, 'Bunk'. What, I wonder, are the chances of anyone repeating the same mistake in a history test? In (chaos) theory nil, but that strange attractor, otherwise known as getting the grade you need, seems to coerce individuals into not investigating this further.)

What are the implications of this approach for practising managers? What difference might chaos theory make to the way organizations operate? Let me consider answers to these questions by looking at both an internal and an external focus. In the former I want to consider how a chaos model of organization might be used to model and subsequently reconfigure the culture of an organization. In the latter I want to consider what a chaos model implies for the vexed issue of long-term planning and strategy.

CHAOS, CONFIGURATIONAL SYSTEMS, AND CULTURE

One of the problematic consequences of this peculiar combination of freedom and restraint, manifest in the strange attractors that inhibit completely random behaviour, is its possible effects upon patterns of intended change. If organizations are completely random in their behaviour, then any change programme is subject to the same issue: how can we change an organization from A to B when, first, it will probably never get to B and, second, if it does, it will be subject to precisely the same kind of vagaries that made A so unstable in the first place? What might this mean for an organization?

Svyantek and DeShon (1993) suggest that current developments in evolutionary theory, aligned with the implications of chaos theory, may be a way forward here. Assuming that organizational culture operates as a strange attractor, they suggest that long-term culture change is extremely problematic, irrespective of what appears to be short-term unpredictability and chaos. Borrowing from evolutionary theory, they suggest that genetic systems can be conceived in terms of two elements:

adaptive (externally focused) and configurational (internally focused). Adaptive systems are open to incremental change in response to competitive behaviour or environmental pressure, but these changes do not have significant impacts upon the individual. This acts as the chaotic and random element. On the other hand, configurational systems are composed of internally balanced gene complexes that are not open to environmental change, unless it is of the most extreme form, wherein the nature of the individual will change. For example, dogs all have the same configurational system, but different breeds have different adaptive systems: Dobermanns guard premises; sheepdogs guard sheep; and Pekinese—well, who knows what they are for. It is possible to develop new breeds of animal through cross-breed mating or gene manipulation (e.g. 'wolfnese' from cross-bred wolfhounds and Pekinese), but these are extremely rare and usually peter out (or at least fall over at lot). Gordon (1991) suggests that organizational cultures can similarly be divided into two elements, with the adaptive system concerned with how an organization competes for customers, and a configurational system based on how it treats its employees. We could go further than this to consider the configurational system itself as an organizational culture—what the organization *is*; while the adaptive system is what the organization *does* to survive: produce car parts, fly passengers, undertake health care, teach schoolchildren, breed Pekinese dogs with Giraffe-like legs, and so on.

In essence, then, the suggestion is that the strange attractor, or configurational system, which manifests itself in the recurrent patterns of organizational behaviour that make up organizational culture, acts as a powerful limit to the changes intended by some change programmes. At a political level, one might argue that the emergence of the Soviet Union from its original promise of a 'workers' state' to a totalitarian dictatorship merely demonstrates the significance of the prior Tsarist configurational system—where authoritarian control held sway for many centuries. At the business level, one might consider any number of organizations that profess to 'empower' their employees in the new participative culture, but which, in reality, are unable to make the necessary changes and slip back into the traditional pattern of authoritarian management. Indeed, one can go further than this to suggest that where organizations attempt change so radical that the boundaries of the strange attractor are broken, then one might expect to see them descend into the kind of disorder normally associated with the pejorative interpretation of the word 'chaos'. In the absence of a method for breaking the configurational system or the strange attractor of corporate culture, organizations might find it virtually impossible to change radically. Hence, most radical overhauls seem to be premised upon a pervasive and pernicious crisis. I will return to this in the next chapter. Organizations, therefore, have the ability to change their adaptive systems virtually at will—by expanding their portfolio of businesses from airline passengers to include record retailing, financial investment, and so on, as the Virgin Group has done during the 1990s, although it will probably retain its configurational system through the strange attractor, which persists in corporate culture, and which suggests that all Virgin enterprises have a core similarity. Naturally, each business and department will be slightly different, but this should not be at the expense of the core similarity. If it is, then we have a case of configurational breakdown, and a breakup of the organization is likely. It is also important to note that this approach suggests that attempts by management to change or impose a culture upon an organization are unlikely to succeed, though it may be that a founder has the necessary butterfly effect early on to impose his or her own configurational system.

How might this be deployed on the ground? How can we know what the boundaries of the configurational system or strange attractor look like? One approach might be to employ a consultant to undertake a cultural audit and provide an external expert opinion on the matter. But there is a problem: how does the consultant know what the strange attractors or configurational system might be? If the world is as fuzzy as I have implied, then expertise is a matter of trust rather than evidence. Unless we can generate the kind of data that allows us to pick out strange attractors—for instance daily temperatures to establish the limits of a region's weather—we appear to have reached an impasse. However, an essential element of chaos theory is the notion of self-organizing; perhaps if we employed the theory rather than simply observed it we may find a way through the impasse. One alternative approach, then, would be to require organizational members to describe their own view of the adaptive and configurational systems—to facilitate chaos theory reflexively by refusing to provide an authoritative top-down solution to the problem and getting the staff of the organization to come up with their own ideas. In this way it may be possible to expose not just what people think about an organization, and not just what they like and dislike, but also what they think are the most recalcitrant or inertial elements. It may be that the ideas that evolve from this exercise are inadequate to the task—but set against a backdrop where 75 per cent of change management fails we are hardly in a position to know that an alternative approach will definitely generate more utility.

Having established that we should involve as many people as possible in assessing what the current state of play is, and how it might be changed, the next stage is to develop a mechanism for compressing the inordinate complexity of any culture—and most organizations will probably have many—down to a more easily accessible form. At this point we can either begin to accumulate vast amounts of data from all concerned on an individual and quantitative basis, or we can again embody the principles of chaos theory by allowing teams to self-organize and generate their own assessments. Since chaos theory is not about random patterns but about complex patterns, we can also fix our own strange attractor in here by requiring the groups to develop their ideas in the form of metaphors for the organization rather than linguistic or numerical descriptions of it. In this way we can provide an easier route into the problem and keep some control over the costs. Let us assume that each team now produces four metaphors or symbols or images which represent (1) an image of the configurational system that embodies the beneficial elements of the organization; (2) an image of the configurational system that embodies the disadvantageous elements of the organization; (3) an image of the adaptive system that encompasses the beneficial aspects; and (4) an adaptive image encompassing the disadvantageous element. Precisely what counts as adaptive (externally facing and changeable) or configurational (internally facing and inertial) ought to be left to the teams involved, since their view on this is probably more accurate and useful than any outsiders. The example shown in Figure 3.1 summarizes one team's efforts from a recent exercise I conducted.

First, the configurational and positive element of this organization (a medium-sized manufacturing company) is represented by the team as an elephant, a solid, thoughtful,

Positive   Negative

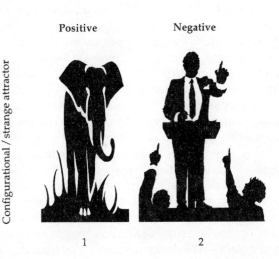

Configurational / strange attractor

1   2

Adaptive system

3   4

FIG. 3.1 Metaphors of Change

dependable, unstoppable, giant of a creature which looks after the members of the herd. It was certainly slow to react and had managed the employees in virtually the same way since time began. It was this very solidity in the face of an increasingly frenetic world that the employees most valued, and this is surely a warning against those who intend to apply draconian change across the board; for the configuration of this firm, as the team saw it, was the primary reason for remaining there and for reciprocating the elephant's loyalty.

On the other hand, the problem for the team with this company, at least in terms of how it handled these same members of the herd, was its dictatorial style, represented by the second, lecturing image. Here, the CEO appeared to dominate the managers, who in turn appeared to dominate the workforce. Although the team felt that there was much it could offer the company in terms of advice on how to run the organization, this advice was seldom if ever sought, and the consequence was an increasing resentment at having its voice ignored. This was especially significant in the general business context where many other firms were listening to their employees instead of shouting at them. Now, the problem lies in the assumption that this is part of the configurational scheme, that is, an area not easily changed because it is seen to be so ingrained as to be a necessary part of the system. The strategy for management then—assuming this is representative of the employees generally—is to begin to move away from the authoritarian mode without undermining the solidity of tradition that the employees respected. A rapid shift to empowerment, curiously, might not be what is required here, since the workforce might not accept that it was intended to overturn convention, and because managers themselves would probably resent any rapid ebbing of their power base.

The third image, jazz instruments, represents the team's assumptions about how the company operated with regard to its customers and products, this time its positive aspects. Here, the team regarded the improvization of jazz as a metaphor for the inventiveness with which the company operated, constantly developing new ideas, new models, and new ways of interacting with the market and customers—though always with the same instruments. On the other hand, the negative adaptive image of a butterfly is closely related to this, since it implies an inadequate level of concentration—as the company flits from one idea to the next, and from one management fashion to the next, without any apparent strategic plan or goal. I would assume that the strategy here is for the company to demonstrate its long-term plan more overtly to the teams, and to explain where the apparent shifts in policy and procedure fit with regards to this plan. To take a spatial metaphor, if the overall goal is visible then it is obvious why reaching the goal may require turning left, right, and even back on oneself to reach it; but if the goal is invisible then the wanderings appear meaningless and random, as the group appears to be buffeted by mere variations in the ground and weather.

The adaptive system, at least within this approach, is the easiest to change, and in the example shown here requires a more overt sharing of the strategic intent—both in terms of how the study is constructed and how it is reiterated. Since the adaptive system is unconstrained by strange attractors, rapid and radical changes of direction should not pose a danger to the organization. However, the same cannot be said for the configurational system, where the elephant and 'master' approach embodies significant strengths and weaknesses, and these are perceived to be different sides of the same coin, not alternative currencies. In this case the loyalty of the management might be compromised by too radical a change in the way the system operates internally (though this, of course, may be the intention of those instigating the change). In short, if the configurational system is perceived in the terms suggested here, then some methods of changing direction may be more suitable than others: elephants do change direction if you wave a firebrand in their face—but they do not forget or forgive who did it to them, and a metaphorical apple may be better in the long run.

CHAOS AND PLANNING

The second practical implication of using chaos theory relates more to the external world of the organization, in particular the problem of long-term planning and the level of requisite control deemed necessary to maintain direction.

Chaos theory asserts that the world is far more unstable, and unpredictably so, than most of us would like to believe. Although at the heart of contemporary chaos theory there *is* a long-term predictability, I want to consider the unpredictable aspects of the theory in this context. From ferry disasters to sports games, the final 'result' is the outcome of literally thousands of decisions and actions that cannot possibly be traced through any causal map. The strange attractor in sport might be the rules of the game, so that although 'anything might happen' in a game, in practice that 'anything' is restricted and constrained by certain precepts: no one knows the result of the game in advance, but it will be ascertained by the number of times a goal or basket or point is scored by each side. In management beyond sport the strange attractor is far less clear, and this means that strategic planning may be little more than an illusion. Some strategic goals may be achieved but, first, many more will not, and, second, the achievement of the strategy may well have been wholly fortuitous rather than the direct causal result of the original strategy.

Despite the development of strategic planning over the last few decades, fire-fighting still seems to be the preoccupation of most managers and executives, particularly in British companies. That even the best laid plans can come to grief through what appear to be insignificant contingencies can best be examined by taking four radically different examples of chaos, or non-linear dynamics, in action.

In the first case, the Japanese battle plan for controlling the Pacific during the Second World War came unstuck as a consequence of several unrelated problems that together led to their defeat at the battle of Midway. Thus, the Japanese were unaware that their secret code had been cracked by the Americans—though sending the American fleet out in precisely the right direction was fortuitous. The Japanese were also unaware that a simple typo in orders for the deployment of their submarine fleet sent them to the wrong location, allowing the US fleet to steam past unseen. They were also unfortunate in choosing an island for the refuelling of their reconnaissance planes that had, unbeknown to them, just been taken over by the Americans. When the invasion of Midway was under way, the Japanese carrier fleet was, by error, not given the necessary information concerning the type of American warships moving towards it, so it did not rearm with the requisite munitions in time to prevent the two squadrons of American fighter-bombers—both of which were independently lost—discovering its position and sinking three of the four carriers. The chaotic and unpredictable nature, not just of human error but of sheer chance too, facilitated the end of Japanese domination in the Pacific; no amount of strategic planning could have predicted, let alone controlled, this sequence of events (Luecke, 1994).

The second example stays with the management of war but takes us back to 13 September 1862, when the American Civil War hung in the balance. The Confederate armies, under Robert E. Lee, had just inflicted defeats on the Union at Richmond and Manassas, and now intended to destroy the Union army, under the command of George B. McClellan, and hence to win independence for the South. However, a copy of Lee's battle plan was discovered, by chance, by a Union soldier and delivered to McClellan, who, ever a cautious general, took so long to take advantage of the information that he failed to destroy Lee's divided army, although the information did prevent Lee from drawing McClellan into a trap. The resulting battle at Antietam involved more Union than Confederate casualties, but Lee's greatest opportunity to destroy a large part of the Union army had gone and never returned. As General Lee admitted afterwards, without the lost order, 'it was impossible to say that victory would have certainly resulted . . . but the loss of the dispatch changed the character of the campaign' (quoted in Sears, 1992: 210). Note here that this is not an example where chance determines what happens: chaos theory is not the equivalent of chance, because chance may be thought of as entirely random. Chaos theory suggests the world is random at the micro- or short-term level, but relatively predictable at the macro- or long-term level. Thus, the finding of the lost order introduces an element of chance into the war that has significant consequences, but it does not determine the results, because, in the longer term, McClellan's distaste for risk-taking and Lee's superior tactical ability—the equivalent strange attractors—enable the latter to make some form of recovery.

My third example is much shorter and significantly less vital for the development of world history. Back in England, some one hundred and thirty years on, a double-glazing company made an unfortunate error when it refused to return the deposit on a cancelled patio door. The customer turned out to be the editor of the *Sun*, a British national daily paper, and the eventual result of a media tirade against the company was that it was sold off to another party (Evans, 1989; quoted in Stacey, 1993: 13).

The final example is even more mundane and concerns the closure of the London Brick Company's brickworks in Ridgmont, UK, in 1981. Having been concerned about the level of pollution emitting from the works, and keen to ensure that any new plant was environmentally cleaner, the local council was suddenly faced not just with an issue over planning permission, but, as a result of the collapse of the brick market, with the possibility of closure and large-scale redundancies. The threat of complete closure was used by the company to persuade a subcommittee of the full council to recommend acceptance of the new plant without the environmental conditions previously required. In the end, the decision went in favour of the company because the opponents of the plan were one short of the number required to send the plan to the full council—which would, in all probability, have rejected the threat. The decision swung on the actions of one councillor, who, despite having been expected to resist the company plan, failed to vote against the plan because he had had to leave the meeting early. While the fate of the warring sides in the Pacific hung on the decisions of a few individuals, so too did the fate of the company (Levačić, 1983).

The 'moral' of all these tales relates to the chaotic links between phenomena and to the capacity for these links to be unpredictable in their effect: the effects may be disproportionately increased or they may simply fade away. Had the typo in the submarine orders not occurred at that particular point in the message, the submarine fleet may have moved to the correct position and the outcome of the battle of Midway may have been very different. Had the double glazing customer been a newspaper-seller rather than an editor, the company may still be owned by the original owners. Now, the question that chaos theory poses for managers is twofold: first, is it an accurate way to describe business and management, and, second, if it is, what are the most appropriate responses that managers can make? The notoriously high failure rate of both new and old businesses (not many of Peters's and Waterman's original Excellent Companies are still Excellent) suggests, if nothing else, that business may not be as controllable as traditional models assume. But this need not necessarily mean that managers are helpless before an environment which is so unpredictable that no amount of planning and no particular approach can cope with it.

If we consider popular approaches to individual planning, given some form of 'accident', we can see two extreme forms of reaction to chaos. First, individuals may abandon previously held plans on the assumption that 'one never knows' and therefore one should 'live for today'. Here, an assumed chaos suggests the complete abandonment of planning. On the other hand, one might want to plan more carefully in the future to ensure that such an accident will not recur. Here, chaos is not to be managed better than before—it is to be eliminated. When we map this on to management we can see the former being concerned with fire-fighting in the knowledge that the only predictable thing about business is its unpredictability. Alternatively, the strategic planning approach does the contrary— unless events are managed, chaos will prevail. Neither approach is self-evidently better than the other: permanent fire-fighting is not only exhausting, it also prevents the manager from looking above the fire to see if something else is more appropriate.

If we cannot predict and control behaviour, then clearly there are problems with conventional approaches to strategic management: notwithstanding 'the best laid plans of mice and men', chaos theory implies that the only way we could succeed at controlling the environment is by severing its links from all other environments and manning the boundaries to keep chaos out. But sealing oneself off from the outside world, while it may give you a breathing space and the illusion of control, simultaneously prevents you from monitoring that very same

world. As the Japanese found to their cost after the expulsion of
foreigners in the sixteenth century, control can be secured over
a local environment, but when the outside world eventually
breaks back in, as chaos theory implies it will, that environment may well find itself several generations of technical and
organizational development behind. Those companies that
take strategic planning and the control of chaos to their logical
end—by controlling the very environment which generates the
chaos in the first place—may find themselves isolated from
other environments, which ultimately engulf the chaos-free
'safe haven' established; the original Ford Model T system, or
IBM in the 1980s, would both be classic examples of this. So, if
the local environment *should* not be closed off, does this simply
mean that managers should fire-fight, since this appears to be
a good way to manage the borders of chaos?

Perhaps we should go back a step and consider *why* managers fire-fight. Is it because this is a constructive way to manage the inevitable chaos, or because the desire to appear 'busy',
and the failure to delegate decision-taking as far as possible,
ensures that managers are engaged not so much in fire-fighting
but in checking to see whether there is a fire, in evaluating its
seriousness, giving subordinates the go-ahead to fight it, al-
locating the necessary resources, watching them do it, and
checking that the flames are out. In other words, managers
don't so much fight the fires as monitor others doing it. Assuming that fires are a natural and spontaneous result of the chaos
system, then clearly some fire-fighting has to occur. Indeed,
using a gardening analogy, there are some forms of plant
whose development is considerably enhanced by fire. Fire-
fighting, then, is not so much a problem to be resolved by more
rigid and rational strategic planning but something that should
be executed by those nearest to the fire itself—the workers on
the shop-floor, the staff on the telephone, and so on. Managers,
in this perspective, should seldom be directly involved in fire-
fighting, but they should be directly engaged in ensuring that
the fires spontaneously generated by a chaos system provide
the maximum opportunities for *learning*. Such learning may
occur through fire-fighting, or through methods for fire-sup-
pression, or anything else, but the point is that it is the learning
opportunities that management has to maximize if the organ-

ization is to develop, rather than allow to deteriorate, by and through self-organizing.

Some interpretations of the significance of this self-organizing element in chaos theory generate radical, indeed, anarchic, approaches to organizations. For example, a conference by the Western States Health Advisory Commission for the Advancement of Women's Health, and another for Intermountain Health Care Laboratory Services, both held in Utah in 1993, began without expert speakers, without central control, and with as many voices as was possible to get into the venue. The consequence, according to the co-ordinators, was a large dose of frustration and anger followed by constructive self-organization and the development of a consensus on the way forward (Prather and Lazar, 1994).

Other interpretations of spontaneous self-organization can be premised upon a much simpler policy of letting the employees off the managerial leash to get on with the jobs they know more about than anyone else. For instance, as Sid Joynson (Joynson and Forrester, 1995) suggests, if the workforce were guaranteed that any improvements they made would not lead to redundancies, most British firms, at least, could probably become between 25 and 50 per cent more effective without spending any money. But for this to occur managers have to slough off their assumption that the absence of (managerial) control leads to chaos in an anarchic sense, and adopt the idea that lifting the lid leads to the self-organizing element of chaos. In effect, that chaos is not the random sequence of unrelated ideas, but an environment constrained by patterns that will emerge *if* they are allowed to emerge and *if* the general desired direction of the organization is both clear to, and clearly accepted by, the workforce.

Chaos theory, therefore, has implications for the very idea of strategic management, visions, missions, corporate culture, and all the rest of the contemporary buzz-words. However, let me summarize the implications here by distinguishing between the way our assumptions about the outside world lead to very different methods for managing organizations. In Figure 3.2, box 3, the assumption that the environment is ordered leads to an approach that configures fire-fighting as a threat, a problem to be solved—hence it implies nothing about

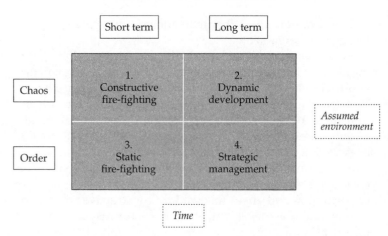

FIG. 3.2   Chaos and Strategy

learning from the fires, merely attempting to douse them. On the other hand, in box 1, the chaos model regards fires as an opportunity to learn—hence it becomes a constructive experience. In the longer term, a controlled environment, as in box 4, facilitates long-term strategic planning, safe in the knowledge that an effective plan, in and of itself, secures that control. For chaos models (box 2), however, the environment cannot and indeed *should not* be controlled, since the chaotic boundary is the leading edge for learning: no chaos—no learning—no learning—no advance. Obviously I have painted the division in very stark terms here, but the point I am trying to make requires managers to think long and hard about what it is they do and why they do what they do, and whether the implications of chaos theory have any relevance for them.

CONCLUSION

This chapter has considered the utility of chaos theory to management. It began by exploring the elements of the theory and in particular the six aspects that I take to be critical: that organizational life is both predictable and unpredictable; that causal analysis is virtually impossible; that diversity rather than homogeneity is a more productive base; that self-organizing principles reduce the concern that anarchy may prevail over chaos; that individual action, in conjunction with the multiplier effect, concentrates responsibility at the lowest point: individuals; and that scale-invariant properties and irreversibility are components of all chaotic organizations.

Rather than examine all these elements in detail, the chapter then considered two particular aspects: first, the role of the strange attractor in explaining the limits to organizational culture change and, second, the role of chance and its relevance for strategic planning. I have suggested that chaos theory does have serious ramifications for the way managers manage, especially in terms of the hierarchical and authoritarian manner in which many traditional organizations are run. If chaos theory does indeed resemble the world rather more closely than systems theory, then we should expect those organizations that are the most chaotic to be the ones that survive over the long term. Since very few organizations, at least very few business organizations, do indeed survive in their original form over the time frame of an average human, it might suggest either that not enough managers have taken the message of chaos to heart, or they are themselves impaled upon the horns of a strange attractor, despite their best intentions, or that something else is busily gnawing away at their carapaces. Now that we have some idea about the significance of fashions in change, and some understanding about the possible limits to change, I want to consider in the next chapter whether an organization can change by concentrating its resources upon the commitment of its members—and whether this is advisable.

4

Managing Change Through Commitment: *Autistic, New Model, or Pandorian Organization?*

> After Prometheus had defied Zeus and given fire to hu-
> manity, Zeus sent Pandora with a jar or box to trick
> Epimetheus, the brother of Prometheus. Pandora was for-
> bidden to open the jar but, after marrying Epimetheus,
> she opened the top and from it escaped the evils that
> plagued the world ever after: sickness, age, sin and death.
> The very last thing to emerge from the box was Hope.

INTRODUCTION

THREE things stand out in considering management in the
1990s: the colossal efforts made to change the way organizations operate, the astonishing degree of failure that accom-
panies all but a handful of such attempts, and the radical
aversion to risk-taking that appears to typify most organizations. If the rejection rate of organizational change was repli-
cated amongst organ transplants, surely most attempts to
change would have been prohibited long ago. One might think
that the high degree of failure has provided us with a veritable
mountain of data to understand the causes; this is probably
right. One might also think that the data mountain enables us
to predict a successful route to change; this is probably wrong:
we know why change goes wrong, but we find it extraordinarily difficult to make changes work.

The problem of change is especially significant now, because, as we saw in the previous chapters, management and
organizations in the Western World appear to be in a state of
constant turmoil, as change follows change in an ever more

frenetic attempt to reverse what it took two centuries to construct. The traditional methods of organizing business, including public services, no longer seem viable to staunch the haemorrhaging of industry to leaner and meaner overseas competitors. This chapter considers the general inability of organizations to transform themselves successfully. Despite all the attempts by organizations, both public and private, to change by increasing levels of risk-taking by managers, in response to the perceived changes in the market-place, the paradox is that there is little evidence that managers are increasing their risk-taking. Even when chief executives publicly exhort their managers to take risks ('if you are not making mistakes you are not learning'), the shift from 'fail-safe' management to 'safe-to-fail' management appears not to have happened in any major way (Pascale, 1994; Stacey, 1992).

It is possible that organizations are actually autistic; in other words, organizations, or rather their leaders, are simply unable or unwilling to listen to what others are saying to them, so that their strategic intentions are rolled out irrespective of the advice that is being offered to them. For instance, one could argue that IBM went through a phase of being an autistic organization, as its market share crumbled and its leadership continued to deploy the failing strategy despite internal and external criticism and advice that the company was going in the wrong direction. One might even consider wide-scale elements of British industry as a whole as being autistic in its failure to listen to advice. For example, the poverty of British manufacturing management (Britain is now ranked 23rd in the 1996 *World Competitiveness Report*) might be related to the poverty of its starting salaries for graduate managers compared to the kind of sums available to graduates entering a career in finance or consultancy. In 1996, for instance, recruiters from six of London's top merchant banks (including Goldman Sachs, Merrill Lynch, and Morgan Stanley) increased their graduate starting salary to £50,000 and their MBA starting salary to £78,000; average graduate salaries at the time in the UK were just £14,000 (*Guardian*, 16 November 1996). One consequence of this is that British manufacturing then has to hire in the expensive consultants whom it could have had as managers with better salaries. Since the problem of elite students avoiding manufacturing careers has existed since the start of the industrial revolution—and since the concern about it has lasted almost as long (see Grint, 1995b: 15–44)—we might wonder whether autistic organizations are a national institution rather than an aberrant and unusual problem.

On the other hand, perhaps the issue is not one of failing to *listen* but rather more one of failing to *learn*. If organizations are ordered in such a way that all mistakes lead automatically to the punishment of the mistake-maker, then individuals find ways, not of avoiding mistakes, but of hiding them. Thus, risk-avoidance becomes a career-protection strategy for those involved in decision-making (Buchanan and Storey, 1995). The result is what Dearlove (1993), calls 'The-sweep-it-under-the-carpet school of management', and the consequence is that any potential learning that the organization can drive from an error is lost—as represented in Figure 4.1. The contrary process

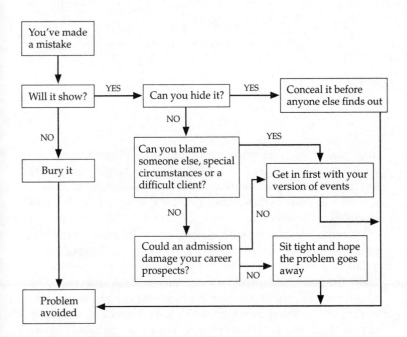

FIG. 4.1   The Sweep-it-Under-the-Carpet School of Management
Source: Des Dearlove (1993: 8)

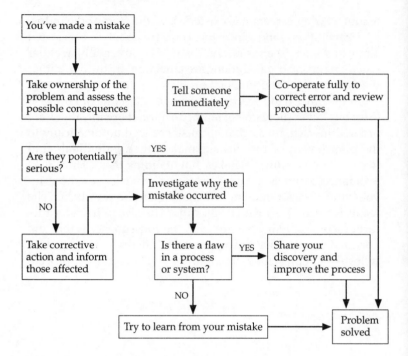

FIG. 4.2   The Learning Organization
Source: Des Dearlove (1993: 8)

implies that learning requires organizations to learn from individual mistakes; indeed, it suggests that even *individual* learning from his or her individual mistake is inadequate because it still fails to inhibit others from making the same mistake. This model is represented in Figure 4.2.

Without organizational learning, organizational change is virtually impossible. It is this loss of learning through risk-avoidance that is captured in the plaque on the wall of Ed Land (founder and president of Polaroid): 'A mistake is an event, the full benefit of which has not yet been turned to your advantage' (quoted in Senge, 1990: 154). However, since it is apparent to most managers that failure is punished more harshly than success is rewarded, the most appropriate career strategy is to avoid 'mistakes' rather than 'turn them to your advantage'. In the words of one anonymous executive involved in change:

[W]e mustn't get it wrong. If it doesn't go right there is a tendency to fix the blame on others ... people operate almost in fear, that it is better not to be entrepreneurial because that way we won't get it wrong ... There are some cult figures. The impression that I would have in some cases, would be that they owe their success more to their astuteness in avoiding blame and taking credit where things go right.

Or in the words of a colleague of this executive:

It seems to me that the most sensible thing to be in these circumstances is risk-adverse in the current circumstances. It would be stupid to be anything else ... The last thing we need are some creative ideas that lose us a lot of money. We can't afford to take risks.

We might call this politically inspired aversion to change 'active immunity', since, like its medical counterpart, it is a conscious response to the threat of the risk 'virus' and is extraordinarily difficult to overcome.

A second form of explanation lies not in the individually rational, and politically inspired, behaviour of individuals seeking to avoid the high level of flak from above, but in the culturally embedded distaste for all forms of overt conflict—despite the evidence which suggests that intentional conflict, and constructive response, may prove beneficial to the organization in the long term (Pascale, 1990, 1994). Under this form we might consider organizational *systems* that reduce risk-taking: for example, a procedure requiring all decisions to be vetted at the top, irrespective of their significance. We might call this form of risk-avoidance 'passive immunity'. In the biological case passive immunity is passed on through the mother's placenta and milk, and this we could take as a crude analogy to the invisible but pernicious resistance to the risk 'virus' that operates as a default preference for the status quo. As another example, the relatively limited success of BPR during the 1990s, as just the latest management fad to sweep through the business world, can itself be explained to some degree by the extent to which senior managers systematically—and consistently—back away from such radical change when any substantial degree of resistance is experienced

(Grint, 1994; Grint and Willcocks, 1995, 1997). As a consequence, many companies appear to be making radical statements about change, but in practice everyone knows that they are unwilling to face the harsh realities of increased competition, and senior management lacks the political will to risk radical change.

Argyris (1992) has argued that the cause of such risk-avoidance lies in what he terms 'organizational defence routines'. These are routinized patterns of behaviour in which potentially threatening or embarrassing situations are overcome by the mutual—and skilful—enactment of avoidance and defensive strategies, such that conflict is avoided or displaced but mutual or organizational learning is consequently lost. Argyris asserts that some of this can be explained by the paradoxical nature of managerial commands such as 'You are running the show, however . . .'. But even when commands appear to be clear it still seems that a yawning gap often exists between the command and the execution. One reason may well be that the culture of the organization is itself antipathetic to all forms of change, or at least to risk.

A third explanation for the paradox may be that although both risk and reward are usually perceived to be individual phenomena, management is essentially a social, or rather a political, accomplishment (Grint, 1995b). Relatedly, what counts as 'a risk', and how the success or failure of the action is assessed and allocated to the person deemed to be responsible, appears to be a consequence of the powerful accounts of leaders rather than self-evident fact. In effect, although success and failure in organizations is invariably a collective achievement, there are strong tendencies, especially within Western cultures, to apportion responsibility at the level of the individual. Since managers rely upon each other and their subordinates to achieve anything, the problem of risk-taking is refracted through this binary prism of collective accomplishment but individual responsibility. The result, then, is not just that managers are rationally protective of their careers (though this fails to explain why any risks are taken), nor even that the organizational defence routines inhibit risk-taking (since conflict avoidance may support it), but that the cultural configuration of management and risk-taking operates to discourage risk-taking and to encourage blame-avoidance and success-ownership after action is sanctioned as 'risky'. The issue, therefore, is that of assessing how actions or prospective actions come to be construed as 'risky', and of evaluating the political machinations by which collective action is converted into individual responsibility. Under these circumstances the likelihood of radical organizational change being successful seems minimal. We should also probably be more concerned with, for example, the significance of the organizational equivalent of 'urban legends' in which certain individuals' actions are held to embody powerful group cultures: morality tales of office heroes and villains, rather than rational analysis of the risk–reward trade-off, may be the more heuristic way of explaining why risk-aversion appears to be such an endemic part of management, and why this impedes organizational change. But since there clearly are occasions when high-risk strategies are successfully enacted, can we learn from the success of change rather than from its failure?

In the next section I suggest that we could learn from a historical juncture that is heavy with contemporary resonances: the development in 1645 of the English New Model Army (NMA). It was the NMA which, above all, turned the tide of the English Civil War against the Royalists, and I consider the extent to which contemporary developments in organizations—which I have called the New Model Organizations (NMO)—are beginning to embody some of the elements of the NMA. I then want to pursue the issue of change by focusing upon another contemporary fuzzy approach—actor-network theory (ANT)—and consider the extent to which this explains the practical failures that accompany most attempts to manage change. In short, can ANT—an esoteric sociological theory that eschews the apparent division between humans and 'things' in favour of a blurring of all boundaries—help organizations manage risks and change successfully? First, however, let us go back over 350 years to consider whether a successful change in seventeenth-century England can provide hints to our future journey.

THE NEW MODEL ARMY

When King Charles I raised his standard in England in 1642, and his parliamentary opponents began to counter-organize and legitimate their call to what Charles considered a 'rebellion', their demands embraced claims to political rights that eventually led from a movement seeking constitutional limits to the royal prerogative to a republican constitution and beyond to a (male-based) democratic society. The Pandora's box that had opened up began a conflict over the legitimate right of rulers over the ruled that had previously been restricted by the dead weight of tradition. From the severance of what some saw as Charles's absolutist crown from the parliamentary body to the absolute severance of Charles's crown from his own body was a step that few, outside Zeus, may have foreseen.

In 1644 it became obvious to many on the parliamentary side that their army did not have the capability to defeat the royalists (see Gentles, 1991, 1992, for a full account of these activities). A year after the victory at Marston Moor, the parliamentary forces had suffered defeats at Roundway Down and Cropredy Bridge, and the leaders of the main army, the Eastern Association (under the Earls of Manchester and Essex), appeared unwilling and unable to achieve victory over Charles I. The parliamentary hawks recognized that all was lost unless a major change in course was enacted, involving very high levels of risk, personal and political. They decided to change both the leaders and the organization of the army by issuing a Self-Denying Ordinance in April 1645, which prevented any member of the Houses of Parliament from holding office in the army for the duration of the war. In effect, it removed the conservative old guard and replaced it with Fairfax, Cromwell, and Ireton. Second, the hawks funded the army on a different—and for once efficient and effective—basis for the first time, paying the soldiers on time and focusing the resources of London on the New Model Army, as it became known. The third development went beyond the leadership and resources to centre on commitment. The English Civil War had, hitherto, not been fought by political zealots but by soldiers whose loyalties lay as much with whoever paid more reliably and appeared more successful as with anything else. However, by this time the religious fervour that a minority of parliamentarians had always had began to spread rapidly and radically. Four of the five new generals were devout Puritans (Fairfax, Cromwell, Ireton and Skippon—only Hammond remained uncommitted), and a high proportion of the junior officers also appear to have been driven by the new millenarian streak that undergirded the Puritans. With regular religious sermons and Bible study, and fasting before battle an increasingly common event, the NMA began to shape up as a different form of fighting unit. It became known as 'The Praying Army' and, at least for the duration of the war, fought within a strict moral and exacting personal code of conduct: blasphemers were bored through the tongue with a red hot poker, drunkards were forced to ride a wooden horse, and sexual offenders were whipped and cashiered. A powerful egalitarian streak began to emerge from the NMA, as evidenced by the General Council of the Army in 1647, which was composed of elected representatives from each regiment and from which emerged an attempt to write a new and more democratic constitution for the country: 'The Agreement of the People'. The zealots of the NMA also became convinced that they were undertaking God's work on earth and that revolutionary events were about to unfold which would herald the second coming of Christ. As Gentles argues:

These creeds enabled the soldiers to overcome their anxiety about their social origins, and their fear about challenging their anointed king. They liberated them psychologically, transformed them into men of iron, endowed them with a ruthlessness, and furnished them with invincible belief that in turning their own society upside down . . . they were performing the will of God. (1992: 118–19)

In short, the very high personal risks shouldered by all the 'rebels' could be dramatically reduced by placing their actions in the context of a movement ordained by God.

The first major battle that the NMA was involved in was at Naseby in 1645, when 5,000 royalists were captured or killed as opposed to 150 NMA casualties, thanks to the formers' incompetence as much as anything done by the latter. This was interpreted by the NMA as an obvious sign from God as to the righteousness of their cause. After Charles had escaped from parliamentary hands and initiated the Second Civil War, the leaders of the NMA, having defeated him again at Preston, fasted for three days before calling for Charles, 'that man of blood', to be held to account; he was (Gentles, 1991: 99). The rest, as they say, is history.

The successful management of change in this episode required three related developments: leadership, commitment, and resources—and all three were premised upon a very high level of risk-taking. The issue of leadership is covered in the following chapter, and I will, therefore, leave most discussion of it until then. However, most leadership books, indeed most writings on the management of change, suggest that the only real problems are to do with the 'people issues'. The issue of resources is an area of critical, yet self-evident, importance. Without money and material resources there is little that can be achieved, but even with it there is still no guarantee of successful change. Resources, then, might be considered in Herzberg's (1966) terms as a hygiene factor—a preconditional state for anything to occur, but insufficient in and of themselves. Take, for instance, a list of the top ten change management risk factors drawn from a leading consultancy group, and applied to the case of the *Titanic*, as shown in Figure 4.3. The change plan will probably fail if one or more of the factors is omitted.

The likelihood of this party of *Titanic* survivors reaching the island is clearly dependent on the resources—no boat means no survival. However, the actual process of achieving the jour-

Top ten critical change issues	Translated for the *Titanic*
An accepted need to change	We all know this boat cannot sink
A viable vision/alternative state	There is a tropical island nearby
Change agents in place	The bosun and ship's officers are keen
Sponsorship from above	Captain's supportive (he's in the lifeboat)
A realistic scale and pace of the change	It's 2 days rowing but we must start now
An integrated transition programme	Some short straws are on board
A symbolic end to the status quo	The captain has dumped his hat
A plan for likely resistance	Keel hauling ropes on board
Constant advocacy	*We* will keep encouraging *you* to row
A locally owned benefits plan	Once there, we will share the treasure

FIG. 4.3 Top ten critical change issues

ney is highly contingent on generating a high level of commitment on the part of the passengers by the leadership. In effect, this plan is premised upon the humans, not on the technology or non-humans. Of course a boat is essential, but this is not the real problem so let us concentrate on the 'people issue'. In the NMA case, this would imply acknowledging that the resources (weapons, money, food, transport, etc.) are important, but we only need to have these in place—once this is achieved, we do not need to worry about them. Instead (and remembering that we are side-stepping the issue of leadership until the next chapter), the issue of commitment is critical. Let us first assess the degree to which commitment exists in organizations.

ORGANIZATIONAL COMMITMENT AND THE NEW MODEL ORGANIZATION

The significance of self-belief in the righteousness of one's cause, and, probably equally important, the assumption that one's actions were either predestined by God or the inevitable result of circumstances beyond one's control, appears to play an important part in the drive to power and action by many people, leaders and led alike (see Grint, 1995b: 210–31). For the New Model Army, 'the warfare of heaven' (Gentles, 1992: 105) appears to have driven it well beyond the limits reached by the royalist armies, and if the majority of the rest of the civilian population was unimpressed by such claims to godliness this was interpreted as being precisely what the Bible had predicted for the chosen *few*. Not only did Cromwell proclaim Naseby to have been 'none other but the hand of God' (quoted in Gentles, 1992: 93), but a large proportion of the rank and file seems to have been similarly entranced by the way God appeared to move with them, and against the king.

It was also what the Vietnamese called aligning oneself with the 'Mandate of Heaven'. This was not necessarily to accept and support any particular political position or interest, but to recognize what was inevitable and to avoid resisting that which could not be resisted. Just as it was futile for the grass to resist the wind, so it was futile to resist whatever heaven mandated. Of course, what exactly heaven required was a difficult question, but just as the NMA took its victories as manifestations of righteousness, so, too, many Vietnamese seem to have taken the defeat of the Americans as predestined (Fitzgerald, 1972: 3–31); commitment was deemed to be more significant than advanced technology.

The search for a level of commitment that would release the 'latent talent' apparently stored up in organizations is something that many have pursued since the idea was first mooted during the Hawthorne experiments in the 1930s into working conditions and productivity (Grint, 1991: 123–6). Here, it appeared that ordinary workers could perform productivity miracles under certain circumstances. The trouble was that, unlike F. W. Taylor's assumption, these miracles did not appear to be explained by conventional scientific procedures. Scientific managers could not delineate the most successful way of producing something and simply tell the workers to get on with it, albeit with economic incentives. Instead, it seemed that workers would only perform productivity miracles when they felt like it; that is, when they interpreted the circumstances as being suitable for miracle efforts. Perhaps these were when they were allowed to work in small groups without coercive supervision—as the Hawthorne experimenters suggested—or perhaps effort only radically increased when the conditions were extreme. Indeed, much of our knowledge about the significance of teams is derived directly or indirectly through research undertaken either during periods of war or for the selection and training of soldiers. Thus, much of the early US research on the motivation of troops under fire suggested that they did not fight for 'great causes' but for their comrades in arms (Holmes, 1987; Grint, 1995b: 132). Hence, one way of inducing high levels of commitment was deemed to lie in the construction of work groups that mirrored fighting units in their size and responsibility: the workers may not work hard for the company or boss, but they were not going to let their colleagues down.

The efforts of people under conditions of crisis appeared to support this—but how could the effort level be maintained in the absence of a crisis? What happened if the situation implied that no amount of increased effort could realize the goal? Persuading soldiers in the NMA that they could defeat the king, and persuading Vietnamese Communists that they could defeat the American forces, provides us with examples of the significance of commitment that defies the 'logic of the situation'. When we consider business applications it has been taken for granted for several years that Japanese success is premised upon a level of commitment from Japanese employees that others, especially in the West, can only imagine (see Grint, 1993a).

Where technological advantages provided the competitive edge for most Western organizations for the most part of the industrial era, this no longer seems sufficient. Now, to quote the phrase, 'People are our most important asset' (though it's difficult to remember seeing an annual account that lists people amongst the assets, let alone tries to put a value on them). Organizational commitment, then, is seen as the new panacea for managerial problems and low levels of productivity.

Historically, this is to overturn over two centuries of tradition: workers were not required to think but to do, just as F. W. Taylor split superordinate thinking from subordinate execution, so the commitment of employees was neither sought nor acquired. Virtually from the beginning of the industrial revolution the 'cash nexus' has been the primary, if not the only, link between management and the workforce. Under this approach employee commitment is structured within a competitive market environment where all involved in the employment relationship are free to sever their economic relationships: employer commitment to employee is based upon the continuation of profitable enterprise, while the employee only remains committed to the employer as long as conditions remain preferential to anywhere else. But since the late 1970s the increasing threat from the Pacific Rim, especially Japan, has been explained as a consequence of greater organizational commitment on the part of the employees (though this too is now under threat).

Most recent developments in the restructuring of organizations to increase the level of organizational commitment have involved concentrating on issues of 'ownership'—though not usually legal ownership—in which employees are encouraged to take more responsibility for, and control over, certain forms of processes. A veritable raft of alternative ideas has emerged, such that organizations that are not involved in 'empowerment', 'organizational culture', 'joint working parties', 'delayering', 'teamworking', 'business process activities', 'customer focused lean systems'—and so on and so forth *ad infinitum*—are perceived as being tardy, unhealthy, old-fashioned, and, more generally, doomed. For the sake of convenience, I will refer to this conjunction of disparate forms as the attempt to generate the 'New Model Organization' (NMO). The NMO, theoretically at least, implies some of the fervour behind the NMA and, like its predecessor, involves—again in theory—a new form of leadership, a higher level of resources devoted to supporting the alternative structure, and a high level of commitment from leaders and led. Model is the operative word here, because there is considerable doubt as to whether the model remains at the level of rhetoric only, and whether the intent behind it is disingenuous.

But where does this notion of organizational commitment spring from—assuming it does not have the religious undertones that inspired the NMA, does it develop from some notion of organizational ownership or organizational citizenship?

Marshall's (1950) evolutionary model of the rise of citizenship is useful here, suggesting, as it does, that citizenship has occurred (at least in Britain) in three distinct waves:

1. Legal Citizenship: that is, freedom of thought and speech and equality before the law, arose in the eighteenth century.
2. Political Citizenship: that is, the right to participate in the exercise of political power, arose in the nineteenth century.
3. Social Citizenship: that is, the right to a minimum standard of social and economic welfare, arose in the twentieth century.

The development of the rhetoric of empowerment could be taken to be the beginning of the fourth wave: Organizational Citizenship. Organizational Citizenship implies the rights that are already embodied in the current organizational rhetoric. In other words, this is not a hair-brained extremist plot to overthrow management's right to manage but a method of enhancing corporate loyalty—and therefore corporate performance—that has been developed by managers and management consultants, not by trade-unionists or their fellow-travellers.

We may also want to add in here that a necessary precondition of the development of any form of citizenship appears to be what Rustow (1970) called 'a hot family feud'. This is a condition of political stalemate between two or more interest groups which (1) cannot continue without tearing the entire society/organization apart, and (2) does not appear to be leading to the elimination of one or other of the parties. The agreement to compromise is therefore premised upon a utilitarian realization—not that compromise is good, but that compromise is better than the elimination of both sides through continuing attrition. Whether the compromise involves a new approach to working with trade unions, as in Rover, or an approach that does not recognize trade unions, as in Unipart, is secondary to the commitment to a new way of working.

In the case of organizational citizenship, the agreement to pursue a different path comes after decades of an approach conventionally known as 'them' and 'us', or class struggle, or whatever you like to call it, which left neither side in complete control nor in a position to expect complete control in the near future. Organizational citizenship, for managers, therefore, may appear as a means for securing the social integration of the shop- and office-floor into the body of the organization. For the shop- and office-floor, organizational citizenship may become a mechanism for securing the right to participate in the running of the organization—at some level.

In the recent academic literature the attempt by management to move into a new relationship with their employees has generated a divided response between those who see it as a hypocritical attempt to screw the workforce in a different, and rather more subtle, way than before; and those who see it as a real attempt to change the basis of the relationship for good— in both senses of the word. But what evidence do we have for assessing whether the NMO has carried with it a high level of organizational commitment? As ever, this is very difficult to say, since we know relatively little about organizations that fit into the NMO approach; indeed we know little about the nature of commitment generally, so let us proceed by considering this first.

THE NATURE OF ORGANIZATIONAL COMMITMENT

Figure 4.4 considers a typology of ways in which to explore the nature of commitment (see Held, 1987: 182). It should be self-evident that the move down the list is one that incorporates both a temporal dimension and a humanistic prescription that resonates with contemporary managerial rhetoric. Thus, one could see a development from slavery at the top, through commitment based on tradition throughout the Middle Ages, through commitment rooted in exhaustion during the industrial revolution, via the absence of any viable alternative until the Russian Revolution, through economic incentives for the most part of this century, and up until the contemporary development of organizations that resemble churches in their requirements for adherence to the (normative) faith.

But the data suggests that there is little agreement about the stage we are currently at or the direction we are likely to move in. The most recent and systematic data on the nature of commitment derives from surveys and case studies carried out by Kessler and Undy (1996) in association with the Institute of

---

Coercion (no choice available)

  Tradition (always been so)

    Apathy (no energy to do otherwise)

      Pragmatic Acquiescence (cannot imagine alternative)

        Instrumental Acquiescence (advantageous)

          Normative Agreement (right and proper)

FIG. 4.4   Forms of acceptance

Personnel Directors. This survey of over 1,000 people, undertaken in 1995, generates a sample with the following characteristics:

- 7% upper management
- 26% middle management
- 12% lower management
- 18% supervisors
- 37% shop-floor/office workers

Beyond the concern that the sample may overemphasize the proportion of managers, the results suggest that one of the critical factors in the successful management of change—the commitment of the shop-floor—is missing, or at least minimally present. In particular, the loyalty of the shop-floor or office-floor worker is generally lower than that of their superiors, and usually less than half the workforce is happy with/loyal to/trusting in/committed to/their organization. All these preconditions for successful change seem to correlate with status. For example, in Figure 4.5, on the basic attitudes to

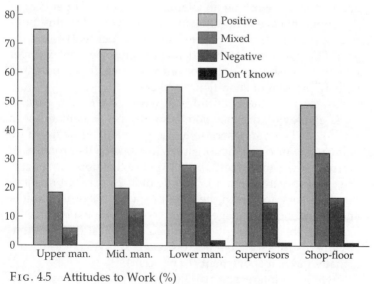

FIG. 4.5   Attitudes to Work (%)
Source: Kessler and Undy (1996)

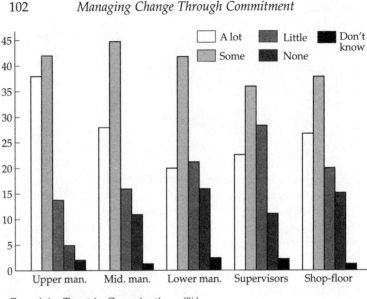

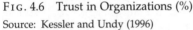

FIG. 4.6   Trust in Organizations (%)
Source: Kessler and Undy (1996)

work (measured by answers to a question concerning 'feelings about going to work on an average day'), over 74 per cent of the upper management 'Look forward to work'; but this 'positive' approach contrasts with just under (49 per cent) half of the shop-floor workers. On the other hand, only 6 per cent of upper managers 'wish they didn't have to go' (negative), compared with 17 per cent of shop-floor workers.

Moving from basic attitudes to work, to consider trust in one's employing organization, a similar result is manifest in Figure 4.6. Here, in response to the question, 'How much do you trust your company/organization to keep its promises to you and other employees?', over 38 per cent of upper managers trust their organization a lot, while only 27 per cent of shop-floor workers do. Given the recent experiences of the middle and lower end of management, it should not be a surprise to learn that the most sceptical people are not just the traditionally distrustful shop-floor and office workers (15 per cent), but actually lower management (16 per cent).

There is an interesting parallel here with Weber's work on Calvinism and fatalism, since he argues that the uncertainty derived from the worry over whether one was 'saved' or 'damned' generated a particular work ethic, which facil-itated—but did not directly cause—industrial capitalism; in short, the nervous Calvinists looked to material success as a 'sign' of 'grace', but, since they were also aesthetic, they could not consume the fruits of their labour and had, instead, to reinvest them. Thus, to force Weber into a corner, and do him a great disservice, was born modern capitalism. However, it also undermined the very church that spawned it. One parallel here is with Hegel's belief that civilizations are under-mined by an untrammelled development of their founding principles. Or, in terms of leadership or businesses, one could argue that many leaders and businesses are toppled by the very strengths that originally ensured their success; hubris—as Greek tragedies so often remind us—is a constant threat to the winners in life. Another parallel here is where the move to-wards 'employability'—that is, the uncertainty of a short-term contract, in place of long-term certainty—undermines the very organizational commitment that the cultural change traditions have been trying to install for over a decade.

The final figure from the survey that I want to consider is related to trust but implies a rather different issue. If we con-sider the linguistic convention, then we put our trust *in* an organization but our loyalty is *to* an organization. That is to say, trust puts oneself at the mercy of 'the other', while loyalty implies that 'the other' is far more dependent on oneself than vice versa. In effect, although trust and loyalty are clearly con-nected, it is possible to consider a situation where people are loyal to an organization but distrustful of it: 'my country right or wrong' would be an example of this. In terms of the survey results, shown here in Figure 4.7, they suggest that 60 per cent of upper managers are very loyal to their organization, but only 35 per cent of shop-floor/office workers are similarly positioned (only one-third of lower managers and supervisors are very loyal). At the other end of the scale, 10 per cent of upper managers either had no or only a little loyalty, while 25 per cent of shop-floor/office workers had no or only a little loyalty.

Does this mean that shop-floor and office workers are simply detached from all organizations and unable to commit

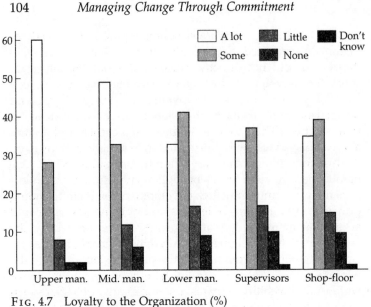

F I G. 4.7   Loyalty to the Organization (%)
Source: Kessler and Undy (1996)

themselves to anything? Figure 4.8 suggests that the strength of commitment can also operate in the opposite hierarchical direction, for here the degree of commitment to an organization is stronger at the lower end of the salary scale, and therefore, presumably, at the lower end of the social status hierarchy. In this case 35 per cent of premier league season-ticket holders earning less that £10,000 per annum regarded their football team as 'One of the most important things in their lives'—twice the proportion of those earning more than £30,000 per annum. Indeed, for Newcastle United season-ticket holders the club is the *most* important thing in their lives for over 46 per cent.

Does this mean that the average NMO is bound to fail because the level of commitment is insufficient? Well, in the absence of comparative data it is difficult to say. A figure of a third of the shop-floor or office workers being strongly loyal may mean that great strides have been made or that massive backsliding has occurred. Worse, even if we take it as a fact that about half the workforce appears committed to their organizations this does not tell us the basis for the commitment, and

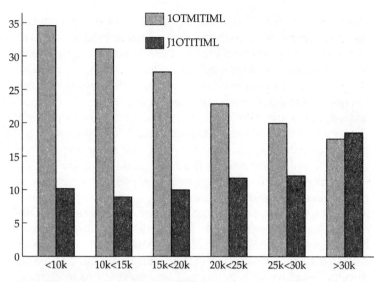

F IG. 4.8   Commitment to a Club (%)
Source: University of Leicester 'Third FA Premier League Survey' (1996)
Key: 1OTMITIML = One of the most important things in my life
J1OTITIML = Just one of the important things in my life

whether, therefore, management can assume the commitment is genuine and permanent or merely short term and instrumental. How, then, can we explain the apparent failure of the NMO to reproduce the kinds of commitment allegedly achieved by the NMA? There are at least three ways of explaining this.

1. *The consultants' tale: (a.k.a. Managerial Séance versus Managerial Science)*

This approach suggests that a normative agreement between the majority of employees and the management is both possible and readily achievable. If the data does not reveal this it is because the data is suspect, or the time necessary to develop the commitment has not yet elapsed. Where there is a 'problem', managers should concentrate on the behavioural not on the attitudinal changes: first, because behaviour is more important than attitude and, second, because Festinger's (1957) theory of cognitive dissonance suggests that the gap between their own behaviour and attitudes is uncomfortable and will persuade the doubters to change their minds and bring their attitudes in line with their actions, rather than vice versa. The persistence of the problem of subordinates' commitment, however, suggests that there is more to this than a failure of tactics. Indeed, as Coopey (1995) has suggested, although the concept of commitment is central to most current prescriptions for organizational transformation, it is often the management culture itself which undermines the attempted transformation. In other words, because management is rooted in structures of personal control and personal career enhancement, the daily actions of management consistently disrupt the rhetorical advances that posit the new order as one of equal status and corporate responsibility. Pascale and Athos (1981) have taken this idea further to suggest that organizations have failed to develop employees' commitment because they have concentrated on organizational 'doing' not 'being'—that is, the focus has been on the way an organization produces something rather than what the organization *is*, its identity, culture, and purpose. If management continues to be wholly instrumental we can expect employees' commitment to remain low.

2. *The dominant ideology*

This sceptical approach, rooted in the work of Abercrombie et al. (1980), to the significance of dominant groups' *ideas*, implies that perhaps managerial rhetoric does not entrance the employees—but it does not matter. Employees' commitment can be secured through non-normative means (wages and the threat of unemployment). However, the rhetoric is still important because it cements the management together into a group and provides *them* with a satisfactory explanation for their actions. In this final approach the rhetoric of commitment is regarded as probably hypocritical—management does not *really* want to empower subordinates—but this gap in reciprocity generates a short-term solution and a long-term problem. For management, organizational citizenship secures stability by integrating employees into the body of the organization. But it also institutionalizes and raises social expectations that cannot be met under the present circumstances. This increasing gap between the rhetoric and reality, the promise and the achievement, generates dissent and allows the subordinates to use the rhetoric of citizenship against their superordinates. Moreover, for European workers, the developments in the European Union, especially over the Social Charter, Workers' Councils, and so on, suggest that if the box is not already open, then if and when it is opened it will be under different (and more propitious) conditions from those that currently exist. There is no going back in time in this sequence: to remove the rhetoric of citizenship is to invite yet further dissent, but to fulfil the expectations is to undermine the privileged position of management. Those who open the Pandora's box of organizational citizenship would do well to ponder their actions.

Yet there is a nagging problem here; I cannot help feeling that there is something missing. It seems clear that the commitment of organizational members is crucial to organizational success, especially organizational change, and from the NMA to the NMO one would be hard-pressed to find successful examples that did not involve winning the hearts and minds of the target population—but something is not quite right. Let me go back to the beginning of this chapter and see where our *Titanic* lifeboat has got to, now that we are aware of the importance of commitment.

We have the most committed crew ever seen upon the water; the captain knows where we are going; the crew 'own' the strategy and are keen to start rowing. The thing that is missing from this is the iceberg: an object that is mainly invisible to the eye, not because it does not exist but because we choose not to look under water. Once the iceberg appears, an array of related problems arise that generate some concern about the efficacy of the commitment solution. If the iceberg sinks the lifeboat, where does the commitment of the crew get us? If the organization has the most committed employees who make the best-quality and most efficiently produced Sinclair C5s, is this going to help it? If our gallant NMA takes the battlefield with everything except weapons, will they secure another stunning victory? This lacuna from the management of change literature suggests that, important though the 'people issues' are, they are not sufficient in and of themselves to ensure success. In the final part of this chapter I want to turn to a theoretical approach that embodies a fuzzy way of apprehending what we take to be reality, and offers the possibility of increasing the chance that organizational change will be successful. Of course, success cannot be guaranteed, but actor-network theory might increase the odds on achieving success.

ACTOR-NETWORK THEORY

Actor-network theory (ANT) (Callon, 1986; Latour, 1986, 1988; Law, 1988, 1991) is one approach which tries to bring into the analysis all the human and non-human, social, and technical elements in a scenario such as this one. Analytic divisions between the human and non-human, the social and the technical, are explicitly prohibited under this theory. In Callon's (1986b: 200) words: 'The rule which we must respect is not to change registers when we move from the technical to the social aspects of the problem studied.' In other words, we should use the same explanatory procedure for all elements in the equation. Rather than saying, for example, that we can take for granted what the NMA cannons and muskets can do—so let's worry about the troops—and rather than saying we know the ship is unsinkable—so let's rearrange the deck-chairs for the dancing—we should insist on holding a question mark over all the issues involved. In effect, we cannot be certain that the cannons will work, we cannot be certain the troops will obey the officers, and we cannot be sure that the ship will not sink, so let's leave the deck-chairs and get the covers off the lifeboats.

The ANT approach proposes that power entails the construction and maintenance of a network of actors; these networks involve both human and non-human 'actors', or 'heterogeneous entities that constitute a network' (Bijker et al., 1989: 11). Such entities (more correctly designated 'actants' so as to emphasize the point that both humans and non-humans are to be included in the analysis) are analysed through the notion of 'generalized symmetry'—the development of an approach that maintains the same terms and methods for different entities; and 'free association'—the rejection of all and every a priori distinction between the so-called 'social' and the so-called 'natural' world (Callon, 1986b: 196).

The actor-network is constructed through the enrolment of allies (both human and non-human entities) into a network by means of negotiations. This process of 'translation' involves four relatively discrete moves and we will use the NMA and the *Titanic* cases to illustrate these. First, the 'problematization' stage identifies key actors who are then persuaded that the solutions to their own problems lie with the enrollers:

NMA: Listen, people of England, if you want to get rid of unfair taxation, and think the King's religious leanings are inappropriate, the only way out is through the NMA—so join up!

TITANIC: Listen, passengers, the only way off this ship is on this lifeboat—get in the queue!

Second, *interessement* involves the gradual dissolution of existing networks and their replacement by a new network woven by the enrollers:

NMA: Look, forget about the possibility of staying at home while the problem resolves itself, and forget the promises that the royalists can make the King behave properly—the only solution is the NMA: join up!

TITANIC: Look, you cannot survive in this water even with a life-jacket, you cannot stay on board and the other boats are full: get in this one!

Third, the stage of 'enrolment' proper occurs in which, through coercion, seduction, or consent, the new network achieves a solid identity:

NMA: Right, then, here's a shilling and a uniform—now if you leave we'll shoot you!

TITANIC: Right, then, your child is on board and that thing behind you is not an ice cube—I'm pushing you into the boat now!

Finally, the alliance is 'mobilized' to represent an even larger network of absent entities.

NMA: Just look at the numbers of our soldiers—and there's another three armies like this round the corner—we cannot lose.

TITANIC: You have to stay on board the lifeboat now—you owe it to your family and to the sailors who risked their lives to get you on board; anyway the water's a bit nippy at this time of year.

Another example would be the success of various green pressure groups in resolving the 'problem' of the depletion of natural resources. In terms of the four stages, first, those with similar interests are mobilized through such interest groups and not elsewhere. So the populations—of both people and natural resources—must be persuaded that the solution lies with Greenpeace (or Friends of the Earth, or Earth First) or a similar organization, rather than with the government or through isolated individual acts of protest. Second, attempts must be made to shatter the networks currently binding the new recruits and to reform them as part of new networks. In an incident in Oxford in 1992, this involved Earth First protesters chaining themselves to the gates of a timber yard accused of importing Brazilian hardwoods. Third, the new network must be persuaded, bullied, or coerced into taking on a stronger identity. The linking of human and non-human through the chains, and the resulting public exposure, can be understood as attempts to construct this new identity. Finally, such a network must operate as the representative of a much larger but absent network. In the case of some green organizations, this might include representing the Earth itself, 'nature', or in this particular incident, the Brazilian rain forests. Of course, such representation can be disputed. Hence, in the Oxford case, the timber company counter-argued that it was promoting the 'proper' use of natural resources, thereby also claiming to speak on behalf of the rain forests (*Oxford Times*, 15 May 1992).

Actor-network theory stresses the contingent nature of networks and network-building. There is a constant need for them to be established and reproduced. In part, this can be achieved through material embodiment. Indeed, networks based solely on human relations tend to be very weak. Hence, an important question is not whether constituent members of a network are human or non-human, but 'which associations are stronger and which weaker?' (Latour, 1987: 140). In the case of hoteliers seeking to persuade hotel guests to leave the keys to their room at the reception desk when they go out, this implies an increasing addition of varying elements to the key: an oral request, an inscribed instruction, and, if these fail, a weight that makes carrying the key around a problem (Latour, 1991). Since those elements that are enrolled into the network will have their own reasons for doing so, the problem for the enroller is to ensure that recruits carry out the enroller's interests rather than their own.

In effect, networks do not maintain themselves, even though a viable tactic for extending the time-span of a network is to inscribe it in material form, so as to make it *appear* irreversible (Callon, 1991). For example, at the turn of the century, in a successful attempt to prevent the privatization of the Metro system, the radical Paris government rebuilt its subway tunnels too small to allow the coaches of the private railroad companies to pass through, thereby literally ossifying its contingent political control. As Latour argues:

They [the tunnels] shifted their alliance from legal or contractual ones, to stones, earth and concrete. What was easily reversible in 1900 became less and less reversible as the subway network grew. The engineers of the railway company now took these thousands of tunnels built by the subway company as destiny and as an irreversible technical constraint. (1988: 36–7)

The point here is not that the tunnels are impervious to alteration. In principle, the situation was reversible, but alteration involves costs, and these costs can increase with time if the network secures greater support.

At a more mundane level one can evaluate the utility of this approach by considering the way office or classroom furniture seems to generate different kinds of cultural resonances. For example, rows of desks facing the front, arrayed in straight lines and separated from each other, imply a hierarchical approach to work and school. However, a circle of chairs in a classroom, or a communal 'hot desk' in an office, has quite different connotations about the role of power and equality.

But in what ways is this approach any different from a more conventional systems theory approach—in which all the relevant systems that exist (technological, social, economic, legal, etc.) are brought into play with each other and their respective values established? In the first place, ANT suggests that we can never really be too sure about the capacities of the elements at work, since they can only be seen to exist in and through the mobilization of the network. In other words, we cannot say that the NMA's cannons, in conjunction with the muskets, cavalry, and infantry will definitely secure success over their royalist enemies because we do not know how well the various components will co-operate with each other. What if the gunners cannot keep their powder dry? What if the horses are starving and not interested in suicide today? It is this hugely contingent and fuzzy series of 'what ifs' that mark one distinction between the deterministic format of systems theory and the indeterminate nature of ANT.

Second, ANT's insistence on using the same analytic frameworks for explaining the strength of the network—rather than its 'effects'—leads us into some rather strange waters. This is evident, for example, in Callon's (1986b) account of the decline in the population of scallops in St Brieuc Bay, in which the scallops are enrolled by various parties to the controversy in their attempts to achieve predominance. For Callon, it is crucial to forget the assumption either that scallops exist independently of the human actors, or that they only exist in and through the action of the humans. Instead, we have an analysis that leads us to ask how the fishermen managed to persuade the scallops to take their side of the story by clinging to their net(work) and not to somebody else's. Wait a minute—does this imply that scallops have interests? Next, we'll have cannons with attitude and evil machines (see Grint and Woolgar, 1997, for an example using textile machines). Now, the important point about this for our purposes is not whether Callon *really* means that scallops have interests, but how we traditionally impute interests to other humans on the basis of similarly flimsy evidence. So, for example, I know exactly what is in the interests of my students or my family; and no, I don't need to ask them because it is obvious—well it is to me, anyway. Of course, I am constantly surprised when they appear not to be

grateful for what I've done for them on the basis of their interests, but that's another matter. This is critical for the significance of commitment, because so often organizational leaders
appear to misunderstand the attitudes of their subordinates.
It may seem, from above, that all your employees are in full
agreement with your proposed westwards move, but since
their lives or careers may be dependent on appearing to agree
with you, would you really expect them to disagree with you
in public? It is far more likely that they will say yes to your face
and no to your back. So if we stand back from the unwarranted
attribution of interests to others and consider the ways which
we can align them with our heterogeneous network, then perhaps, first, our misunderstandings will be less significant in
their significance and, second, it may not matter that they do
not agree with us, and be far more important that their actions
are in alignment with the established strategy.

CONCLUSION

We have come a long way in this particular journey, via the
seventeenth-century English Civil Wars through the *Titanic*
disaster, and up to the most recent survey of attitudes to work
and organization. The journey has sought to explain the failure
of organizational change and also the success. We know a great
deal about failure and we can probably make generally accurate predictions that anybody pursuing a change strategy that
encompasses the top ten forms of failure is unlikely to succeed.
On the other hand, it is far more difficult to predict what will
succeed. If we cannot predict success with any accuracy, is the
effort of analysis worth it? From the case of the Civil War we
can surmise that some elements of leadership, followership,
and resources are crucial, and we can also suggest from actor-
network theory that relying upon the human element alone is
a far riskier prospect than one of buttressing the weakness of
the flesh with the strength of concrete and steel. You probably
will not manage change successfully without a high degree of
commitment from the staff involved, but even this is not going
to ensure success if your product is poor, your customer

service inadequate, or your finances weak. In other words, as actor-network theory suggests, you have to get the entire complex of elements operating as a network and moving in your direction; commitment is necessary, but not sufficient.

We also should be clearer about the import of learning from mistakes. Given the apparent inability of many organizations to learn at all, perhaps this should be the final point: perhaps it is the fear of failure that inhibits the very experiences we need to learn. You cannot learn to ride a bike from watching a video or reading a book: you have to get on—and you have to fall off—to know what the union of human and machine will or will not do. Scraped knees are not an unfortunate consequence of poor learning, but an essential process through which we learn. The alternative is not to learn safely, but simply not to learn. The autistic organization cannot just be something that other people work in, because so many of us experience the generation and repetition of so many mistakes that one wonders sometimes how on earth anything ever gets done. However, leaping from an autistic to a new model organization on the basis of a disingenuous promotion of the notion of commitment is the kind of risk-taking that ought to be avoided, as Pandora's case reminds us.

Now that we have uncovered some possible benefits and disadvantages with commitment as a panacea for change, in the next chapter I want to consider the extent to which leadership can displace the problematic fuzziness of subordinates with a transparent way forward.

5

Deep Leadership: *In Theory*

We speak of *deep* night, *deep* autumn; when I think back to
the year 1943 I feel like saying *deep* war.

Ilya Ehrenburg (quoted in Overy, 1995: 63)

INTRODUCTION: READERS OR LEADERS?

IN the last chapter I considered the difficulties of change management and suggested that we might learn from historical
circumstance if the intention is to change an organization rapidly and radically. In this chapter I want to focus on the
significance of leadership rather than change. Very often the
two appear to be irredeemably linked: leadership in itself implies change. Here I want to examine the significance that
different contemporary theories attribute to leadership. In traditional models, leaders are the critical *sine qua non*, but some
current approaches attribute very little to leadership, or reconstruct the meaning of the term to change the entire debate.
Leadership is amongst the most prescriptive areas of management knowledge, and organizational theory is often the least
prescriptive; in this chapter I want to answer two related questions: first, what practical difference, if any, does a particular
theoretical account of personality make to our assumptions
about and measurement of leadership, and, second, what difference does a particular theory of organizations make to leadership? In effect I want to turn the debate into one of leadership
praxis—theoretically informed practice.

Between 1986 and 1996, using the Business Periodicals
Ondisk system, which covers the vast majority of relevant titles
in English, there were 17,800 management journal articles written that concerned leadership. On average, that means about

1,780 per year, or 148 per month, 37 per week, 7 per working day, 1 per hour. You do not have to be a genius to work out that in this life you can either be a leader or you can read all about them—but you cannot do both. Indeed, just reading about them would take so much time that it would not be possible to do anything else but read—there would be no time to write anything or teach anyone what you knew. Socrates maintained that he was an extremely ignorant man, despite his great knowledge, because he knew just how much he did not know. Leadership writing appears to fall into the same category: if you want to remain knowledgeable about leadership you should stop reading here and never read anything else on leadership.

In fact, despite an enormous outpouring of material in the second half of the twentieth century, we appear to be little closer to understanding leadership than either Plato or Sun Tzu, who began the written debate several thousand years ago; certainly, Chester Barnard's (1946) concerns that we should stop focusing wholly upon the formal leader seem to have gone largely unnoticed. Since the post-war period we appear to have gone full circle: from assurances that personality traits were the key, through equally valid counter-arguments that the situation was critical, to a controversy over whether the leader was person- or task-oriented, and back to hunting out the charismatics whose visions and transformational style would explain all (see Bryman, 1992). During this latter period there has also been a prescriptive urge to push leadership in an empowering direction, so that 'superleadership' (Manz and Sims, 1991) can ensure that leaders work to free up the skills and potential of their subordinates rather than to throttle initiative in bureaucratic and functional hierarchies.

Leadership is a topic that has been studied extensively through numerous interdisciplinary approaches, including political theory, management, psychology, sociology, and education. Yukl (1989) provides a survey of the theory and research on managerial leadership, yet he acknowledges that there is precious little consensus on precisely what it is, how or whether it can be instilled into individuals, or even how important it is. It is difficult to settle upon a consensual definition of leadership, let alone a consensus about the substantive phenomenon itself or its effectiveness (Lieberson and O'Connor, 1972), nor how leadership can be taught—if at all (Conger, 1993). As Stogdill (1974: 259) argues, 'there are almost as many definitions of leadership as there are persons who have attempted to define the concept' (quoted in Yukl, 1989: 252). Yukl's own diagnosis of the field goes deeper than the question of definition to assert that 'most of the theories are beset with conceptual weaknesses and lack strong empirical support. Several thousand empirical studies have been conducted on leadership effectiveness, but most of the results are contradictory and inconclusive' (ibid.: 253).

Despite the jaundiced feel of much leadership writing, and notwithstanding the danger of adding yet more trees to the bonfire of the leader readers, there is something of value that needs to be understood in this field. I have chosen not to consider the great bulk of leadership material here because, first, it has already been covered in a massive tome (Bass and Stogdill, 1990), and in succinct ways (Wright, 1996; Yukl, 1989); and, second, because I have already covered some of this material in previous publications (Grint, 1995b; 1997).

In the next section I want to look not at which theoretical debate on leadership is the most accurate, but at the practical consequences of two different approaches to personality: Procrustean and Heisenbergian—and how these may affect our choice and retention of leaders.

THE PROBLEM OF PERSONALITY

By tradition, only through accurate appraisal can an organization ensure that the right people get into the right jobs at the right time. Two very different approaches to this kind of problem have emerged in the 1990s. On the one hand we have Sulloway's (1996) attempt to predict the degree of conservatism and rebelliousness in individuals by considering the position of their birth as the most important element: first-borns emulate their parents, the rest have to find a different niche to occupy, and that often requires some degree of rebellion. All recruiters have to do, then, is assess the degree of rebellion appropriate to each job and screen out all those who don't fit the picture—this is nothing new, after all, Moses had a similar problem a few years ago (for an extended review of appraisals see Grint, 1993b).

An alternative, and rather more contemporary, procedure is the 'balanced score card' (Kaplan, 1994; Kaplan and Norton, 1996) approach to appraising and monitoring management. This is rooted in the concern that a narrow focus on the bottom line leaves many other managerial skills or competencies unmeasured and inadequately supported. In contrast, a balanced score means just that: a balance of measurements across different fields of management so that issues such as customer care or concern for employee development, or whatever you want to consider as critical, can form the basis of the appraisal system. Naturally, the method can only work properly if you select the 'correct' elements to measure—whatever elements you choose to measure become the elements that managers 'manage'. In other words, if your organization chooses to measure you on the degree of innovation that you bring to the party—but not on your leadership skills—then managers will tend to concentrate on innovation and forget leadership; in short, the measurement system creates rather than simply reflects the world it measures. In theory, the more holistic measurement system can be applied across a range of areas, not just annual appraisals but also selection, retention, and removal appraisals. Indeed, we can go further than this to consider the way the 'audit' has become a device that has prospered at the expense of trust: now, virtually everything that moves seems to be audited, but the advantages from this are far from obvious. Granted, we may now be able to measure more things as a result of some creative auditing construction, but does the audit 'devote more resources to creating quality rather than just to police it?' (Power, 1994: 49). Moreover, does the new policing undermine the trust that used to exist? If we audit institutions, does this imply that we don't trust them to work as effectively as they can? If we audit individuals, does this suggest that they need only concern themselves with the elements that are being audited? Anyway, who audits the auditors—and who audits the people who audit the auditors?

Audits carried out not of organizations but of individuals are hardly less important, but they often operate on even more unstable foundations than do their organizational equivalents. Conventionally, we insist that however obscure organizations are we do at least know what people are like, what their characters are, and whether their personality is appropriate for particular jobs. Virtually all of these are firmly established in common-sense assumptions about human character or personality—it is essentially rooted in the three Ss: the stable, symmetrical, and singular (see Burr, 1995, on essentialism in personality, and Grint and Woolgar, 1997, on essentialism in technology debates). Thus, our personality remains roughly stable across time ('she's been like that since she was born'), the facets of personality are symmetrical ('she's outgoing, adventurous, risk-taking, outspoken'), and the crystallization of the facets constructs a singular character which is unique ('I've never met anyone quite like her'). This is just as well because it allows us to monitor and measure individuals and plan their future in the organization. Using psychometric tests (have you ever wanted to be Genghis Khan?—a lot, a little, not sure, not much, who hasn't, who is she, are there two of us? etc.), experiential tests (here are two pieces of stick, a rubber, a piece of string, and a pair of shorts—can you (a) build a raft to get an entire regiment of cavalry across a raging river, and (b) not get the rubber wet), and a whole host of other systems for getting boy scouts out of horses hooves etc., we are now in a position to establish precisely what kind of person you are, what you will do in most circumstances, and whether you fit into the kind of organizational scenario we can accurately predict in five years time. If this is accurate then we seem to have solved a major organizational problem: how do we know what kind of people we want, and how can we be sure that we get them?

Let us suppose our scenario is likely to be rather desperate five years down the line. What we need, then, is to find someone who is absolutely ruthless, who will have no qualms about sacrificing some of our people for the sake of our vision, a gifted strategist, and an individual who is willing to risk everything to win everything. This is easy: we need a civilian version of General Patton, the US Second World War commander who did not know the meaning of defence, who loved war, whose daring knew no bounds, and who was willing to sacrifice huge numbers of US troops to defeat the German army. We only have to watch George C. Scott in his portrayal of Patton in the film of the same name to recognize this man.

Or do we? What if Patton (and everyone else) is infinitely more complex, less stable, and less unique than we think? What if Patton cried a lot, hated the destructive consequences of war, took the lead only because he thought he could achieve the goal with fewer casualties than anyone else, and was really a romantic? This is certainly part of the case made by D'Este's (1996) biography of the commander. So which portrayal is more accurate: the film which was based on the book by Patton's rival and 'enemy' Omar N. Bradley or the biography by D'Este? More importantly here, where does this leave our traditional assumption? Is it not the case that Patton's 'reconstruction' is not unique at all, but happens to virtually every well-known figure over time as different and conflicting accounts are produced? Even the most hallowed hero can find life difficult once they are dead. Take, for example, Douglas Bader, Second World War British fighter ace, legless hero of Colditz, and looking remarkably like Kenneth More in the satellite TV's promotional programme *Reach for the Sky*. In the Battle of Britain everyone knows that Bader's crippled legs mirrored a crippled country, but he won over adversity just as Britain did, and had a pretty spivving time as a guest of Colditz. Well, not according to research undertaken fifty years later, which alleges that he was an incorrigible egoist who exaggerated the number of planes shot down, ruined several escape attempts by Allied pilots from Colditz, and made 'teamwork' something that other people did for his benefit (*Secret Lives*, Channel 4, 9 December 1996).

If this is the case, if people's personalities are considerably less robust than we conventionally assume, then we have a problem because we have undermined the basis for recruitment, retention, and removal: how can we be sure we keep, promote, and reject the right people if our methods of assessment are so subjective and unstable? One response is to deny the counter-evidence as significant: OK, Patton cried now and then, but deep down, 'in reality', he was a ruthless hardman.

Or is it the other way round, that deep down, 'in reality', he put on a hard man image because he thought that was necessary to win the war, but actually he was a big soft romantic underneath all the bluster, just like many people. How can we tell which is the real Patton here? Indeed, why do we assume there is a 'real' Patton here—if by 'real' we mean stable, symmetrical, and singular? Why can't Patton be a complex mixture of quite different elements, or act in very different ways under very different circumstances, or, more radically, be the different person that different people see, rather than the person that fits the traditional norm?

Let us return to our stable personality: when we see the boss sacking an employee for some minor infringement we know just how hard-hearted she is, but when she brings her baby into work she seems quite different, almost pleasant. Moreover, when someone unearths her school report it is quite difficult to imagine the 'shrinking violet of 2b' against the assertive CEO now standing before us. Yet, according to my colleague, she isn't assertive at all, she's downright aggressive. Could she be all these things to different people? Could it be that there is no solid centre here, no core characteristics that remain unchanged across time and space? Or perhaps it is the people who interact with her who construct the character? If this is so, is there no essential 'essence' to people, but merely a character that is constructed through various relationships? Which characterization prevails over time tends to depend upon who has the power to reproduce it; thus, accounts of popular figures may change with each biography, but you would be hard-pressed to find a positive account of someone who ended up on the wrong side of war or who upset the establishment. The consequence of this is to bring us back to the issue of pattern discovery. If the world really is full of patterns waiting for us to discover, then we can expect personalities to be patterned and we need to keep refining our measurement systems until we come up with a method for discovering the pattern. On the other hand, if we impose patterns upon the world to make sense of it, then the patterns we seem to 'discover' are actually imposed by us. Hence, if we adopt a framework that divides people up on the basis of being 'extrovert' or 'introvert' through responses to questions, we will probably be able to say that one third are extrovert, one third introvert and one third confused. But if we develop a 'pattern discoverer' which has 240 different personality types, we are more than likely to find that there are indeed 240 different personality types.

What are we to do if this constructivist critique is valid? If we are what (powerful) people say we are, but are probably a whole lot of other things too, then perhaps we need a system, not for abandoning the whole idea but for mirroring the constructivist account. That is to say, if most appraisals are normally undertaken by a single person—your boss—who considers you a Beta 2.4 on the personality Richter scale, but you do not think this is accurate, you can always deny the validity of the appraisal. But it is unlikely to do you much good and may even confirm what the boss always thought—that you are an awkward so and so. And if the organization misses out on your talents because of this appraisal then everyone suffers the consequences of a flawed system. If, however, appraisals are conducted on the basis of a potentially multiple result—you appear to be a different person to different people—then perhaps the organization can get a rather more sophisticated picture of your identity, and make use of those hidden talents that the boss has always ignored. For example, Captain John Smith, a leader of the colonists in Jamestown, Virginia in 1607, was uncertain about the future and chose to plant corn and build fortifications rather than search for gold and find a route to the Pacific—as he had been employed to do by the Virginia Company of London which financed the expedition. The Virginia Company's appraisal of Smith was that he had failed, and he was removed in 1609. If the company had chosen a different method of appraising him Disney would be considerably worse off today. In another example, in 1862 the Revised Code of Regulations, drawn up by the Newcastle Committee after a review of the English and Welsh education system at the time, suggested that children were still failing to learn properly. The response was performance-related pay, with 1*d*. for each child above a hundred one-third of which was deducted where that child failed any of the exams in reading, writing, and arithmetic. It is little wonder that teachers, under these circumstances, responded by concentrating almost wholly upon the three 'Rs' (shouldn't this be the 'A', 'W' and

'R'?—just look at how far standards have fallen since 1870). A rather more interesting appraisal system developed much earlier, with students attending lectures at Oxford University paying a fee on their way out of the lecture—if they thought it was good enough (thank goodness this idea is no longer considered appropriate). More recently, in the 1990s, prospective teachers at Highfield Junior School in Plymouth, England, have been appraised by the children they are about to teach. This rather radical approach to empowering subordinates appears to have changed the decision-making process rather little, since the last three student selections have been the same as those made by the formal selection committee (MacLeod, 1996).

Such 'under-performing' teachers, and poor Captain Smith, became early victims of the behavioural appraisal approach—what you do as opposed to what you are like. Its primary alternative, the trait approach, which was developed initially by the US and UK military after the end of the Second World War, tends to be restricted to non-managerial appraisal schemes. In the USA, at least, trait-based appraisals received a considerable attack at the hands of McGregor (see McGregor, 1978) and, despite some subsequent recovery, such systems have generally slipped into the background over the last two decades, as researchers have found few significant correlations between 'positive' traits (responsibility, friendliness, etc.,) and 'constructive' behaviour or action. Moreover, the behavioural approach is preferred on the grounds that behaviour can, it is argued, be objectively observed, while traits are merely subjective assessments. Other appraisal schemes include: written reports (500 words on why X should not have your job); peer-ranking (why Y (your best friend) is better than X (who regularly beats you at squash)); 'critical incidents' (what did X do when you dumped responsibility for making 500 employees redundant on X's lap); management by objectives (why did X not achieve the impossible sales target you set last year); and, finally, the ultimate challenge in appraisal schemes—the NMJ (Not my Job) scheme (X is so good at doing that subordinate job that X really should stay there and not take my job). Such approaches include a wide variety of forms of appraisal, which range from written to oral and whose focus alters from process to content and all points between.

Yet scepticism appears to remain the order of the day, and this relates to both the process of undertaking and responding to the appraisal, and the well-known 'distortions' that are likely in the assessment itself. In the latter category the most popularly acknowledged 'distortions' are manifest in several forms:

1. The **Halo Effect** is the result of an assessment which is based on one specific criterion that distorts the assessment of all the other criteria.
2. Alternatively, what might be called the **Crony Effect** is the result of an assessment distorted by the closeness of the personal relationship between the appraiser and the appraised.
3. A variant of the Crony Effect is the **Doppelgänger Effect**, where the rating reflects the similarity of character or behaviour between the appraiser and the appraised.
4. The **Veblen Effect**, where all those appraised end up with moderate scores, is named after Veblen's habit of giving all his students 'Cs' irrespective of their quality.
5. The **Gender Effect** comes from the tendency for women to receive lower ratings.
6. The **Ethnic Origin Effect** is when a similarity of ethnicity between appraiser and appraised tends to lead to higher scores.
7. The **Age Effect** age emerges when increasing age correlates with decreasing assessment.
8. The **OGIITTA Effect** (Oh God is it that time again?) results when the appraisal form is completed between meetings and whilst making two simultaneous phone calls.

If such biases are common and if the theoretical underpinnings of the models are suspect can we construct an objective alternative?

The unprincipled certainty of Procrustes

Procrustes, the mythical robber of Attica, solved the subjective problem of individual difference by *making* the body of his victims conform to the length of his bed. Thus, he chopped off the limbs of tall victims and stretched the limbs of small ones. The consequence was that he could be certain that the victim was the same length as the bed, but the victim necessarily died in the tortuous process.

McGregor's transcendence of the problem was to delegate responsibility to the individual subordinate who sets the goals and assesses progress towards them (1978). Since no superordinate can know as much about a subordinate as the subordinate does, McGregor argues that top-down assessments are necessarily problematic. The solution preferred by others is to adopt 'multiple rater' evaluation through which the errors of the few can be compensated for by the good sense of the many. This is usually based upon the Procrustean technique of eliminating the highest and lowest rater and flagging any rating that remains non-consensual as being 'unreliable'. Given, for example, an appraisal using five raters, we must assume that where 60 per cent of the raters agree then their judgement is regarded as 'fair' and 'accurate', but when less than 60 per cent agree then the rating is biased and unreliable. Note here the way that individuals are assumed to have permanent and axiomatically coherent behavioural traits. The possibility that an individual is interpreted differently by his or her colleagues is necessarily regarded as an 'unreliable' rating. In effect, the system imposes a uniformity upon the raters and the ratee, and where they dispute the uniformity, it rejects their assessment as unreliable! Here there are clear signs of the effects of a Procrustean approach to appraisal: where the character of the appraisee fails to fit the character moulds constructed by the appraiser, the latter slices off aspects the former until the fit is perfect. The problem is: what happens if we get a picture of an individual who simply does not fit the Procrustean bed that our appraisal system has created? We might chop off the 'outliers' that suggest the individual is not as coherent as the consensual accounts imply, but does this give us a more realistic or a less realistic picture of the individual?

Now the critical issue is what might be called 'the Spartacus syndrome', which previously faced Marcus Licinius Crassus after defeating the slave army led by Spartacus in 71 BC. While Roman historians pretend that Spartacus fell in the final battle, the Hollywood historians have a much better ending, with Crassus demanding that Spartacus give himself up from the remaining captured rebels or they will all be crucified. Almost before Crassus has stopped talking, the entire population of rebels is on its feet attempting to establish their credentials as Spartacus—either through some form of bizarre group identity crisis or, much less likely, in a vain attempt to protect Spartacus from personal retribution. (Since Spartacus is the one who looks like Kirk Douglas with the dimple in his chin it should have been obvious.) Now the serious point to this Roman excursion is that it poses a similar problem for establishing the 'real' identity of everyone else. In effect, will the real individual please stand up? Of course, it may be that the measures are simply too crude to capture the 'real' person here, but might it not also be that the only way we are going to develop a single unitary and coherent model of this individual is to force him or her into the Procrustean bed of 'the average'. But given the possible diversity of views, he or she may appear to be anything but average; indeed, he or she appears to be a different person to different assessors. Nor can we simply assume that there is a direct correlation between position in the hierarchy and perspective. In other words, it might seem that one explanation for the diversity can be explained by simply matching up the views of subordinates as against peers and bosses, with all subordinates assessing him or her as 'poor' and the scores advancing with seniority. In fact, this is a rare occurrence.

The problem for the traditional approach, then, is that the individual may appear to have several very different images and these are not necessarily complimented by that person's self-image. The impossibility of being able to reduce the complex and uncertain nature of any individual to a series of scales on a tick list of characteristics or behaviours strongly suggests that the quest should be abandoned rather than refined yet more: the results appear to be necessarily uncertain. If our appraisers provide different accounts of the appraisee, whom do we believe to have the most accurate appraisal? Perhaps we would do better to reflect more carefully on the practical consequences of our personality theory.

The principled uncertainty of Heisenberg

If the Procrustean solution does major damage to the complexity of people—or at least others' assessments of them—perhaps a Heisenbergian approach is more feasible. Here we simply assume that a person appears good to some but poor to others—that there probably is not a 'real' person in here trying to get out, but rather a complicated individual whose skills are not consistently appreciated by those around him or her.

Heisenberg's uncertainty principle suggests that there are various pairs of properties that cannot be measured accurately at the same time, notably the position and velocity of a subatomic particle; if we can measure the velocity of the particle we cannot know its position—which is essentially indeterminate. Indeed, the very process of measuring one affects the other to make the dual measurement not merely more difficult but theoretically impossible. This is rather similar to one of the most obvious yet least appreciated aspects of motivational schemes—that occasionally, just occasionally, they work. If we pay people to concentrate on quality, the quantity tends to drop, and if we pay them by quantity, than quality seems to drop. The problem is that both are important but they appear to be mutually exclusive: the more we concentrate on one the more the other seems to move, and vice versa.

The use of Heisenberg's uncertainty principle is not meant to be a literal translation from quantum mechanics to quantum management, but a metaphorical one. However, it should be clear that I have fundamental doubts about our ability to measure accurately many aspects of human performance, though I do not doubt that measurement systems have consequences—sometimes unintended—for the actions of managers. This does not necessarily mean that we should abandon the appraisal system, but that we should think rather more creatively and reflexively about what it is that we are measuring and what the effects of the measurement might be.

The alternative is somewhat more radical, and suggests that we should accept the plurality of appraisal constructions and make positive use of them. In particular, we might try to embody the principles into the appraisal scheme rather than consider them as a persistent and ineradicable nuisance. One such scheme involves inverting and destabilizing the traditional direction of appraisals altogether: 360° appraisal.

Hence we have two radically different theories and methods of measuring phenomena which have clear practical consequences: for Heisenberg we can never be sure in our measurement, but we do little damage to whatever we are attempting to measure. For Procrustes we can always be sure, but the process of measuring destroys the object being measured. If our theories of individual identity have such radically different implications for leadership, is the same true for theories of organizational identity?

FROM INDIVIDUAL TO GROUP, FROM PERSONALITY APPRAISAL TO ORGANIZATIONAL ANALYSIS

In the next part I want to move beyond the utility of personality theory and consider instead the utility of that phenomenon which leaders are alleged to lead: the organization. As before, I run through the theories and analyse the practical consequences of the theories, but in this case I consider four approaches to leadership: structural contingency theory: the leader as fitter; population ecology theory: the Darwinian cull; institutional theory: the fashion victim; and constructivist approaches: the deep leadership mirror. I will spend less time on the second, the population ecology theory, because it suggests a very limited role for leadership, and rather more on the latter two because these most approximate the fuzzy world we are especially concerned with here. One of the clearest, but most controversial, accounts of contemporary organizational theory is Donaldson (1995), though he does not attempt to explain the significance of the theories for leadership.

Structural contingency theory: the leader as fitter

The central idea underlying the structural contingency theory is that the environment generates certain forms of structure that provide for specific ways of operating successfully, and limit other alternatives. At its crudest, one might suggest that the conditions of market success are determined by the symmetry between what the market demands and what the organization provides. This is not just to do with the provision of goods or services, but also with developing the architectural foundations of the organization, and, in particular, establishing what the environmental independent variable is which determines success, survival, and failure. For example, an environment of extreme stability is, as Weber (1978) and later Burns and Stalker (1961) suggested, particularly appropriate to the development of a bureaucratic form of administration. On the opposite side, an environment of extreme instability requires a flexible and dynamically changeable organization architecture: decentralized control, widely dispersed power, and the encouragement of local initiative might be what this environment requires.

The role of leadership in this approach is twofold: first, to analyse the environment correctly—no mean feat, despite the apparent simplicity of the task; second, to adjust the organization to fit into the shape required by this analysis. Leaders, then, have to play the role of a 'fitter': they must ensure that the square organization is rounded sufficiently to fit into the round environment. In fact, one could say that the fitter is close to a Darwinian evolution accelerator—they must assess the need for evolution and ensure it occurs within the smallest possible framework so that the discrepancy between the environment and the organization is not large enough to render the latter extinct.

As ever, the role of the leader is not as easy as it sounds because assessing exactly which factor in the environment is the critical one that will encourage adaptation is seldom obvious. For example, Blauner (1964) suggested that technology played the role of differentiator: those organizations with the appropriate technology would survive, those without it would not. Since there was, at least according to Blauner, a correlation between a particular form of technology and the level of alienation, one would expect leadership styles to vary with technology. Hence, large-scale assembly lines generated high levels of alienation and, consequently, 'social control rests less on consensus and more on the power of management to enforce compliance to the rule system of the factory' (1964: 177). There was, therefore, little point in empowering subordinates or operating a form of participative leadership because the technology coerced the leaders into a particularly coercive approach. Only one solution to the problem of alienation appealed to Blauner, and that was to develop the technology as rapidly as possible so that other forms of organization and management would be possible. In effect, the leader-as-fitter would have to try and redesign the production system within the tight confines set down by the market so that Blauner's 'inverted "U" curve', which saw alienation and skill as negatively correlated across time, would ensure that a highly skilled, minimally alienated workforce was the result.

As Donaldson (1995: 36) notes, organizational change is more likely where there is an evident misfit between the environmental requirements and the organizational form, and where—as a consequence—the organization's performance is notably poor. Moreover, the model implies that a change in the significant variable—in Blauner's case technology, but in Chandler's (1962) it is the level of product diversification, and in Pugh and Hickson's (1976) Aston Studies it is size—does not in and of itself automatically generate structural change. If it did then there would be no need for leadership. Rather, the changing conditions undermine the symmetry between environmental requirements and organization fit such that the level of asymmetry or misfit becomes increasingly obvious and leads to performance problems. Once the latter occurs, and the leader recognizes the problem, then he or she can take the requisite action to bring the alignment back into shape.

Where does this theory fit into the fuzzy world that we began this book with? In brief, it does not. The model assumes either a clarity of view that the fuzzy approach denies, or it implies a degree of control that the fuzzy world also denies. In the structural contingency theory leaders are able to analyse the world accurately and have the ability to change the design, structure, culture, and anything else they choose to change. As Joan Woodward argued at the conclusion of her major work, the consequence of not being clear about what caused organizations to fail or succeed (in her case it was the technology) was that organizations relied on 'the possession of the elusive, almost mystical qualities of leadership, and long experience' (1965: 256).

Moreover, the most appropriate leader may also change with the conditions. The most obvious connection between this theory and leadership approaches clearly lies in the contingent approaches to leadership. Fiedler (1967), one of the leading authorities on contingency approaches to leadership, developed one of the first and most influential contingency theories of leadership, where 'the context of an organizational environment . . . determines, in large part, the specific kind of leadership behaviour which the situation requires'. Asserting that the model 'can predict the relationship between certain leader attributes and organizational performance at a given point in time with a reasonable degree of accuracy', Fiedler developed his model based on two different forms of leadership behaviour. The first centred on relationship-motivated leaders, the second on task-motivated leaders. Task-motivated leaders perform best where the situation is one either of high or low control, whereas relationship-motivated leaders work best when the control situation is of neither extreme. There are, then, no universally 'good' leaders, but when the situation is one of extreme uncertainty or extreme certainty then task-related leaders are more successful than relationship-oriented leaders. The trick is to match up the personality characteristics of the leader with the situational characteristics.

The characteristics of the situation are not all externally impervious, of course. Through securing greater training and experience, notably of routines and locally situated knowledge, leaders can reposition themselves within the situation. It is also the case, argues Fiedler, that the degree of organizational turbulence will have an impact upon the situation. Indeed, one might go further than this to suggest that if the environment is constantly turbulent then what may be an appropriate form of leadership today may be inappropriate tomorrow.

So did Fiedler's claim to have developed a predictive theory of leadership resolve the problem? Yes and no. Yes, many subsequent accounts provided support to the basic model (Fiedler and Garcia, 1987) but no, a large overview of the data suggests that a significant minority of cases fall outside the predictive model (Bass, 1990).

Hersey and Blanchard's (1982) 'situational leadership theory' is a slightly more complex version of this kind of approach, in which the particular style of 'appropriate' leadership depends not upon the external situation but upon the nature of the followers. Where followers are defined as being of 'low maturity' they are required to have high levels of supervision at the task level but a low level of relationship-oriented supervision. As the maturity of the followers increases, the shift towards lower levels of task-oriented supervision and higher levels of relationship-oriented supervision occurs. The same kind of problem that affects Fiedler's approach affects the assessment of 'maturity', and several recent attempts to verify this model empirically have been less than successful (see Norris and Vecchio, 1992). Moreover, it would be worth starting from first principles, as described by many of the neo-human relations authors of the 1960s and 1970s—if you treat employees as children they might very well respond in childish ways. Hence, to take as given a certain level of employee 'maturity' is itself to beg the question of leadership: what kind of leadership treats adults as having low levels of maturity, other than a leadership which is itself 'immature'?

A further possibility is that the criteria for leadership can change to the extent that our interpretation of prior leadership itself alters over time. It is not, then, that leadership is contingent upon the situation—in the sense discussed above—but that as time elapses so our interpretation of the leadership at a particular time alters. Thus, for example, whether Winston Churchill was the 'appropriate' leader for the British during the Second World War is less contingent upon the wartime conditions and more contingent upon the predilections concerning leadership espoused by particular groups at a particular time. In other words, Churchill may have been be regarded as a great leader during the war itself, and subsequent to it, but during the 1990s, when racism has become much less socially acceptable, he may appear as a man who was primarily driven, and therefore tainted, by a racism that undermines the claim to 'great' leadership status—even during the war (Ponting, 1994; Roberts, 1994). Indeed, if much of the early inter-war work on leadership stressed traits, and the irrational desire of the mass to be led by a charismatic leader, we can see the 'style' approach of the early post-war period (which tended to support participative and democratic leadership styles over laissez-faire and authoritarian styles) as the democratic response to the military defeat of 'irrational' political leaders (Brown, 1964; Likert, 1961). The shift from 'leaders' to 'situations' continued through the 1960s, ending up with the work of Fiedler (1978) and the whole contingency approach to organizations and leadership, in which the most appropriate form of leadership could only be derived from a careful analysis of the particular situation.

A related form of leadership analysis, cognitive resources theory (Fiedler and Garcia, 1987), stresses the relationship between crises and leadership styles, in that experience is more significant than intelligence for periods of crisis and the reverse operates in periods of stability. These contingent approaches to leadership nevertheless seek, and usually fail, to provide dependable predictors of the 'correct' leadership behaviour for certain situations. As Yukl declares: 'With few exceptions, it is still not possible to make confident predictions about the optimal behaviour pattern for a leader in a given situation' (1989: 263). One might add that if leadership behaviour could be predicted in a given situation then the whole notion of volitional leadership becomes redundant. The predictive model could simply be wheeled on stage and anybody capable of following the rules would be able to lead successfully.

Two further implications of this assumption are that once the model is perfected, competitive advantage in any area would be difficult to establish and, perhaps equally interesting, human leaders could be replaced by computerized leaders (who would be less likely to fail to follow rules and more likely to analyse complex 'rule rich' scenarios correctly). Come back 'Hal', all is forgiven.

Stewart (1982) has also offered a version of the contingency model of leadership. She argues that the kind of managerial leadership necessary is dependent upon the nature of the work being undertaken: its predictability, the speed of execution required, and the degree of initiative allowed. The broad implication of such contingent or situational models of leadership is that the form of leadership required under condition X may not be the most suitable for condition Y. This is clearly considerably more flexible than many of the other models we have already considered; so is the solution to the determinist conundrum a contingent determinism? Note here the repetition of determinism, for herein lies the weakness of the contingent account. What appears as a flexible explanation for differential leadership skills is actually just a more sophisticated form of determinism. It is not that several forms of leader appear to succeed in the same situation, but that, given a specific situation, a specific form of leadership is *the* most suitable. In effect, the situation determines the leadership—but not vice versa. This might be satisfactory—but only if we could agree upon the two things: first, which leadership was most appropriate in each situation; second, what the situation was. Do situations remain impervious to interpretive readings? Do we all *know* what a situation is really like, or do we have to interpret innumerable variables to come up with an educated guess? If we still have to interpret the situation, and the appropriate leadership for it, then we are still unable to claim that the key to leadership has been secured. The problem is simply that the situation is just as much of a social construct as the essence of leadership—so that rendering a clear response to the environment is only possible if we ignore the fuzzy nature of that environment.

Let us move on to an alternative that, if accurate, solves a lot of these problems, but renders leaders incapable of doing anything about it: the population-ecology approach.

Population ecology theory: the Darwinian cull

While the role for leaders in the contingency approach discussed above is extremely complex—and, well, contingent—the role for leaders in the population ecology model, usually associated with Hannan and Freeman (1977) and Aldrich (1979), is mercifully simple: there isn't one. For while the contingency theorists are advising leaders whether or not to lead in the situation and what to do in specific circumstances, the population ecologists elbow the contingent fitter aside and replace him or her with a far more deadly figure: the Grim Reaper. Population ecologists hold, in their most extreme form, that selection not adaptation is the mechanism for distinguishing between successful and unsuccessful organizations. If an institution has the requisite fit between environment and organization then it will survive; if it does not it will die, leaving the survival of the fittest. This quasi-Darwinian (quasi because organizations are often 'taken over' by or merge with others rather than simply die) rebuff to the adaptive contingency theorists does not focus upon individual organizations, let alone individuals, because its interests and models are rooted in populations of organizations. Here, organizations do not adapt to changed conditions, they die and are replaced by other organizations that are better aligned with the requirements of the environment. Thus, death not change is critical because organizations rarely, if ever, change sufficiently to remain alive under changing conditions. Instead, new organizations spring up to replace the old, as novel market niches are created by the maelstrom of dynamic change. This, it is argued, explains the enormous cull that regularly occurs as organizations fall in thousands, only to be replaced by others wishing to take their chance in the great 'selection'. Moreover, because organizations cannot evolve fast enough to remain alive, each newcomer has a limited life span. As long as the environment remains stable, the new organization may survive, but once the environment changes the very structures and procedures designed for survival under a particular form of environment hinder the possibility of the organization surviving.

Of course, this approach has drastic implications for leaders. If the organization is failing because it no longer fits the environment, the difficulties of managing change (political resistance, general inertia, short-termism, incomplete information, etc.) imply that leaders should not stay to try and turn the oil tanker, but jump ship and start again.

Once again, this model does not sit easily with the fuzzy world we have considered. There is nothing fuzzy about it. On the contrary, the bleakness and clarity of the vision is painfully apparent: not only can you see what is happening but there is nothing you can do about it. The Grim Reaper appears silhouetted against the changing world, but you may as well commit suicide as wait for the inevitable swish of the scythe. At best, all a leader can do is know when to jump ship, when to build a new one, and when to reconcile him or herself to imminent immolation.

Before you, dear reader/leader, dive into the bath with the live toaster, or reach for the lifejacket tucked under your seat, let us hold back a while and consider a rather more active and positive account of leadership: institutional theory

Institutional theory: the fashion victim

The population ecology model effect may be the equivalent of what happens to some rabbits when faced by a stoat: the former appear to be frozen in fear and are unable to take any kind of avoidance action as they wait for the inevitable. On the other hand, institutional theory may explain, as was suggested in chapter 2, why otherwise rational people throw perfectly good clothes away and buy a whole new wardrobe because the previous clothing was the wrong colour or the wrong shape. In short, institutional theory may explain why people no longer wear flared trousers—because it is unfashionable to do so (unless you are at the leading edge of fashion, as most academics apparently are). If we are as wasteful as this implies, if we do act like veritable flocks of sheep when it comes to clothes and so on, then might this account for the way leaders undertake the kind of actions they think are expected of them, rather than the kinds of action they think are necessary?

This is a particularly nefarious approach to leadership because it suggests that the actions leaders take may not be those that are the most rational in the situation, and, furthermore, that leaders are often so rooted in their own cultures that they cannot see the normative influences that coerce them: what is normative appears rational. Some of this approach has already been explained in chapter 2, so here I merely want to reiterate the significant points for leadership.

First, although the theory has been developed for explaining action at an institutional or organizational level, it should be clear that individuals can hardly be isolated from such pressures. Hence, the institutional isomorphism suggested by

DiMaggio and Powell (1991), and Meyer (1983) might explain how leaders increasingly resemble each other where they operate in related fields. For example, (virtually) all chief executives in London, New York, Tokyo, and so on, wear suits of limited variety, usually dark and often pin-striped. They also work similar hours, and work in similar buildings within similar organizations that are modelled on each other. These leaders all have 'visions' that are all remarkably similar—'We want to be the best'—and their operating styles ensure that it does not really matter whether they all change round tomorrow: their organizations would probably carry on regardless. Very often, leaders will mimic each other because they are uncertain what else to do in the face of considerable uncertainty. For instance, they may institute a fresh round of change not because they know the change will have positive economic pay backs, but because everyone else seems to be doing it and it is necessary to appear to be up with the leaders in whatever way they can (see Kling, 1992, and Bansal, 1995). At other times, leaders will be coerced by laws or traditions that demand they act in certain ways—for instance, there used to be a time when British government ministers would resign if their department had acted incompetently. These days, the traditions seem to flow in the opposite direction: on no account and under no circumstances should anyone resign for any reason whatsoever.

Rather more often, leaders are coerced into a pattern of familiar action by health and safety standards. Or it may be that compliance is only at the level of ritual. For example, let us pretend that the day before a quality assurance audit occurs the standards required are resurrected—and the day after the audit they are put back in their boxes. Next, we will be painting only those parts of the building that presidents or the British Queen walk round—which must have a very strange effect on the latter for she must surely think that everyone in Britain walks around with a Union Jack in their pocket, has a line of children in front of them, has nothing else to do, wears a perfectly clean set of overalls, and has a permanent beaming smile.

Also interesting is Meyer and Scott's (1983) loose-coupling theory, which describes organizations as comprising an operating core and a management organization. Since the two are only loosely connected, and the operating core works virtually autonomously of the management core, one might wonder what management is supposed to do. Perhaps this explains where all the people on royal walkabouts come from, but the real answer, according to Dilbert (see Adams, S., 1996), is that the act of removing managers and leaders from the productive process is, in and of itself, sufficient justification for the development of a division of labour, for management is 'nature's way of removing morons from the productive flow'. However, on the assumption that Dilbert is wrong, the theory asserts that management's task is to interface between the organization and the outside environment. That is, to provide an array of myths and rituals that satisfy outside bodies—investors, the state, consumers, etc.—(see Donaldson, 1995, chapter 4, for a fuller review of the theory itself).

What does the theory imply for our fuzzy leaders? Well, it may be that they are only in a fuzzy world because society expects the world to be fuzzy. That is, if we keep telling each other that the world is ever more turbulent, and science ever less dependable, then we will eventually come to believe these things and act accordingly. On the other hand, we should also note that a leader who ignored the requirements of fashion would be unlikely to survive long. Which global corporation, for example, would employ a new chief executive who wore flared trousers, or a dress with a bustle, or who didn't have a vision, or who went home at 3 p.m. to pick up the kids, or who refused to be paid more than the average salary of the shop-floor or office workers? All of these things may be rational, but they are not what is expected. The wider implication of this model, then, is that the kind of leader varies not with the situation but with the expectation. Leading counter-intuitively, then—assuming intuition is also prone to normative influences—is likely to fail. Let us now turn to a theory that takes the counter-intuitive as a starting place: constructivist theory.

Constructivist approaches: the deep leadership mirror

Constructivist approaches are rooted in a concern for the way that language acts to create the world rather than to discover it (see Burr, 1995; Grint, 1995b; Grint and Woolgar, 1997; Kelemen, 1995). As I suggested earlier in this chapter, individual identities are constructed through the accounts provided of others—we do not 'discover' others but construct them through our accounts of them. In other words, language acts as an essential barrier between us and the world: essential because we cannot know the world without language, and a barrier because we are unable to know the world directly, except through language. This has consequences not just for our faith in the 'truth'—for we are unable to verify truth claims except through the language which makes the claims—but also for the way we know what is happening in the world. In this section, therefore, I want to explore the implications of constructivism for leadership itself. How can one lead anything in such a fuzzy environment, when life appears to comprise an infinitely deep mirror?

Probably the most popular assumption is that this relativist approach provides no basis for leadership other than some form of Machiavellian 'might is right'. The relativist's or constructivist's dilemma seems to imply that, in the absence of any objective or true criteria for evaluating anything (truth, science, morality, etc.), everyone's account is equal and therefore anything goes. Hence, we cannot criticize a leader who ignores conventional morality, or even the law, because there is no firm foundation for that morality or law. Here we might substitute the slogan: 'If it works, don't fix it' by one that reads 'If it works, use it'. This is actually not what the model implies. Instead, the Orwellian approach to animal equality is a better representation: for 'all animals are equal but some are more equal than others'. The issue is not that we cannot evaluate between leaders because they are all equal, but why do some leaders appear to be able to succeed while others fail? The crucial point, therefore, is not differentiating truth from lies, but more from less persuasive accounts; it is a contingent but not an arbitrary issue. Indeed, it is not a trivial point to note that an account tends to carry more weight if it is issued higher up the organizational hierarchy: not because it is more truthful, but because the higher status allows such people to define what counts as true.

Furthermore, the implication of this is that what counts as

leadership cannot be derived from an 'objective' analysis of any particular action, but must be contextually read. Such a contextual reading does not imply that, given an 'objective' assessment of a culture, one can 'objectively' assess the form and quality of leadership. Rather, it suggests that what counts as leadership lies in the accounts of those who are assessing the actions of the individual. Leaders, then, are constructed through the accounts that are provided of their actions, but, in order to resist other accounts, which may seek to delegitimize their position, pro-leader accounts must be constantly reproduced.

Another implication of this is to cast doubt on the essentialist model of leadership, in which leaders, whether born or taught, embody leadership qualities that can prevail in (almost) all situations. On the contrary, the argument implies that leadership is a social construction that needs constant action for its effective reproduction. In effect, it casts considerable doubt upon all trait approaches to leadership in so far as they assert that leadership lies *within* an individual rather than being the product of action by a network. Such essentialist models are, nevertheless, very popular. Indeed, one could argue that they are positively fetishistic in their concern to lay blame and praise for all kinds of events at the feet of individual leaders.

On the theoretical front, it has been suggested that leadership, defined as a process/act of achieving change through others, must exist throughout the organization and at all levels for anything to occur (Grint, 1995b). Since the commands of a formal leader are seldom—if ever—sufficient in and of themselves to achieve the aims behind the commands, it is clear that many people must be continuously engaged in acts of leadership. The formal roles of leaders are, therefore, an inadequate foundation upon which to study leadership because leadership seems to be necessarily systemic or 'deep' if it exists at all. 'Deep leadership', then, disputes the *individual* or *shallow* orientation of most leadership theory—in which leadership is restricted to the narrowest possible number of formal office-holders—and asserts that it should be configured as a *social* or *collective* phenomenon. It is 'deep' because it pervades the entire organization. If leadership implies the act or process of changing others' actions, then leadership exists when CEOs persuade entire organizations to change direction, and it exists when the office cleaner persuades the office workers to reuse paper wherever possible to limit environmental damage.

The significance of the theoretical switch from 'shallow' to 'deep' leadership is complemented by the current trend towards empowerment. Empowerment should, in theory, make itself manifest in an expansion of leadership activities at all levels. A deep leadership approach, in contrast, holds that leadership processes occur through an organization at all levels, irrespective of trends such as empowerment. However, given the increasingly dynamic nature of the world's economy, it would seem appropriate to consider the extent to which deep leadership—assuming it exists—has actually expanded over the last decade.

Heifetz (1994), for example, combines a relatively novel theme—about forcing subordinates to reflect upon their influence in the achievement of goals—with a relatively old theme—about the difference between situations that require mechanistic responses, which he calls 'technical' issues (often called 'management' elsewhere to distinguish it from 'leadership')—and those that require 'adaptive' responses (often called 'leadership' elsewhere). Heifetz, like Weber, also distinguishes between the exercise of 'authority'—sometimes labelled power derived from formal role—and the exercise of 'leadership'—sometimes labelled power derived from informal role. Hence, for Heifetz, the critical issue is whether people have the ability and skill, or whatever, to intervene in situations that are not routine, and in which the answer cannot be derived from previous experience, and where part of the role of the leader is to reflect the problem-solving back into the followers. In sum, the leader must not take on the mantle of magician him or herself. Storr (1996), for instance, notes how 'gurus'—like Bhagwan Shree Rajneesh, Jim Jones, and Shoko Asahara—appear to own the problem of purpose and provide meaning for their followers in a way that galvanizes their physical and mental powers as well as enervating their critical moral faculties. In contrast, a constructivist approach encourages us to look beyond the formal positions of authority and to consider both the way leaders are constructed through others and the way leadership may well be a fundamental form of action throughout the organization. In short, constructivism constitutes leadership as a recursive mirror.

CONCLUSION

We began this chapter by considering whether late twentieth century developments in organizational theory might facilitate the construction of an alternative perspective on one of the most significant and enduring problems of management—how to recruit, reward, and retain the right people. Traditional appraisal systems tend to operate along Procrustean lines, that is, they cut the shape of the individual to fit the prescriptive model developed. Since individuals are held to exist within the three Ss model (stable, symmetrical, and singular) the slicing up of the individual is merely a method of gleaning the truth about the person, of separating the wheat from the chaff, and of solidifying the 'real' character underneath all the data. If this model was satisfactory, then we would not have a problem. If we can all rest assured that traditional appraisal systems have ensured that we have the right person for the job in the vast majority of cases, then we do not need to seek out an alternative which may be legitimated by some obscure theory. But do we? Is your boss the right person for the job? What about your colleagues—can we be sure that we did not overlook someone and select the 'wrong person'? Having secured the right person, are we sometimes stunned by the apparent change that occurs between the day of the selection and every day after that? When you go home at night are you the same person that inhabits your body at work—would your children, friends, partners, and spouse recognize you? Perhaps. After all, if you were completely different, if you were akin to Dr Jekyl and Mr Hyde, then maybe someone would say something. But the paradox is that we regularly witness people acting quite differently in either contrasting or in similar situations, but rarely consider what this implies for our notions of identity or how the flexibility may have a bearing on organizational effectiveness and efficiency. What I have outlined and suggested in the first part of this chapter is that we consider switching from the unprincipled certainty of Procrustes to the principled uncertainty of Heisenberg if we are not to damage both the individual and the organization; to paraphrase a famous saying: the analysis of individuals is too important to be left to the experts.

The second part of the chapter extended the theoretical critique of traditional approaches to leadership by suggesting that a much more systematic analysis of leadership is required. In summary form, this 'deep leadership' hypothesis suggests that leadership processes and practices, not roles, are critical (Hosking, 1997; Knights and Willmott, 1992); that leadership is deeply and systemically present throughout all levels of the organization and not just at the formal top of the hierarchy; and that the fixation with formal leaders or 'shallow leadership' and not informal or 'deep' leadership is also rooted in an epistemological approach (which has methodological consequences) that perceives leadership to be only the effect of leaders and never the consequence of followers. Of course, it may be that leadership is an ineffective phenomenom in terms of the survival of organizations—as population ecology models suggest—or that leadership is merely the requirement of normative pressures—as institutional theory suggests—or that it is merely a myth whose purpose is to ensure the survival of the leaders themselves (Gemmill and Oakley, 1992). However, the point is that traditional—that is, 'shallow' leadership theories—employ correspondingly 'shallow' methodologies.

Naturally, deep leadership may not be recognized because researchers are not looking for it. This is the equivalent of the drunk looking for lost keys at night under the lamp because the light is better. If researchers are convinced, a priori, that leadership is something which only executives and managers do, then, by definition, they are not going to assess the actions of subordinates. Indeed, it may be that the most inefficient organizations are those in which subordinates *refuse* to undertake actions defined here as those of deep leadership. The practical significance of the theoretical switch from shallow to deep leadership should now be clear, for only *if* organizations can harness deep leadership are they likely to be able to fulfil the oft-mentioned claim that 'people are our greatest resource'.

With a few notable exceptions (Manz and Sims, 1991, and Sims and Lorenzi, 1992), the research interests of academics have generally been restricted to the elite group at the top of organizational hierarchies, particularly CEOs, chairs, and senior managers. Some efforts have been made to investigate middle managers (Dopson and Stewart, 1990) and, in previous eras, some research into the leadership roles of shop stewards (Batstone et al., 1979) and platoon commanders (Fiedler, 1967) was executed, but there has been virtually nothing that has researched the subject from this deep leadership perspective. Even those theoretically close to this approach tend to concentrate on those at the top of the hierarchy who empower others, rather than those who are allegedly empowered (see Kouzes and Posner, 1987, and Manz and Sims, 1991, for example).

Moreover, the fascination of most leadership writers with the formal and heroic model of leaders—in which leadership qualities are strictly limited to, and embodied within, particular individuals—appears to relate to a research approach that itself mirrors, and hence reproduces, the assumption that since we assume that only formal leaders are capable of leadership, we only consider their actions and interpret their effects as the consequence of individual attributes (see Bryman, 1992). For example, as Rosener (1995) and Calás and Smircich (1991) have suggested, very often leadership and masculinity are regarded as indistinguishable, such that when women undertake leadership actions these may be disregarded. It may well be that if we spread the research net wider not only would we capture leadership processes through an organization, but we might also be in a better position to see the extent to which leadership is a consequence of other people's assumptions and attributions of effects to leaders: followers make leaders (Lilley and Platt, 1997).

The approach also seeks to examine the extent to which individuals who are regarded as being leaders—whether formal or informal—are able to affect and effect their own version of events. It might be, for instance, that the crucial difference between leadership and non-leadership does not lie in the particular act or process, but in the ability of some account-providers to prevail over other account-providers. Is leadership, rather like history, just the acts of victors? It may even be that acts of deep leadership are indeed identical at all levels—but only formally recognized where they coincide with formal authority. Or, alternately, it may be that leadership styles and processes do differ between the levels of hierarchy so that there are qualitative differences between the leadership on the shop-floor and leadership in the boardroom. Either way, we need to make inroads into this area if we are ever to get beyond the infinite mirror and the law of Socratic ignorance with which we began this chapter.

In the next chapter I want to continue the search for systems that reduce uncertainty by considering an example of the extent to which constructivist theory can illuminate the cow and eliminate the bull, taking a case from the late 1990s of organizational risk and managerial failure: mad cow disease.

6

Mismanaging Risk:
The Madness of Cows

'Was the cow crossed?'
'No, your worship, it was an open cow.'
A. P. Herbert, 1935: 'The Negotiable Cow', in *Uncommon Law*

In the last chapter we considered two elements of leadership which are radically dependent upon the particular theoretical approach used: the extent to which uncertainty could and should be eliminated from appraisal systems through recourse to various forms of allegedly objective approaches, and the extent to which one's theoretical perspective on organizational autonomy alters the role of leadership. It has been suggested throughout the book that under conditions of uncertainty—which appears to be the norm for most organizations and managers—responsibility for organizations tends to be located in the hands of individual leaders, even if their power to control the organization is extremely limited. This chapter takes the uncertainty problem one stage further by examining whether we are likely to be able to fall back upon the utility of scientific knowledge in a situation of extreme organizational uncertainty and risk. In other words, if we are going to experience greater uncertainty and environmental turbulence in the future, can we assume that a more scientific approach will necessarily help managers to manage? Convention has it that where the world appears fuzzy, the application of science can distil the ambiguous continuum into an Aristotelian binary of truth and error. Thus, in the case of mad cow disease, science can gradually dispel our ignorance and provide a solid foundation for managers to take rational decisions. Once we are certain that we know all about the problem we can also address the issues of culpability and prevention: who or what was to blame, and how can we eradicate the problem? A binary principle already operates in this arena: either individuals were at fault, or the system is the problem. The former assumption is examined here through an 'action approach', the latter through a 'structural approach', and, within each, the alleged party (individual or system) is either guilty or innocent. The former (action) approach suggests a high degree of individual choice, the latter (structural) approach suggests a high degree of determinism. What can a fuzzy approach offer us here? Constructivism asserts that the critical issue is epistemological—how we know things to be as they are claimed to be. It is rooted in a scepticism of 'truth claims', but has, as I have argued throughout this book, significant practical consequences. The entire debate hinges around modernist notions of science and technology and proffers an alternative route into the complex issues that confront all those engaged in the 'environmental debate' (see Bansal and Howard, 1997, for an extended review of this).

But why and where do mad cows fit into conventional management? Surely this is either a biological or a political problem, but not really a managerial issue? As we have previously seen, one of the points raised by approaches that are critical of conventional theories is the whole idea of categorization and boundary construction. By categorizing mad cows as a biological problem we immediately divest ourselves of any responsibility for it, and look to biologists to solve it for us. By categorizing them as a 'green' problem we refer to politicians and the environmental lobbyists. Each categorization induces different ideas about culpability and problem resolution, but the significant point is to note how these categorizations do not lie within the problem but within our method of categorization. If we consider the extent to which farm animals form an important element in agriculture, and that agriculture is a major industry in all countries, then what happens to mad cows, and why they are 'mad', becomes a business problem as much as anything else. If, for example, a certain famous 'natural' water-bottling company suddenly found its water supply contaminated, then an *environmental* problem becomes a major *business* headache. In other words, not only can managerial problems in allegedly marginal areas prove enlightening for all

Travels—and had to be socialized by social restraints. Either way, nature was now irrevocably separated from humanity, although many early European accounts of the native populations of the Americas suggested that their state of nature provided the necessary but oppositional touchstone through which the Europeans constructed their own identity as 'civilized' people (Hall, 1992).

Third, the growth of the market economy, presaged by Adam Smith (1974), implied that the operation of the economy was itself subject to natural 'laws'. Of course, where such 'natural' economic laws did not exist—in 'uncivilized' lands—then humans had the 'natural' right to introduce them: enter the colonies. Even those politically opposed to the imperialist developments, like Karl Marx, were nevertheless unaware of any possible limits to natural resources and considered nature merely as a resource to be exploited for the benefit of (all) humanity.

Such domination can be perceived through the relationship of humans to the animals that they eat. Indeed, Fiddes (1991) has argued that the slaughter and eating of animal flesh is a powerful symbolic re-enactment of human domination. After all, we seldom eat animals killed by accident or killed by other carnivorous animals—they somehow seem to be 'dirty' if we accidentally run them over in our cars, but 'clean' if they are wrapped in cling film and look as distanced from a once-living creature as possible. This is rather similar to Thomas More's early sixteenth-century identification of cleanliness with godliness in *Utopia*, where:

There are special places outside the town where all the blood and dirt are first washed off in running water. The slaughtering of livestock and cleaning of carcasses is done by slaves. They don't let ordinary people get used to cutting up animals, because they think it tends to destroy one's natural feelings of humanity. (1965 edn: 81)

All of these arguments have recurred within what has been termed a modernist debate, that is, a debate in which the progressive domination of nature through the rational application of science is the measure of civilization. Indeed, McKibben's (1990) consideration that we in the West have now reached the 'end of nature' (in so far as our relationship with nature is no longer direct but always mediated by technology) is the logical end point of this approach (see also Yearley, 1992). However, even though many current green movements are antipathetic towards such an anthropomorphic view of the world, the main attempt to limit damage to the environment has occurred through the same modernist channels. In effect, while the debates about pollution are as acrimonious as ever, the actions of most greens have been premised upon the use of the very same scientific techniques which allegedly instigated the problem in the first place. In short, the business applications of science may have polluted the world, but only the business of applied science has the ability to stop the pollution, and only through greater scientific knowledge can we begin to construct sustainable developments (see Hajer, 1996 on this approach). For example, drought may be caused by farming or land-use patterns, and it is not always possible to (re)irrigate such lands since this tends to increase the level of salinity in the soil unless the soil is well drained (an expensive option) or irrigated with relatively 'pure' water (another expensive option). However, during the 1990s plant physiologists and geneticists have been experimenting with enzyme inhibitors to develop salt-resistant strains of plants, such as *Brassica napus*, a genetically engineered form of oilseed rape (*Guardian*, 18 April 1996). 'Eco-Realists', such as Easterbrook (1996), suggest that human-induced pollution is declining through the application of science, and, anyway, such pollution is marginal compared to the self-destruct systems operating within nature itself. In a similar vein there have been claims for several years that developments in information technology will eliminate the need for many to make physical journeys, so that we can shop and work from home, etc. Let us hope so, because if everyone who wants a car gets one we may have to live in them.

There are several different responses to this modernist approach. Arguments by the likes of Ulrich Beck (1992) suggest that we have now moved from one form of society to another, in which the very foundation stone of the way we live has changed. Whereas the challenge of the eighteenth, nineteenth, and twentieth centuries was to accumulate wealth, the challenge from now on will be to avoid risk, for we are about to enter the 'Risk Society'. By this, Beck means that disputes kinds of apparently unrelated problems, but the very categorization of problems as 'relevant' or 'irrelevant' is part of the technique by which agendas are set and power deployed. As one might expect from the implications of chaos theory discussed in chapter 3 just because the government is allegedly in power does not mean that it can control the course of events—as the unravelling of the mad cow problem will reveal. But there is another lesson for all organizations here, and that is to beware of the power of boundary construction generally. For example, those organizations that are intent on bench-marking their way to the top would be wise to avoid assuming that only organizations in precisely the same market are going to prove useful for them—far from it: some of the most valuable comparisons can only be made when the notion of comparison is unhinged from the idea of similarity. In sum, if you think that mad cows and the response of the authorities to them is only of relevance to farmers then perhaps you should think again.

FROM THE STATE OF NATURE TO THE END OF NATURE

After the battle of Agincourt in 1415, at least in Shakespeare's version of *Henry V*, the Duke of Burgundy rails against the effects of war and beseeches the Kings of both France and England to look upon the battle as an opportunity for peace to prevail, to drive out the savagery of war with the abundance of peace; he longs for the lush garden of France to recover and for the rusting 'coulter' (plough) to be put back to work—to tear up the weeds of war, to 'deracinate such savagery'. Deracination—to pull up by the roots or to remove from a natural environment—embodies the traditional approach to nature in the West: without human control over it, not only can nature not be exploited to the benefit of humans but nature is actually an anarchic formation which benefits only 'weeds', those parasitic, displaced things that have no place in a 'properly' ordered world. So keen were the Victorian naturalists in Britain on making sure things were in their proper place—in this case ferns in copper pots by the fireside—that many hillsides lost all their ferns to the collectors (Prance, 1996: 22). European colonists in North America seem to have 'civilized' the 'wilderness' they 'discovered' with a similar kind of ruthless reordering of the natural world (Nash, 1983). Of course, the 'natural' world was itself, at least in part, the consequence of prior human reordering by earlier human populations. For example, many of the western prairies were not 'naturally' devoid of tree cover, but kept clear by regular burning to ensure the growth of vegetation congruent with maintaining a stock of game animals for hunting (Pyre, 1982). After the European colonization, 'naturally', the ecology would again have been altered by the invasion of 'alien' plants, animals, and diseases brought by the colonists (Crosby, 1986). The displaced ferns and the clearings of the American 'wilderness' can, as Williams (1972) has argued, be related to several developments, all linked to the Enlightenment events that appear to be responsible for a gradual change of perspective from one where society and nature were essentially intertwined to one where society succeeds in dominating nature (see MacNaghten and Urry, 1995).

Three issues are particularly important here. First, as science and the rational analysis of the material world developed, so the focus shifted from explaining how humans and nature related to each other in religious terms to explaining how the various elements in nature acted. In effect, the question shifted from why the world of nature was as it was, to how it worked.

Second, political debates erupted concerning the significance of the relationship of humans to nature, not in terms of explaining the relationship but in terms of how humans were different from nature. Thus, Rousseau (1968) argued in the mid-eighteenth century that humans in their 'natural (pre-social) state' were originally good, but had been infected by human institutions. One can read here a contemporary parallel with Lovelock's (1987) Gaia hypothesis, where the world is perceived as a living organism, previously unspoilt in its 'state of nature' but now rebelling against the destruction wrought by humanity. In the mid-seventeenth century Hobbes (1968), on the other hand, argued the opposite: that in the 'state of nature' humans were 'naturally' evil—the 'Yahoos' of *Gulliver's* become oligarchical over time. Or, in this (olive)green version, 'the iron law of olivarchy': all anti-modernist protest organizations become modernist over time. So what often starts out as an emotional rebellion against the consequences of 'science' is ultimately forced to take on the clothes or camouflage of the scientists if they wish to be successful. To put it another way, if you want to persuade the government to stop building nuclear plants on your doorstep then mere protest is unlikely to be effective—after all, such a project means a considerable number of jobs and a consequential increase in local spending. However, if you can garner the resources to fund a research project undertaken by 'legitimate scientists', which 'proves' a link between such plants and cancer amongst the local population, then you have a much better chance of success. The moral of the tale is clear, and it is one reason why so much effort is now spent by green protest groups in monitoring pollution in as systematic and scientific way as their resources will allow: facts count.

Now the rub: Greenpeace's scientific assessment of the dangers of dumping the Brent Spar oil rig at sea in 1995 was probably wrong—but it worked in so far as Shell changed its mind. A similar controversy raged through Britain in 1996 and concerns bovine spongiform encephalopathy (BSE), popularly known as 'mad cow disease'; the next section outlines the story before we begin to assess the utility of competitive forms of analysis.

RELATIVELY MAD COWS

In the mid-1980s a Kent cow developed strange patterns of behaviour that involved stumbling, falling, and a general inability to balance; it was diagnosed as BSE, or mad cow disease. A further twenty cases discovered in 1987 and this rose eightfold by the following year, when a committee under Sir Richard Southwood, Professor of Zoology at Oxford, met and recommended that all infected cattle be destroyed and that the feeding of cattle or sheep protein to other cattle or sheep be halted. It also asserted that, although no one knew what caused

BSE nor how to cure it, it could not be passed on from cows to humans and had very little to do with human health. The numbers of cattle with BSE, and of those slaughtered, are shown in Figure 6.1.

This is not the first time that Britain has been at the centre of a cattle 'plague' of one sort or another. As Atkins and Brassley (1996) note, trans-species diseases 'plagued' the nineteenth century in particular and bovine tuberculosis (TB) was held responsible for 800,000 human deaths before it was finally eliminated in 1960. Compulsory slaughter was first carried out to fight the rinderpest outbreak (cattle plague) in 1865—though the then Archbishop of Canterbury suggested that a 'Day of National Humiliation' might work better (ibid.: 15). Then, throughout the late nineteenth and early twentieth century, TB in cattle continued, despite a rash of parliamentary acts designed to stem the disease. The compulsory mass slaughter of infected animals had first been mooted in the 1890s, but the policy was not executed until 1960 (sixty years after Finland had dealt with a similar problem by a mass cattle slaughter).

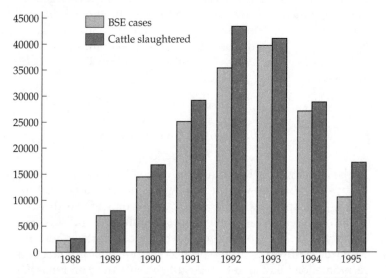

FIG. 6.1 Cattle with confirmed BSE and Cattle Slaughtered, 1988–95

Source: MAFF

which were previously centred over the distribution of 'goods' are increasingly likely to be centred over the distribution of 'bads'. Where most people used to worry about whether they had food, shelter, and work, in the future they will be more concerned with whether they are eating 'mad cow', or drinking poisoned water, or breathing polluted air. As Beck argues, such risk is not new—people have always been poisoned by pollution or died in high-risk adventures—but there are differences now. First, the risk has changed from being personal to being universal. In Beck's example, Columbus took a voluntary personal risk in his adventures, but we face an involuntary and global risk from the likes of Chernobyl. On the other hand, Chatterjee and Finger (1994) and Yearley (1996) have suggested that local, rather than global, action is the only practical way forward for environmentalists—especially in the absence of meaningful and powerful transnational environmental organizations. Second, the risks have changed from being visible to being invisible: it was clear to all that the streets of most medieval towns were littered with filth, but we cannot see the deadly viruses that infect our food and air, nor the immediate risk of pouring 20 tons of aluminium sulphate into drinking-water—as occurred in Camelford, England, on 6 July 1988, where the cluster of leukaemia in the town has generated considerable public alarm (*Observer*, 14 July 1996). Third, previous risks were the consequences of an undersupply of hygienic technology, whereas today's risks are a consequence of an oversupply of production. For example, on 28 May 1996 the British Ministry of Agriculture, Fisheries, and Food (MAFF) announced that nine unnamed brands of baby milk had been found to contain phthalates—synthetic chemical compounds—which were in excess of the European Union (EU) precautionary limit, but below the safety limit. Phthalates may reduce fertility if present in sufficient quantities, but since, according to the government, there was 'no risk', there was 'no point in naming the brands' (*Guardian*, 29 May 1996).

We might add a fourth ingredient to Beck's list of differentiation, and that would be that the late twentieth-century crop of ecological threats are not just unseen and unknowable but, by their very randomness, pose a serious question about the ability of humans *to control* nature. Thus, not only are we threatened by natural mutations that appear to outstrip our knowledge of disease eradication, such as 'superbugs' that live on, rather than die from, antibiotics, but we appear to be essentially unable to control nature and secure the kind of progression to a better life that science once promised us (see Vidal, 1996). The question then is can modernist science dispel modernist risks? We are, according to Beck, 'living on the volcano of civilization'.

A fifth form of change could also be added to Beck's list, and that is an increasing doubt about the ability of science to generate knowledge that the public accept as 'true'. So whether the risks are actually increasing or not, and whether they are changing in form, is compounded by an increased scepticism on the part of the public that scientists know what they are talking about with any certainty. We only have to run through the changes to 'healthy eating' since the 1970s to know that, almost by definition, whatever is regarded as healthy today will turn out to be unhealthy tomorrow. Indeed, the business of dieting in the 1990s is a huge industry and, as Klein (1996) suggests, since the rate of obesity seems to increase in direct proportion to the number of people who diet to lose weight, perhaps we should do the opposite: eat fat to get thin.

On the other hand, there is, of course, a range of pressure groups, such as green political parties, Friends of the Earth, Greenpeace, and the like, which have for several years been attempting to influence the direction taken by governments and by businesses in an effort to persuade them to protect the environment. Many of these groups began life as protest movements, and the direct action of those like Greenpeace carry resonances of these origins. However, while direct action still occurs within movements dedicated to animal rights, or 'deep green' groups committed to the prevention of the development of new roads, etc., many of the more established groups have become considerably more professional and scientific in their approach to the environment. In other words, they have modernized themselves. Students of democratic parties will recognize a parallel debate here, as democratic organizations take on the clothes of their autocratic opponents to engage with them on a more level playing-field—what Michels (1949) referred to in 1915 as 'the iron law of oligarchy': all democratic institutions collapsing, as the consumption of its own beef had dropped 70 per cent. In Britain, without any immediate prospect of the export ban being lifted, Prime Minister John Major announced a policy of non-co-operation with the EU. By the first week of June the government had produced a 120-page report detailing the cause of the problem—meat from infected animals had been mixed with 'ordinary' feed—and announced that the eradication programme would eliminate BSE shortly after the year 2000 (when 1,000 cases would remain). Two weeks earlier an Oxford University team estimated that between 15,000 and 24,000 animals would develop the disease between 1996 and 1999 (*Oxford University Gazette*, 16 May 1996).

The culling programme came unstuck when several slaughterhouses pulled out of the contract—on threat of exclusion from their ordinary trade with supermarket chains, which did not want their customers to consume beef slaughtered at the same places that dealt with infected animals. By 18 June, Hogg had rejected the possibility of any further cull to placate the still hostile EU, saying that such a measure would require a further 67,000 cattle to die (cattle born between 1989 and 1990). Two days later this number was added to the growing list of animals needing to be culled, and the number of legislative bills blocked by the British government at the EU had reached 100. A further two days saw the end of the first crisis, when an agreed plan to slaughter 120,000 cattle in all was exchanged for a lifting of the British legislative blocking at the EU and the removal of the ban on certain beef by-products. The agreement was either a 'victory for common sense' or a 'disaster', depending on which paper one read, but the formal ban on beef exports remained and on 12 July the European Court of Justice rejected the UK government's bid to overturn it, for 'despite the harm being done to Britain's beef industry the ban was a legitimate measure to protect public health' (quoted in *Guardian*, 13 July 1996; see appendix 2 for the estimated costs of the BSE crisis). It added that no requests had been made to import British beef from non-EU countries since the ban.

By 1 August the government admitted that the 'impossibility of maternal transmission' had now moved from 'transmission impossible' to 'transmission possible': cows could, after all, and despite all the evidence, pass BSE on to their calves. This had followed a 1991 statement from David Maclean, then the Junior Agriculture Minster, who had asserted that it was of 'no significance to public health' and chief veterinary officer Keith Meldrum's comment that, 'if transmission does occur it is unlikely to be a major feature of this disease', and a 1994 statement from an Agricultural Ministry spokesperson that 'the theory of maternal transmission is basically rubbish'. Luckily the Spongiform Encephalopathy Advisory Committee (SEAC) agreed that this *still* did not pose an increased risk to public health (quoted in *Guardian*, 2 August 1996). Indeed, on 3 August MAFF suggested that after a series of experiments there was no evidence that BSE could be transmitted from mother to calf by milk, and that no further experiments were being undertaken; in fact, MAFF asserted on 5 August that 'claims about new tests are rubbish. There are no plans to conduct any more.' (quoted in *Observer*, 11 August 1996). Unfortunately for MAFF, the German authorities remained unimpressed and on 5 August they called for a selective cull of calves of BSE-infected cows (*Guardian*, 6 August 1996). A week after the MAFF denial of the milk experiment the ministry decided that, after all, there was an experiment under way.

An independent group of Oxford University scientists then claimed that as many as 700,000 BSE-infected cattle may have been fed to humans before the bans became effective (*Guardian*, 29 August 1996). However, the good news was their claim that, even without culling, the disease would die out naturally by 2001. Even better news followed on 26 November when Professor Anderson, from Oxford's Zoology Department, suggested that this figure could now be brought forward to mid-1998 because there were possibly as few as 150 cattle left in Britain that were less than 30 months old and likely to develop BSE (*Guardian*, 27 November 1996). Doesn't time contract when BSE takes hold? Two weeks later news of a further cull of 100,000 older cattle was leaked to Channel 4 (12 December 1996) and admitted by Douglas Hogg on 16 December, in the hope that further elements of the European ban would be lifted. We shall meet the problem of unconditional gestures in the final chapter on negotiating.

The government's position on the protection of the consumer and the safeguarding of the beef industry has, with

The Gowland Hopkins Committee in 1934 summed up the position thus:

The total eradication of bovine tuberculosis is generally agreed to be the only complete solution to the problem of tuberculosis milk . . . But any such scheme must take account of conditions peculiar to Great Britain. In the first place, the incidence of tuberculosis among our cattle is so high that the wholesale slaughter of infected animals . . . is out of the question. Not only would its immediate cost be prohibitive, but it would also seriously contract the supply of milk. (quoted in Atkins and Brassley, 1996; 16)

As we shall shortly see, the 1990s BSE case is uncannily similar in the litany of mistakes made by politicians.

Feeding herbivores boiled-down animals, although a relatively novel idea, started to happen in Britain and Europe in the 1960s. However, in Britain alone the rendering process was operated at temperatures of less than 100 °C—despite warnings from Bram Schreuder, of the Institute for Animal Science and Health (IASH) at Lelystad in Holland, that this process was dangerous and that Britain should switch to the level of 130–140 °C used elsewhere. This warning, in 1980 (six years before the first case of BSE), was ignored (*The Economist*, 30 March 1996) (see appendix 1 for the timetable of related events).

Most—but not all—bacterial and viral diseases survive by using their own proteins and are destroyed by boiling them at 100 °C; it is these proteins that the victim can destroy through its own immune system. However, encephalopathies, such as BSE and its human equivalent Creutzfeldt–Jakob disease (CJD), depend on their victims' proteins and therefore remain invisible to the host's immune system. Encephalopathies seem to be caused by a misshaped protein, called a prion, which does not contain any genetic material, but enwraps a healthy protein, thereby forming another malignant prion, and so on in a chain-reaction, until the brain tissue of the host becomes sponge-like. The only known form of transmission across hosts is the consumption of infected nerve cells. The pattern of transmission across species is complicated: mice can be infected with BSE, but hamsters appear to be resistant.

However, despite earlier claims that transmission could not occur from cattle to humans, the possibility that humans can develop CJD from BSE was raised by the work of James Ironside, (*The Economist*, 30 March 1996: 25–7), and on 20 March 1996 a scientific committee of the government admitted that there might be a link between the two diseases. (Estimates of human deaths from CJD vary from zero—because, the optinists claim, it cannot be caught from BSE—through 'hundreds', to all those who have eaten beef in the last ten years.) Four days later MacDonalds stopped using British meat in its burgers. The following day Douglas Hogg, the British Agriculture Minister, suggested the slaughter of 4.5 million cattle to his cabinet colleagues, but the plan was thrown out. By 27 March 1996, the EU had imposed a ban on the export of British cattle, a ban that was, according to Keith Meldrum, Britain's chief veterinary officer, 'hasty, ill-prepared, disproportionate and unscientific'. Douglas Hogg even proclaimed that 'British beef can be eaten with confidence' and that the government had 'no intention of adopting any such measure [mass slaughter]'. Nevertheless, beef sales plummeted, the British beef industry appeared doomed, and the government ordered the temporary removal of cattle of more than 30 months old from the food chain. Within a week this had become a permanent ban under an emergency control order, and the government became committed to compensating cattle-owners (*Dispatches*, Channel 4, 5 December 1996). Since the claim was that cows cannot pass BSE on to each other, the cull of 42,000 cattle announced on 24 April, and which started on May 3, should have removed the problem—that is, until the publication of advice by the Scottish Office on the same day which suggested that, since two-thirds of cows with BSE were born after the infected feed was banned, they may be able to pass it on to their calves through maternal transmission, though 'not at any significant level' (quoted in *Guardian*, 4 May 1996). Again, on the same day, the EU's worldwide ban on the export of British beef was challenged in the High Court by the National Farmers' Union and the International Meat Traders' Association, which argued that the ban was 'disproportionate', 'a misuse of power', and had been ordered 'merely for political expediency' (*Guardian*, 2 August 1996).

On 17 May Douglas Hogg offered to increase the cull of cattle to 82,000. By this time the German beef industry was also have also altered radically, the consequence is the development of new problems 'out there' and a new response, as seen in green parties which have only a very loose identification with social class (see Scott, 1992). This particular approach has a long and substantial history of support from Marx to Dahl, and it does assume a direct connection between external 'reality' and consequent mobilization by those affected by the 'reality'.

The focus on external causation and away from the volitional acts of individuals also implies that the responsibility for error shifts from the individual mistake-maker, and the scientific resolver of the mistake, to the institutional facilitation and resolution of crises. A persuasive account of another disaster waiting to happen—the Challenger space shuttle, which blew up in 1986 killing all seven crew—can also be developed through a structural account. Conventional accounts of the disaster focus on the faulty construction of the 'O'-rings, which sat between sections of the solid-propellant rocket-booster and failed to prevent the escape of gas created by the ignition. Here, a 'technical mistake', presumably made by an individual, led to a catastrophe, as the importance of the launch took precedence over the potential safety problem. But a space shot like Apollo 11 involved over 5,600,000 parts, so even a 99.9 per cent success rate leaves you with 5,600 defects. Hence, the system itself is problematic, irrespective of the action of individuals. And when the opportunity for large profits is added into the mixture (NASA paid $120 for nuts and bolts that cost $3.28 in the local hardware store), you have a disaster waiting to happen.

Vaughan's (1996) account of the same disaster stresses instead the way the entire NASA culture operated to normalize such problems, to the extent that the management ignored advice to the contrary. It was not, then, that a rule had been broken by a deviant individual, but that the organizational culture redefined what counted as a rule that could be broken. It is this 'normalization of deviance', an issue still concerned with the structure of the organization, therefore, that can explain how such catastrophes regularly occur. In the BSE case it is not that a deviant individual mixed the wrong feed by mistake, or that an individual scientist made a mistake, but rather

that the institutional system under which farmers operate acts
to encourage the 'normalization of deviance'.

The opposite may also occur. That is, the scientific establishment may close ranks to ostracize those who actively challenge
the norm. We can see this historically in attacks upon Galileo,
as well as in contemporary (1990s) developments over Denis
Henshaw's research which suggests there may be a plausible
link between overhead power lines and cancer through the
concentration of radon and other potential carcinogens around
the cables themselves. In this case, Henshaw has been accused
by the public relations officer of the National Radiological Protection Board, Matt Gaines, of 'setting up his case for more
[research] funding' (quoted in *Times Higher Education Supplement*, 29 March 1996). Whether or not there is a link is not the
point here. What matters are the consequences for the institution of its culture. In Sweden the possibility of a link has led to
'cautious avoidance': they do not build very close to power
cables. In Britain, because there is no scientific consensus on the
'truth', building continues under power cables. If house-
buyers' behaviour mirrors beef-eaters' behaviour, then the absence of irrefutable evidence will not stop a fall in the value of
houses built under or very close to power cables.

Another structural way of 'hunting-the-scapegoat' is to consider the extent to which political muscle encourages forms
of farming that are likely to do the most damage to the environment. For instance, under EU agricultural subsidies operative
in the 1990s, the highest subsidies provided are often for those
crops that require the most chemical additives; for instance,
growing linseed (£520 per hectare). Now, the bizarre issue
here is that the EU also pays farmers not to produce anything
at all. In the 'set-aside' scheme a farmer can claim £340
per hectare for not growing anything. Why, you might be
wondering, does the EU pay farmers for doing nothing? In
theory, it is because European farmers currently overproduce
and there is no market for the resulting crops. Under almost
every other system overproduction leads to contraction, wide-
spread unemployment, and plant closure. But in farming we
insist on paying farmers compensation for overproduction—
and it is the structure that generates the results, not the acts of
individuals.

some exceptions—such as the 1980 IASH warning on 'cold' rendering—been driven by a reliance on the scientific experts. However, a major problem for the government has been the extent to which knowledge has proved to be scientific, true, and trustworthy; these are not all the same. For example, the British government has been insisting for a long time now that British beef is safe to eat because: (a) the infected offal is no longer in the food chain (this assumes that every slaughtered animal is inspected by a responsible person who can prove that no trace of offal ever slips back into the food chain, however accidentally); (b) the disease does not occur in the non-offal meat (this assumes that the previous 'truth'—that humans couldn't get the disease from cows at all—is not a testimony to the accuracy of the current scientific truth); and (c) that even if the scientists were wrong, the chances of any particular person contracting the human form of BSE, CJD, are infinitesimally small. In fact, the chances of that person being born are much smaller, but this doesn't stop people being born; the chances of winning the national lotteries in most countries are also smaller, but it doesn't stop governments encouraging people to take a (lottery) risk that may just come off, at the same time as suggesting that we take a (mad cow) risk that is inconceivable.

The apparent absence of leadership and responsibility mirrors that which transfixed Exxon when the *Exxon Valdez* oil-tanker ran aground in 1989, and no senior executive talked publicly for a whole week after the disaster. In contrast, when the Piper Alpha rig blew up in 1988, Occidental's head, Hammer, flew straight to the scene of the disaster and minimized the damage to the company through his public appearances. Unless those responsible for similar environmental disasters take immediate actions that exceed expectations, and unless mistakes are admitted, it seems unlikely that crises wither away quietly and much more likely that the media will ferret around for further damning evidence (Pedler, 1996).

In what follows I take three different approaches to the issue of environmental 'pollution' to demonstrate not just that theory can add something of value to the debate on the environment, but to reveal some of the differences that theories make for managerial practice. At a very general level, these encompass: a structural approach, in which the structures in the environment or organization coerce individuals into certain forms of behaviour; its opposite, an action approach, in which the focus is upon the conscious action of individuals and groups in the construction of their world; and finally, we look once more at how constructivism poses the issues. Constructivist accounts sidestep the debate of the other two approaches and, as I have already suggested, concentrate more upon the epistemological areas of knowledge construction and verification. The discussion draws liberally upon different examples of ecological concern, but also spends a considerable time running back, or perhaps that should read 'wobbling' back, over the 'mad cow' problem in Britain.

STRUCTURAL APPROACHES

Structural approaches tend to locate the causal explanation for events in the structure of the environment or organization or whatever phenomenon is believed to lie outside the individual. Structural accounts are usually relational, that is to say, it is the relationship between elements that generate the motivation to act. Thus, my action is determined by my place in the social order and the direction of my organization is determined by its relationship to its environment. In the most extreme form of this kind of perspective, the views, interpretations, and motivations of actors are deemed irrelevant to the unravelling of events. The implication is that individuals and groups act when external pressures coerce them.

In this form of argument the *cause* of the social protest about BSE lies in the environment which manifests BSE itself. Thus, phenomena external to the protesters cause the protest to occur: excessive road-building causes road protest in the same way that increased environmental pollution generates green parties. This 'structural' response is the equivalent of seeing trade unions and labour parties as the response to the early growth of the industrial working class in the nineteenth century. Since, by the 1990s, the working class has been fragmented into a myriad of different forms, and since its problems that can be solved, but a consequence of a politically and economically biased system that protects the landowner at the expense of the non-landowners.

Action approaches, then, tend to reject the idea of external forces coercing individuals, and focus instead upon the sense-making activities of actors. Under this form of explanation it is the interpretive actions of people that explain what is going on, and not any system that determines their action. Moreover, the action approach also recognizes the responsibility of actors for their own action. Thus, individuals can no longer blame the system for the problem but have to bear the consequences of individual deviance, such as a Worcestershire farmer fined £10,000 for selling cattle in 1995 without revealing that the herd had been previously infected with BSE (*Guardian*, 16 April 1996). Relatedly, we hold managers personally responsible for deviant or illegal actions, even though the market system in which they operate might induce them to act illegally in order to maintain competitive advantage.

Much of the debate about BSE hinges on boundary destruction, in particular the destruction of 'natural' boundaries by deviant individuals. If we return to the discussion about 'nature' we will see that there is a degree of 'naturalness' and 'innocence' attached to the state of nature before the arrival of humans. Thus it is only when humans begin to interfere with the naturalness of the world that things go wrong. In the mad cow case the boundaries that nature imposes upon its fauna suggest that some are vegetarians, some carnivores, and some omnivores. When any of these categories cross the boundaries, trouble ensues. Hence, vegetarians are regularly assailed by omnivorous humans for their 'unnatural' behaviour. But the most sacred boundary is not where carnivores are forced to eat vegetables, but when vegetarians are forced to eat meat. Enter the sheep-eating cow complete with certain damnation written across its forehead. So we do not need all the scientists to prove any links because the problem is a simple but dastardly transgression of a moral boundary by deviant individuals.

Such a boundary explanation also serves the interests of the government well, since it provides an explanation that also implies that BSE—while caused by the virus breaking the boundary between sheep and cow—cannot be transferred

across the 'stronger' boundary between humans and any animal. A guilty individual obviously caused the problem by
breaking the boundary taboo between animals, but people
cannot break the animal–people boundary because they are
'naturally' impervious. Well, they were until a US experiment
suggested that scrapie could not be to blame because it had a
completely separate pathogenesis from BSE. In other words,
BSE may be a new disease and not one inherited from sheep
scrapie after all (*Newsnight*, BBC 2, 4 July 1996).

At one level, this looks like a structural explanation: the
structures that divide different categories of creature are intended to ensure the replication of all, and when these structures are breached then the problem occurs. On the other hand,
we have to consider the extent to which the boundaries are 'out
there' in the system itself, or merely a consequence of our
own interpretation. For example, are humans 'naturally' omnivores? And if they are, does this make vegetarians 'unnatural'?
If cows eat animal by-products is this morally wrong or bio-
logically wrong? If we could prove the practice to be safe, and
a survey of all cows resulted in no objections, would this make
it all right?

It is also possible that persuasive scientific evidence about
risk reduction can lead to an unintentional increase in risks
where the actions of individuals interpret policies in ways
contrary to those intended by the systems' designers. For example, Adams, J. (1996) has suggested that the consequence of
seat-belt legislation, intended to reduce accidents, may well be
the opposite. If we all drive Volvos that are built like tanks,
and are belted and air-bagged in a cocoon of safety, we may
well start driving more dangerously because we think we are
safer. Of course, the opposite is true for pedestrians who may
be regularly mown down by such 'safe' drivers, as the 'risk
compensation hypothesis' kicks into effect. The consequence
in the BSE case might be that a massive increase in the consumption of alternative products itself generates a health
risk, as the demand for lamb persuades farmers not to check
for contamination from Chernobyl, or chicken riddled with
salmonella, or if large numbers of people become vegetarians
without knowledge of the necessary vitamins previously
derived from meat.

The same has occurred with BSE. If food factories produce contaminated produce they are closed down, period. But for farmers with contaminated cows an array of compensatory payments are being devised. Thus, we have a system that encourages farmers to farm as intensely as possible, using the maximum amount of chemical agents, and which encourages them to adopt 'novel' cost-reduction strategies, like feeding sheep infected with the scrapie virus to cows. If ever there was a case for going back to less intensive farming to protect 'nature', it is this. But the main point here is to note how the system is held responsible for the problem: we cannot blame farmers for being rational, can we? After all, they are in the farming business to make a profit and the system determines where the highest profits come from. In short, the generation of the problem lies within the structure of the system and so must its resolution.

ACTION APPROACHES

An alternative approach is to shift from this 'structural' to an 'action' approach, in which it is the action of an individual or group which brings about the focus on the issue and not vice versa. For instance, an action approach implies that individuals do not wait passively for the system or environment to indicate what to do, but play an active role in moulding that environment: don't wait for your customers to tell you what they want, tell them what they need.

In the social class case it could be argued that people do not have objective social class positions which determine their political response, but that they come to identify themselves with a particular social class as a consequence of taking certain actions. If I consider my identity to be determined by my work, then perhaps I regard myself as first and foremost a member of the working class. But in this perspective the division between social classes is not 'out there' but in academic and government papers, which try—and sometimes succeed—in imposing their pattern upon the population. If, though, I decide that my identity actually relates to my skin colour and/or gender and/or sexual orientation, then the term social class may have no relevance to me whatsoever. In the green case this would be to suggest that people do not join green parties because the environment is being polluted, but that they are persuaded that the environment is being polluted—and that something can be done about it as a consequence of the actions of the green party. It is, in effect, not pollution 'out there' that coerces people, but people's action that allows pollution to be 'discovered' and stopped. For example, dead fish in a stream do not persuade people that the stream is polluted, because it may be that God has struck all the fish dead, or that all the fish are old, or that there is no explanation and therefore nothing that can be done about it. But if we are persuaded that the site of a chemical factory near the stream is the cause of the pollution, then we can interpret the evidence of dead fish in a different way. The data remain the same: the fish are dead, but the explanation changes and, as a result of the changing explanation, we may decide to act. The consequences of this shift are profound because it now seems that the more green parties and research we have, the more likely we are to 'discover' an increasing level of pollution. This is the equivalent of flooding an urban area with police and 'discovering' a massive increase in the crime rates over the last year—when there were no police and no means for the population of alerting the police as to alleged criminal acts.

For green activists the problem has always seemed to be that many issues are regarded as single issues: once the mad cow problem is identified and action taken, the population can relax and forget about the environment. But note how this suggestion reproduces the structural account—the outside reality causes the mobilization of the population. An action approach might suggest that environmental and other social 'problems' are related. In short, that the siting of the most polluting plants in the poorest countries, and poorest areas of a country, is not coincidental but a manifestation of a link that exists between poverty and pollution. Hence, what appears to be a single issue—pollution—could conceivably be the foundation for a politically oriented group to mobilize the local population and *to create*, not simply wait for, the agent of social change (see Szasz, 1994, on this). Mad cows might not be just an 'accident' risk of transmission cannot be excluded', the ban should stay (see Macrory and Hession, 1996). In other words, the dispute surrounds the significance of scientific proof: does no evidence for a link mean that there is no link? This particular problem has enormous ramifications for all kinds of businesses: does no unequivocal evidence of leukaemia in the surrounding area mean nuclear processing plants are safe? Does no unequivocal evidence of a direct link between respiratory diseases and traffic mean that we should maintain vehicle production? Does no unequivocal evidence of a direct link between health problems and the use of VDUs mean that we can continue to use our computers without fear for our safety—or are the potential costs of an equivocal answer too economically damaging?

Political and economic 'realties' also impeded the development of research into BSE. As Anand and Forshner (1995) argue, the intervention of politicians into the debate in a normative role is seldom constructive (Gummer, the then British Minister of Agriculture fed his 4-year-old daughter a beefburger on television at the time when we now 'know' it was probably not a good idea). Without a scientific background politicians tend to leap into action to defend scientists (when the evidence suits them) and then find themselves in a rather awkward situation when the scientific evidence is inverted. Yet the inviolable role allotted to science also means that research monies into environmental issues tend to be distributed only to natural scientists and not to social scientists, who might be able to offer alternative advice to that which has, in the BSE case, landed several government ministers in the veritable mad cow-muck. As Anand and Forshner conclude: 'the residual impression is one of individual competence shackled to systems which were unhelpful to the maintenance of confidence in the beef and related industries. This food scare, like the "salmonella-in-eggs" crisis, illustrates the fact that in the absence of complete information, negotiation, and to an extent persuasion, play a key role' (1995: 231).

The critical issue is that the government appears to insist that such environmental problems are wholly technical and can, therefore, be resolved by scientific experts. In this case Dorrell, then the British Health Minister, insisted that he could do nothing because he was merely reflecting what the scientists said. Yet we 'know' that the BSE problem has little to do with the technical problem because we don't actually know much about the disease. Hence, for instance, interest shown in a new claim by Wisniewski that scrapie may be transmitted by hay mites (*Observer*, 21 April 1996). That is the problem—it is an issue of risk management not science. We need to consider what makes institutions generate patterns of action that lead to or exacerbate problems, not merely find the individual culprit or ask a scientists for the 'true' picture and assume this will persuade a rightly suspicious population which, like mad cows, seems to have been fed something rather dubious. Since opinion surveys suggest that 66 per cent of the British public already mistrust government scientists, there seems little point in genuflecting towards them as an act of scientific faith (Pedler, 1996).

This is an important point, because in the absence of any information how are we to know that a problem exists? In other words, it is only through the actions of the media in some form or another that information exists and a scare is 'created'. One implication here is that control over information is crucial for those involved in data suppression or whistle-blowing activities. Any review of the BSE scare should acknowledge how important the construction of the scare through the mass media is: no information—no scare.

CONCLUSION

In this chapter I have sought to demonstrate that the relationship between the environment and humans is not something that can be taken for granted or left to the (scientific) experts. Nature is simply too important to be left to the scientists. Using BSE as a case study, three different perspectives have been brought to bear on the problem to suggest that the difficulties faced by those charged with protecting the environment are not simply reducible to securing a better purchase on 'reality'. Different theoretical approaches embody different epistemological frameworks, and a reversion to the 'iron law of olivarchy' can only provide for a limited advance in our

But what happens if no knowledge exists of the external picture? What if we are not told about mad cows or ozone holes and the like? Do pressure groups form to defend interests when there is no information to show that their interests are being affected? Can individuals be held responsible for their action if they literally do not know what they are doing? Since the degree of veracity with which the various proclamations about mad cows seems to correlate as much with my choice of shirt as with anything else, should we look elsewhere for another way of reflecting upon the problem of the environment? In the last section I turn to a contemporary form of analysis, constructivism, to see whether this may shed new light on the topic.

A CONSTRUCTIVIST APPROACH

As I have already explained, the constructivist approach adopts a sceptical attitude towards knowledge of all forms, in the assumption that we can never achieve an account of the world except through language. Since language is not a mirror of the world but a producer of it, we are constantly faced with developing our ideas about the world through a permanently opaque fog of words. We can, in effect, never get to the world as it is, but only to an appreciation of that world through language. For example, we cannot touch mad cow disease and know that it is mad cow disease. However, we can be persuaded by 'experts' that a wobbly cow is indeed suffering from the disease or that the tissue under the microscope is an example of BSE—but these two cases require us to be persuaded: the 'facts' do not speak for themselves. Naturally, we can dispute what the 'expert' is saying, but since we don't have an equivalent level of expertise (otherwise we wouldn't need the 'expert') we are really not in a position to generate legitimate alternative explanations of the phenomenon. In other words, the things which exist do not have an 'essence' that speaks to us directly, and therefore some human has to intervene and, through the medium of language, persuade us as to the 'truth' of the matter under consideration.

The modernist account, grounded in 'hard' science, suggests that we can 'know' the 'truth' about BSE and quantify the risks. But the trouble seems to be that the population at large simply does not believe the 'truth', as revealed by the scientists. Perhaps, then, the issue of risk ought to be relocated away from the mathematicians and towards the context in which the risk occurs. Since the 'truth' of BSE appears to have mutated almost as many times as the disease itself, on what criteria should people heed the advice of the scientists? We know politicians are economical with the truth, but the whole of the modernist era has revolved around scientific truth. In the BSE case the original research into it concluded that beef offal should not be banned from human consumption because 'it was most unlikely BSE will have any implications on human health' and because, in the words of the chair of the committee Richard Southwood, 'We felt it was a no-goer. MAFF already thought our proposals were pretty revolutionary' (quoted in Wynn, 1996). In effect, it would appear that the scientists' policy proposals were shaped by the political 'realities' as they perceived them, at the same time as the political realities are shaped by the scientific 'truth'.

This is not to say that all scientists believe the same thing. Far from it: Richard Lacey, a microbiologist, suggested in the House of Commons in 1990 that a generation of people might be killed if his worst fears were realized, a comment that stung Wiggin, the chair of the House Select Committee on Agriculture to say that Lacey was 'losing touch completely with the real world' (quoted in *Times Higher Education Supplement*, 19 April 1996). Yet it may have been Lacey's comment in the *Sunday Times*, recommending that people under the age of 50 should not eat beef, that inaugurated the scare. What marks Lacey out from many on the 'other side' is his refusal to fall into the 'proof' trap. As he says: 'You can't prove that smoking causes lung cancer in an individual . . . what you are talking about is epidemiological association' (quoted in ibid.: 19 April 1996). This is similar to the debate surrounding the British government's attempt to overturn the export ban on beef; it felt that because 'a definitive stance on the transmissabiliy of BSE to humans is not possible', the ban should be lifted. But, the view of the European Court of Justice was that, because 'the

12 August	new milk tests are being carried out by the government agency responsible
22 August	it is claimed that 2 million infected cattle have already been exported to Europe
29 August	it is claimed that 700,000 infected cattle have already been fed to humans; it is announced that BSE will die out in cattle by 2001
19 September	this last claim is denied
22 September	the second claim of 29 August is definitely denied
8 October	government offers a £45 million beef-aid package to farmers
28 October	140,000 young cattle considered for culling
26 November	it is claimed that BSE will die out in mid-1998; £3.3 billion aid package to farmers announced
16 December	13th CJD victim dies; 100,000 extra 'old' cattle cull accepted by the government

APPENDIX 2: ESTIMATED COSTS OF
COMPLETE CULLING

Estimated costs of existing BSE crisis: £3.2 billion
Estimated cost of culling entire herd: £15–20 billion

> Slaughter of every animal: £10.2 billion in compensation
> Costs of slaughter itself: £2 billion
> Cost of redundancy of all involved: £1.1 billion
> Maximum fall in GDP of 1.2%
> Current account deficit up by £6.5 billion

(All this is premised on no outbreak of CJD, *The Economist*, 30 March 1996; 8 months later, by November 1996, 14 new cases had been confirmed.)

knowledge of the environment. Whether business is attempting to deploy an environmentally friendly strategy, or green activists are trying to inhibit the intentions of business, the problem of what *should* be done is essentially located in how we *know* what should be done. This is not to suggest that the ambiguities of knowledge impel us to take *no* action at all, but to suggest that companies and individuals consider carefully the lessons of the BSE quagmire and note how an overreliance on the truth of scientific knowledge can itself lead to a series of actions that look remarkably like the actions of a mad cow. Or, as the realist mad cow said, 'I can't catch BSE because I'm a sheep.'

But where does this case study fit into the world of chaos and strange attractors discussed in chapter 3, or the change models considered in chapter 2? The chaos approach is, unfortunately perhaps, all too applicable. In the short term the government had little control over events, which appear to have spiralled out of control almost from the first day—whatever the government did or said, somehow or other events conspired against them to undermine every attempt to restore order to the situation. And therein lies the strange attractor and the link to the autistic organizational model of chapter 4. For here is an organization (the British government) in which the apparently chaotic state of its strategy reveals a fundamental irony: it is consistently inconsistent—the strange attractor sits waiting to pull back to ineptitude every attempt to resolve the problem because it is an inherently autistic organization. It is autistic not in the sense that it does not listen to anyone, but that irrespective of what anyone says it always acts in the same arrogant way, which involves subordinating everything to a quest for political advantage and damage limitation. Here lies the final lesson for organizations: the strange attractor that bedevils them all—but also makes them work—is that they are all irredeemably political arenas.

In the final chapter I want to review the main arguments of the book and take us to the heart of managerial practice: negotiating.

Appendices

APPENDIX 1: TIMETABLE, 1980–96

1980	IASH warning on 'cold' rendering
1986	BSE discovered at the same time as research into the problem drops by 25 per cent
July 1988	government bans feeding of cows and sheep to other cows and sheep
August 1988	government insists on slaughter of infected animals
January 1989	Southwood Committee Report: most infectious tissue (brain, spinal cord, tonsils, etc.) banned from food for human use (by this time approximately 446,000 infected cattle consumed by humans)
1991	maternal transmission announced as being of no significance to public health
1994	maternal transmission theory condemned as 'basically rubbish'
January 1994	*Dispatches*, Channel 4 ('BSE: The Human Link', 26 January) documentary claims a possible link between BSE and CJD
November 1995	stripping meat from cattle backbones illegal (by this time approximately 700,000 infected cattle consumed by humans)
March 1996	new variant of CJD (nvCJD) discovered; EU ban on export of British beef
April 1996	cull of 42,000 cattle announced
May 1996	cull of 82,000 cattle announced; Britain blocks EU legislation
June 1996	cull of 120,000 cattle announced; EU agrees to lifting ban on beef by-products; Britain desists from inhibiting EU legislation
July 1996	European Court of Justice rejects Britain's attempt to have the world ban on beef exports removed; evidence emerges that sheep can catch BSE from cattle
1 August	maternal transmission claimed to be possible
5 August	'Claims about new milk tests are rubbish', according to the government

on the basis of irrefutable scientific evidence, but on the basis of trusting that my guess is more or less accurate.

The suggestion here, then, is that everything is indeed negotiable—but that a primary aim of negotiators is to ensure that as many aspects as possible, which they consider to be advantageous to them, are taken by the other side as non-negotiable. This may take the form of the political concrete which encases the Parisian metro system and prevented the private railway companies from buying up the system at the turn of the century that we saw in chapter 4. Or it may be in the form of a non-negotiable statutory law—for instance, driving above the speed limit. Yet we know that not everyone is prosecuted for speeding, because the boundary is negotiable (if it wasn't we would all be in prison)—which does not mean that when a speeding car hits you, whether or not it damages you is negotiable. The issue is that what the injuries are, and what can be done about them, is negotiable. ('I think I need a second opinion doctor.' 'I can't help you I'm afraid, but, if you can afford the fees, a clinic in the USA can.')

One implication of the assumption that everything is negotiable—but don't let your opposition know it—is that negotiating is critically rooted in power. Traditional notions of power—that it is a possession and that it flows down the hierarchy—is that conversations between individuals are merely the utterance of orders:

'Gerry, get this order out today please!'
'Yes, Margaret, right away.'

Note here the point that Margaret's position implies that she herself has to do nothing—she merely tells Gerry what to do; thus her power is deployed through the language, it is not physically enacted.

Yet the Foucauldian notion of power suggests that power is a relationship not a possession. Here's the second scene of this drama:

'Gerry, get this order out today please!'
'Sorry Margaret, I've got other priorities; yours will have to wait.'

In this scenario Margaret's power remains linguistically configured but its execution is entirely dependent on Gerry acced-
ing to her demand. Should Gerry refuse, as he does here,
Margaret's power trickles away in the deteriorating relationship. The suggestion here is that power should be considered
as a relationship both because it can only be delivered through
a relationship and because its execution is dependent on subordinate action not superordinate demand. If this is the case then
power relationships are essentially relationships of negotiation. If this was not the case we would find it easy to control
our own children. Why, the very words 'go to bed now!' would
have children across the country racing up the stairs even
before the breath has left their parents' lips. Some hope. Instead, children—those allegedly weakest members of society—
are adept at negotiating (this is best observed when going
round the supermarket, where infants scream the place down
until given a packet of crisps; or during a dinner party, when
children appear demanding a chocolate—or else; or when trying to organize a family holiday). Somehow, adults appear to
lose their negotiating skills as they mature, to the point that
many find any form of bargaining or haggling over prices
extraordinarily difficult and embarrassing.

This suggests that we need not envisage negotiating as
simply the traditional picture of collective bargaining between
managers and unions, though this is clearly part of the assumption. Rather, and more radically, it implies that virtually
all forms of management are forms of negotiating. Of course,
it may not appear like this to subordinates (or even superordinates). After all, when the boss says 'jump', you either
jump or you are out—aren't you? Well, no you are not. You can
always say no—and suffer the consequences, which are unlikely to be instant dismissal for such an offence—but this is
not negotiating, it is a refusal to negotiate. Instead, it seems
more likely that most superordinates engage in a form of conversation that does not (normally) involve the words 'must' or
the coercive equivalent; it is far more likely that the words
'please' and 'would you mind' or 'can you' will be used. It may
be that subordinates just simply comply—but this is usually
a choice made about the consequences of not complying
and part of a longer form of strategic negotiation: 'If I do as

7

Negotiating:
Groundhog Ground Rules

Let us never negotiate out of fear.
But let us never fear to negotiate.

J. F. Kennedy, Inaugural Speech, 20 January 1961

IN this final chapter I want to provide an overview of the preceding arguments, but not one that simply regurgitates it in a conventional summary. Instead, I explore the material through a discussion of negotiating. Stewart's (1976) claim that a large proportion of managerial work is conversational has considerable support (see Boden, 1994, for a more radical view of this), but what is less clear is what kind of conversations managers have. Strauss (1978: ix), suggests that social order at any level (from family life through hospital discipline to international relations) is unthinkable without negotiations; indeed, his thesis is that order itself is better conceptualized as 'negotiated order' in so far as some form of negotiation is always critical to organization. This does not mean for Strauss that everything is or has been negotiable—(cf. Kennedy, 1982). As Strauss concludes (1978: 259): 'I am not claiming however that certain things are always negotiable . . . I only say that the limits require exploration.' We have seen throughout this book not only that the limits are indeed fuzzy, but that the entire edifice of the limits is constructed through various powerful actors' accounts. In other words, that part of the negotiating strategy may well be to proclaim that some things are non-negotiable. We might, for example, consider that the starting salary of newly graduated MBA students is negotiable, but that the MBA itself is not negotiated. Yet MBA courses are remarkably divergent so they must be negotiable. However, the time taken to undertake an MBA is not negotiable—or is it?

Is it a coincidence that many MBAs tend to operate within calendar time, that, for example, MBAs take exactly one year to complete? But has anyone ever explained why calendar years are the basis for educational qualifications rather than the time adjudged necessary to acquire a specific amount of information? And who says what counts as specific? We can go further than this.

Let us take the most non-negotiable event that will happen to us: death. Surely I cannot be serious if I am going to claim that death is negotiable? But, as I have argued in chapter 1, even the greatest non-negotiable event now appears to be negotiable: the point at which death is said to occur is increasingly fuzzy, as technological innovations generate further possibilities for dissolving the boundary between life and death. This does not mean that we can cheat death by dint of a powerful thought process, but it does mean that the declaration of death is the consequence of a negotiated process. If this most extreme case is negotiable, then we can rest assured that other—hitherto non-negotiable—items are also. For example, we know that the price of a car is negotiable, and it now appears that the power of the engine is too: my car is supposed to be able to accelerate from 0 to 60 m.p.h. in 12.3 seconds according to the manufacturer's test, 12.8 seconds according to one leading car magazine, 13.1 according to another, 13.2 according to the television guide to cars, and 14.2 whenever I myself try and drive it flat out: so which of these figures is the right one? If technology is non-negotiable, if its effects can be derived from observation truthfully, then where does the variation come from? More importantly than this, the critical figure for me in buying the car is the government's own figures (13.5), because for some obscure reason I trust government scientists more than I trust any of the others.

Perhaps we cannot trust our own eyes then? Well, even opticians are irredeemably constrained by their patients' reactions to a series of test when they are trying to prescribe for them. It is, for instance, always difficult for me to tell when one potential lens does enable me to see whether the black ring is more or less visible. I hazard a guess at the correct answer, but it remains a guess and the optician prescribes my glasses not the boss asks for the next year, I can then negotiate a decent rise or promotion.' Moreover, a large element of most managers' jobs is not the delivery of orders to subordinates, but the negotiation of work with their peers and bosses. Dealing with colleagues of the same or similar status reduces the utility of 'command' systems, even when they are successful, and opens the relationship up to a far more complex and sophisticated system of negotiating. The same occurs for those who struggle with managing upwards: the tradition may be that the path to success is laid by doing what the boss says, keeping one's nose clean, and avoiding errors, but there is precious little evidence that those at the top of the corporate hierarchy got there by the customer service axiom used by the Trustee Savings Bank (TSB)—say yes all the time; it is much more likely that the top dogs are those who have blown their own trumpet at the right time, avoided the blame for failure, claimed the kudos for successes, and networked with the right people. Even in the most extreme of organizations, such as Nazi concentration camps, it was seldom the case that simple obedience ensured personal survival. In Levi's (1993: 95–6) harrowing account of Auschwitz, he concludes: 'to carry out all the orders one receives, to eat only the ration, to observe the discipline of the work and the camp . . . only exceptionally could one survive more than three months in this way.' As a colleague of mine once suggested in a fit of Machiavellianism: the route to the top is not to make the right friends but to make the right enemies. Whether this is good or bad advice, it does embody a significant element of managerial success: other people. Without networking, little is achieved, and, as chaos theory reminds us, the world can be so unpredictable that the more friends in high places we can accumulate the more likely we are to survive the organizational storms that will inevitably sweep over us throughout our lives. However, the implications of actor-network theory should also remind us that people are seldom enough. We may have the right personal alliances up and running, but if the company is not being well managed we may find ourselves acquired by a rival for whom our network is irrelevant. Moreover, unless we can accumulate the non-human elements to our network—and hold them in position—we may still fail. If my computer or car or phone fails at an inappropriate time, then the deal may be lost; if the paint shop breaks down, I cannot shift the products in time; and if I don't get my home page on the internet sorted out, I shall lose all those orders. Even if we get all these elements to work, the bottom line that will ensure my own survival is not simply a red or black number, a loss or a profit, because the accountants have, despite Aristotle's best intentions, ways of making good and bad numbers appear rather better or considerably worse. In short, management is a very fuzzy business.

In what follows I want to complete this journey along a continuum where there is no clear beginning or end, by laying out some ground rules for negotiating. Negotiating is the *sine qua non* of fuzzy management because it is the primary practical method of dealing with uncertainty and ambiguity in all its forms. I will use an everyday example to illustrate these ground rules, because to locate them in a particular form of business often implies that they are only appropriate there. For example, that negotiating is really only for the purposes of collective bargaining. Furthermore, by setting the example in a location that is faced by many people, my intention is to illustrate the extent to which the principles that may resolve wars can also be used to organize a multimillion trade agreement, the price of a new car, and a way of getting your children to do their own homework (don't you get embarrassed when all your efforts amount to a measly 'C' and 'you can do better than this'?).

I set out these ground rules by replicating the format of the film *Groundhog Day*. In the film the leading actor (Bill Murray) finds himself locked into a time warp in which he revisits the same day over and over again until at last he manages to escape by transcending his original personality. In this version of the replication game, we revisit a garage to establish whether we could have achieved more by adopting some basic ground rules for negotiating. Our hero, Gavin, has just bought a new car, but, one month into ownership, it is low on power, has an unstable engine temperature, and feels distinctly unreliable. Gavin drives back to the garage where he bought it from and awaits the mechanic's verdict.

Scene 1, take i: 'Gavin Bluster goes negotiating'

MECHANIC: It's a bit dodgy, mate. I reckon the head gasket
has blown.

GAVIN: Well it's a disgrace. I know my rights and you've got
to fix it immediately or I'll ring the BBC. You people think
you can get away with murder and I'm not putting up with
it.

MECHANIC: Ring who you like, mate. It's not my fault, I only
work here.

GAVIN: Don't you take that attitude with me young man. Do
you know who I am?

MECHANIC: Oh no, not another lost person, why don't you
ring the police and ask them if they know who you are?

GAVIN: Right that's it, get the manager out here now!

MECHANIC: He's on lunch, mate. Should be back about three.

GAVIN: I have never been so insulted in my life. You are just
a bunch of crooks!

MECHANIC: Take your car, mate, and shove it. No one calls
me a crook!

[*Gavin storms out, takes his car to another garage, but it breaks down
on the way*]

One of the most difficult aspects of negotiating is in assessing
the impression you make on others. In this instance, dear
old Gavin was under the impression that his authoritative
stance would secure the correct outcome. Unfortunately, the
mechanic took it to be a General Bluster impression and re-
acted accordingly. It seems obvious that we are aware of this,
since we constantly monitor the reactions of others; indeed,
this is precisely what negotiation is all about. But, as we saw in
chapter 5, it is very difficult to assess ourselves if the reaction of
others seems quite varied. Furthermore, it is not obvious that
even a consistent reaction on the part of others would be interpreted as such by oneself, or that the consistent message would
mean the same thing to oneself as it did to those who generated
the message. This is similar to the shock most people receive
when they first hear themselves on an audio recording. We
know what we look like because we can see ourselves in the

mirror, but whose is that voice? If the owner of the voice has difficulty picking out him or herself, we can be sure that monitoring the reactions of others may be a little more complex than we first thought, especially if the others insist on the distortion of response that Argyris (1992) labels 'skilled incompetence'. Here, we typically use very sophisticated methods to avoid saying what we really think, but are concerned that this might injure 'the other' or damage the relationship. Even when Gavin intends to create a particular impression the consequences seem unintended, as his scene-setting opening rapidly and radically irritates the mechanic.

When we see negotiating as an instance of chaos theory in its short-term unpredictability, then we should be careful that the butterfly Gavin releases does not eventually blow him out of the garage. What Gavin also does is break the golden bridge rule. This follows from Sun Tzu's (see Grint, 1997) proclamation that unless you provide your enemies with a bridge over which to escape they will fight to the death. In this case Gavin has pushed the mechanic into a corner from which he cannot escape except through fighting back, and the consequence is that Gavin now has an unroadworthy car and no immediate means of repairing or replacing it. This is rather like the difference between farming as a metaphor for negotiating, and hunting as a metaphor for negotiating. In hunting the issue is for the quick and total destruction of the target—the only thing you need from the target is its death to ensure your survival. But in farming you cannot farm the land to death, since this will, ultimately, lead to your own extinction. Hence, just as you will need the current and future support of the opposition in the negotiation in most cases, so it would be inappropriate to force them into a corner or publicly humiliate them. Not only will they come back looking for revenge when the tables are turned, but, even if they don't, a negotiation that is a clear-cut total victory to your side is hardly likely to endear the deal to the other side's members. In other words, should you manage to persuade the trade-union representatives that a 5 per cent pay cut is a better deal than a 5 per cent pay rise, in all probability the union representatives would not be able to sell the deal to their members. Finally, Gavin is faced with the personal equivalent of an autistic organization—the mechanic is simply not going to listen to him if he continues with his current approach—so what else might work? Can Gavin take advantage of the significance of commitment and the management of change discussed in chapter 4?

Scene 1, take ii: 'Gavin Apology goes negotiating'

MECHANIC: It's a bit dodgy, mate. I reckon the head gasket has blown.

GAVIN: Oh dear, well thanks for looking at it, here's a spare ticket for Saturday's match for your trouble.

MECHANIC: Thanks very much, mate. It's a sell out so none of us could go and we are all fanatics here—you haven't got another have you?

GAVIN: No, sorry, but when can you fix it?

MECHANIC: Next week's the earliest.

GAVIN: I've got to get to Durham tomorrow—that's why I can't use the ticket—will the car be all right?

MECHANIC: Yeh, probably.

GAVIN: Well, I hope so. Perhaps you could get the manager to have a look at it just in case?

MECHANIC: No need, mate, I've already had a look and the symptoms fit the blown gasket, but it'll be all right for now.

[*Gavin drives to Durham the next day, breaks down halfway and is towed back*]

Gavin Bluster has turned into Gavin Apology and the result is very similar. Once more, the opening gambit has set the scene, only this time it is a diametrically opposite approach. The quietism of Gavin certainly defuses any potential conflict, but at his own expense. Furthermore, the offer of a ticket that Gavin thought would buy the goodwill of the mechanic has failed to secure the resolution of the problem. This is a classic negotiating mistake: unconditional gifts are almost always the stimulant to further demands and not a stimulant to reciprocity. This is not a high trust situation where reciprocity may normally result from unconditional gifts; if the gift is not conditional the receiver has little or no incentive to respond in kind and rather more to seek further unreciprocated gifts. In wage-bargaining this often takes the form of management of-fering the unions a 'sweetener' to start the negotiation off in the 'right' spirit, or, contrarily, the unions unconditionally with-draw the threat of a strike for the same reason. In either case the usual response is for the receiver to thank the giver and proceed on the assumption that the giver is obviously in a weak position and is already ceding ground.

Gavin's attempt to get a second opinion could have saved him a long walk here, but he failed to be assertive enough to secure it. The symptoms of the car may well fit the gasket problem, but they may also fit a range of other explanations. What the mechanic is in danger of doing is operating a Procrustean appraisal system, only this time it's to a car not a person. From another viewpoint the appraisal may suggest a cracked cylinder head, but Gavin has allowed the authorit-ative announcement to become a 'fact' by failing to question its authenticity: 'expertise' has blinded him and, since he is not an expert, he is not able to assess whether the expert is right. Perhaps Gavin could have prepared a little more effectively.

Much the most underestimated element of negotiating is the preparation and, to quote one of my teachers of the martial arts (Ross Jackson), failing to prepare is preparing to fail. It is not just in the conventional arena of collective bargaining that negotiators take too little time to prepare, discussing tactics in the taxi on the way, but also in the more mundane everyday negotiations over taking damaged goods back to the shop or negotiating over a disputed telephone bill. How often do we dig out that copy of the *Consumers' Guide to the Law* that we bought once, before getting to the shop only to find that we are not really clear about our rights? Yet it is amazing how much a quote from the 1984 Goods and Services Act can improve your position: as Foucault reminds us, power and knowledge are irresistibly intertwined.

A variant of this appeal to the law as a method of buttressing one's position is the difference between what Fisher and Ury (1982: 86–8) call 'positional' and 'principled' negotiation. Positional bargaining involves sticking to a position irrespect-ive of anything else. This is often tied to a belief in the objectiv-ity of value and reproduces the Aristotelian binary principles we have met many times before: the house is objectively worth x and therefore not worth $x + 1$ nor $x - 1$; so, for instance, your house is actually worth £100,000 because the expert surveyor/ valuer says so—even when no buyer can be found for it. Principled bargaining is premised upon an attempt to divorce the negotiating from these erroneously objective values, and set the negotiation against an independent base (not 'objective', as Fisher and Ury imply). For example, I may agree to set the value of my house on the basis of averaging three quotes from estate agents. This average figure is clearly not 'objective', but it sets the framework for the negotiation on a plane beyond the restrictive space enveloped by ideas about 'true' value and back into an arena rooted in the skill of the negotiators. To negotiate on this basis, though, requires some preparation— and we have already suggested that preparation is usually the first casualty of negotiations.

So why don't we prepare enough? Probably for all kinds of reasons: we are just too busy to find the time; why bother preparing when the whole thing is sewn up in advance? Why bother preparing for something you cannot prepare for? And, very importantly, preparation implies that we cannot 'shoot from the hip', that is, we are locked into a macho negotiating culture where fist-waving and table-thumping are considered the most appropriate skills—not sitting in the library reading up on the topic beforehand. Take the parents' race on school sports day as an example of the latter problem: how many parents wear loose-fitting clothes, trainers, and spend ten minutes before the race warming up and stretching? No, far better to run in shoes without any grip, in tight jeans, and just to go out there and do it. Do it, in this context usually means one-third of the competitors either fall over at the start or before the finish, and of the other two-thirds most will spend the weekend nursing strained ligaments or muscles or backs—but what a race!

Preparation, then, is critical if you are to avoid injury in the parents' race or in the negotiation. But what kind of preparation is good preparation? Perhaps the most important point is to establish what it is that *you* want from the negotiation. Beyond this, you need to consider what it is that you are prepared to settle for, and what you can trade to get it. If you have nothing to trade, then perhaps you should not be negotiating at all. If you can secure your aim without negotiating, then why bother going through the effort? Why not just require it? In many areas of life we do not negotiate: for example, we tend to pay the advertised price for petrol, but bargain over the price of cars, and part of the skill of the salesperson is in persuading us that we cannot bargain over the advertised price.

So let us persuade Gavin to go to the library and read up on his rights as a consumer, and ring up the makers of the vehicle and see what their position is before he enters the garage that sold him the car.

Scene 1, take iii: 'Gavin Assertive goes negotiating'

MECHANIC: It's a bit dodgy, mate. I reckon the head gasket has blown.

GAVIN: So, when can you fix it?

MECHANIC: Next week's the earliest.

GAVIN: Thanks, could you get the service manager for me please?

MECHANIC: He's on lunch, mate. Should be back about three.

GAVIN: OK, I'll see the garage manager then.

MECHANIC: Oh, well, actually I think I know where the service manager is. I'll go and find him.

SERVICE MANAGER: Yes sir, how can I help you?

GAVIN: I have a problem. I bought this car from you last month and your mechanic tells me there is something seriously wrong with it and that you cannot fix it until next week. I need this car, or an equivalent, for tomorrow and you are no doubt aware that, under the 1984 Goods and Services Act, you are responsible in law for the provision of serviceable merchandise and are liable to repair it under warranty in a reasonable time period. I do not consider 'next week' a reasonable time period, and I've got to get to Durham tomorrow—will it be all right?

SERVICE MANAGER: Yeh, probably.

GAVIN: Do you know what's wrong with it?

SERVICE MANAGER: The head gasket's blown.

GAVIN: So you are absolutely certain that the cylinder head hasn't cracked—because if it has then I could seriously damage the engine driving it—couldn't I?

SERVICE MANAGER: No, it can't be the cylinder head because, well, in truth, they never crack on this engine.

GAVIN: You can guarantee this can you?

SERVICE MANAGER: Well, not so much guarantee it—look, how about you coming back next week and using one of my small courtesy cars for the trip while we fix your car?

GAVIN: OK, fine.

[*Gavin breaks down on the way home but gets a tow in and borrows a courtesy car for his Durham trip*]

Well that's a bit better, Gavin. At least you stopped him on the truth bit. After all, this is a very fuzzy area; it isn't transparently clear what is wrong with all cars all of the time. On the contrary, cars appear to be positively Heisenbergian sometimes: when I drive it, it makes a terrible noise—rather like a 'part(icle)' is about to shear off, but as soon as the mechanic looks at it the noise disappears and he 'waves' the car off. Anyway, if we could guarantee that things would not go wrong (as opposed to guaranteeing to repair or replace them), then the vehicle-rescue services would be out of work. You were also a little more assertive without being aggressive. But you were a bit flaky on the courtesy car, you had to make two extra trips and then took a car that was too small for your needs. Never mind, at least you used the preparation time wisely to mug up on the legal rights of consumers, and that seemed to work. How can we improve on the bargaining?

Most assumptions about negotiating tend to suggest that it's merely a form of argument in which the person with the loudest voice, the best logic, or the most intransigent action wins. But if we could assess the outcome of a negotiation before it began by assessing the various strengths on both sides, then there would be little use in negotiating. On the contrary, the strange thing about negotiations is how much the end result is affected by the negotiation itself, by the actions and utterances of the participants rather than by their positional power. Nor is it the case that we can win simply by mustering the strongest arguments. Very often we go into a situation armed with ir-refutable arguments, only to be irrefutably refuted. In fact, I can't remember the last time I managed to persuade someone that I was right and they were wrong, at least not to the point where my opponent would pronounce in public: 'Gosh you are absolutely right, how could I have been so stupid, I only wish I was as clever as you.' Come to think of it not only does this statement ring foreign to my ears, but I don't recall ever having said it, or something like it, either.

Part of the misunderstanding about negotiations may lie in the focus on the opening statements and the arguments that invariably follow it. Take, for example, a typical salary claim put forward by one of the unions in the education sector. The union side starts off by laying out the 25 per cent decrease in relative pay that its members have suffered over the last seventeen years, and demands an immediate 15 per cent pay rise to start making up for lost ground. The employers respond sympathetically, but claim there is no money in the coffers and offer 3 per cent. We are now entering a form of bargaining that might be called 'pantomime bargaining':

'You can afford 15 per cent.'
'Oh no we can't!'
'Oh yes you can!'—and so on.

A second version of this game might be called chaos bargaining: This is how it goes:

'You can afford 15 per cent.'
'Oh no we can't!'
'Oh yes you can, I mean, I see you driving off in a BMW every evening so you must be rolling in it.'
'My personal income has nothing to do with this negotiation.'
'Oh yes it does. You managers are all the same, living off the backs of honest workers.'
'Honest! Then how come we lose 10 per cent of the stock every year?'
'Are you accusing my members of being dishonest?'

In this case the unpredictability of the situation can lead the negotiation virtually anywhere. Indeed, even when using iden-tical case studies on many situations, I have yet to see anything like an identical scenario played out because the butterfly or multiplier effect tends to undermine the planned direction of the negotiation. Under such circumstances the negotiation may actually spiral out of control and disintegrate unless one of the parties is able to utilize a strange attractor to get the process back on the road. Such strange attractors may take the form of a verbal reminder—'Look, can we get away from personal argument and remind ourselves why we are here?'—or it may require a more formal mechanism to restore order: an adjournment, for instance, in which both sides take a break to cool down and try to find a way out of the quagmire they have landed themselves in.

This game is likely to continue until one side or the other makes a move that signals their intent on achieving a bargain rather than winning an argument. The latter is a critical trap for many unsuspecting negotiators: they become embroiled in an argument that is not only unwinnable, but which actively inhibits their search for a negotiated deal. Let us role Gavin back in for this one at the end of the last take.

Scene 1, take iv: 'Gavin Argument goes negotiating'

GAVIN: You can guarantee this can you?

SERVICE MANAGER: Well, not so much guarantee it—look, how about you coming back next week and using one of my small courtesy cars for the trip while we fix your car?

GAVIN: No. I want a guarantee.

SERVICE MANAGER: I can't give you one.

GAVIN: I'm not leaving without one.

SERVICE MANAGER: You cannot leave with one.

GAVIN: I'm still waiting.

SERVICE MANAGER: Can you turn the light out when you've finished waiting, I'm off now.

GAVIN: I want to see the sales manager who sold me the car, or the mechanic who prepared it.

SERVICE MANAGER: Bye.

[*Three weeks later Gavin has not got a guarantee, and he's missed all his meetings, but at least he hasn't let the service manager win the argument*]

Now what is going on here? Gavin tried at the very end to open up the possibility of another manager or the mechanic taking some (deep) leadership action to resolve his problem, but he was too late. He has also forgotten one of the cardinal principles of preparation: what do you want out of this? Is winning the argument his prime intention? It seems that Gavin has allowed himself to be manœuvred into an Aristotelian cul-de-sac where all thoughts of negotiating in a fuzzy environment are surrendered to the primary binary: if you win, I lose. It certainly looks like a 'positional' stance rather than a 'principled' stance. If so, he should join a debating society. Or is he really interested in getting a roadworthy car to get him to Durham tomorrow? If it is the latter, then how can we get Gavin out of the argument phase and into the negotiating phase? The answer is to hoist a signal that implies you may be willing to trade here—but there are no details of this trade, it is inherently fuzzy, and it will only work if the other side agrees to trade too. This is signalling language. It may involve a desire to start from a principled position (look, can we agree about the legal position here and start on that basis?), but it need not.

Scene 1, take v: 'Gavin Signaller goes negotiating'

GAVIN: You can guarantee this can you?

SERVICE MANAGER: Well, not so much guarantee it—look, how about you coming back next week and using one of my small courtesy cars for the trip while we fix your car?

GAVIN: No. I want a guarantee.

SERVICE MANAGER: I can't give you one.

GAVIN: I don't think we can come to an agreement about this without a guarantee. However, would you be interested in loaning me one of those second-hand cars in the car park instead of a courtesy car?

SERVICE MANAGER: Er, I might be able to do something there, as long as we can come to an agreement on the conditions.

DIRECTOR: Cut!

Now Gavin has a bite. He has not given anything away, even though he moved first—another mistaken element of the macho school of negotiation in which whoever twitches first is the loser. On the contrary, as many self-defence experts know, there really isn't time to wait for the other to move first, you have to get your retaliation in before the attack starts. Note also that the service manager has not given anything away either, there is no resort to a binary 'take it or leave it', and he has begun to use the golden conditional: 'if'. In the absence of an 'if', there is often little incentive for the other to move.

At this point in the negotiation, Gavin's signal ('would you be interested . . . ?') has secured a return signal ('I might be able . . .') and we are entering the bargaining stage. Note, though, how Gavin's signal comes after a negative statement ('I don't think . . .')—this is very common and it acts to prevent the signaller from looking as though he or she is caving in under pressure. Yet the negative element of the signal often tends to be the only element heard by the opponent, and the signal may consequently be lost in the chaotically driven downward spiral that ends in another argument rather than a bargain.

This is not the point at which a compromise is necessarily the solution. Gavin wants an equivalent car now to get him to Durham and back. The service manager wants to loan him a smaller courtesy car next week. The compromise would be to loan Gavin an equivalent car until he's halfway to Durham, or a car that is bigger than the service manager intended but still too small for Gavin. This would resemble an attempt to resolve the Israeli–Egyptian conflict over Sinai, discussed at Camp David in 1978, by splitting the disputed land in two. But the issue remained unresolved because Egypt wanted all the land back and Israel wanted security. The solution was for Egypt to take the land but with a demilitarized strip and over-fly rights for Israel. This is not a classic compromise where neither side gets what they really want; it is a win–win negotiated settlement where both sides get what they want—because they want different things. Let us return to Gavin to see what can be negotiated here.

Scene 1, take vi: 'Gavin Fresher goes negotiating'

GAVIN: Would you be interested in loaning me one of those second-hand cars in the car park instead of a courtesy car if I leave my car now?

SERVICE MANAGER: Er, I might be able to do something there, as long as we can come to an agreement on the conditions.

GAVIN: Well, you know my problem. I need the same size car as mine and I need it today and tomorrow.

SERVICE MANAGER: Sorry, that's impossible. I can't solve your problem because none of the cars are taxed and the Post Office is shut.

GAVIN: Damn! I'll have to wait then.

SERVICE MANAGER: Sorry sir, I'm afraid there's nothing I can do now to help you.

It looks like we have hit a couple of problems here. Gavin has not got into the conditional habit (no 'ifs' in his bargaining), so that doesn't give the service manager any incentive to bargain with him, and he has reverted to stonewalling. Second, the service manager has now recruited a new ally to his side: the missing tax that prevents the car from being used on the road. This piece of paper is remarkably resilient—as the actor-network theory implied non-humans may be—when tied into a network. Gavin is floored by this because it appears an irrefutable and completely non-fuzzy argument, and no amount of shouting is going to conjure the relevant tax disc out of the air.

There are two particular techniques that might help Gavin out here: questioning and silence. Too often, negotiations deteriorate into arguments and failure because the participants forget how useful it is to deliver the message in different formats—including a message of silence. Thus, if your opposition states something that looks blatantly unfeasible to you, you may be tempted to point this out in no uncertain terms. Here's a company with a problem of lateness in the morning:

MANAGER 1: Why don't we get them all to sign on in the morning at 8 o'clock?

MANAGER 2: Look, it's obvious that wouldn't work because

there are 250 people involved. How can they sign on simultaneously—there isn't the physical room!

The consequences of this are an embarrassing public rebuff to manager 1—who will not forget it in a hurry. A more constructive way is to put the same issue into a question:

MANAGER 1: Why don't we get them all to sign on in the morning at 8 o'clock?
MANAGER 2: What would be the consequences of this at the point where they all sign on?
MANAGER 1: Well they would all have to queue up and—hmmm, perhaps there is another way.

In this case the second manager takes responsibility for the problem and withdraws it without being unduly embarrassed or coerced.

The utility of questions over assertions is another way of ensuring that the negotiation does not get side-tracked, but it must operate in both directions. In other words, the more likely you are to attack their proposal or argument, and the more likely you are to defend yours against attack, the more likely it is that the negotiation will lead anywhere but to a deal. This is crucial when negotiating with an inexperienced negotiator whose model of strategy is essentially macho, because the tendency to spiral downwards into acrimony is very strong. Unfortunately, this model has become something of a cultural norm and, as we saw in chapters 2 and 3, cultural norms or fashions are enormously powerful features of most organizations.

The tactic of silence is also useful. If you have ever been involved in a business meeting, or university seminar, or tutorial in which no one speaks for several seconds, you will probably appreciate how powerful silence can be as a technique for pressurizing the other side into speaking. This is also drawn from a cultural norm, but it operates directly against it, because the norm is to engage in reciprocal conversation with another. It is for this reason that speeches and lectures that last for more than a few minutes have an unrivalled capacity for sending the listeners off to sleep—at least this is my experience! It also alerts us to another issue in managing change: if you want to signal a radical change in the way your organization is being run, then you may have to construct counter-cultural processes and events: abolish the privileged parking for executives, abandon the executive restaurant, stop making the staff clock in when managers don't need to, get all the managers wearing workwear and so on.

Finally, Gavin has failed to secure any degree of commitment or ownership from the service manager. He constantly talks about his car as *his* problem and the sales manager is happy to agree to this non-ownership—of course, without commitment to the issue the sales manager lacks the incentive to do anything about it and will not generate the necessary resources to resolve it. This, as chapter 3 suggested, is not just a problem for Gavin in getting his car fixed, it is a problem for all managers in getting anything fixed.

Can Gavin make better progress using these additional techniques?

Scene 1, take vii: 'Gavin Improver goes negotiating'

GAVIN: Would you be interested in loaning me one of those second-hand cars in the car park instead of a courtesy car if I leave my car now? I mean, there has to be a way to solve the problem that you will have if I end up a very dissatisfied customer.

SERVICE MANAGER: Er, I might be able to do something there, as long as we can come to an agreement on the conditions.

GAVIN: Well, I need the same size car as mine and I need it today and tomorrow.

SERVICE MANAGER: Sorry, that's impossible. None of the cars are taxed and the Post Office is shut.

GAVIN: So what do you suggest?

[*silence prevails*]

SERVICE MANAGER: Well er—I don't really know.

GAVIN: I tell you what. I can't drive my car to Durham because it probably won't make it. I'm prepared to take one of your small courtesy cars home today *if* you get one of these larger cars taxed by tomorrow morning for me to use to get to Durham.

SERVICE MANAGER: But I don't have a courtesy car today to give you, I told you that before.

GAVIN: If you don't pull your finger out I'm going to write to the TV and your company CEO about your attitude!

SERVICE MANAGER: Don't you threaten me, mate. I'm leaning over backwards to help you. It's not my fault your car is broken, it's the manufacturer's. I'm just doing my job, trying to keep the business afloat.

Aggh! He was doing so well. Ironically, this is not uncommon. Things go perfectly to plan and then, crash, a message is interpreted as hostile, even if it isn't meant as such ('But I don't have a courtesy car today to give you, I told you that before'), which is followed by a threat and the inevitable counter-threat: chaos theory now takes over. Moreover, the service manager is reverting to a statement of position which is of no interest to Gavin at all. Does he care whether the garage is making a profit? Does he care whose fault the problem is? Does he know that, by law, it *is* the garage's responsibility if they have sold him the goods? Let's leave the service desk a moment and go round to the sales area, while Gavin and the service manager cool down. Gavin enters the showroom where ten shiny cars await his inspection, and an eager sales representative appears.

Scene 2, take i: 'Gavin Unimpressed goes car buying'

SALES REPRESENTATIVE: Good morning Sir! Can I just say that, although all these cars are extremely good value, this [*pointing at a large executive saloon*] is most definitely the one for you.

GAVIN: Oh yes? Why is that then?

SALES REPRESENTATIVE: Because I've already sold two of these this week and if I sell one more I get my monthly bonus of £1,500!

This is absurd. No self-respecting sales representative is going to make this basic mistake—she knows you have to sell cars to customers on the basis of their needs not your own. But how often do we hear managers come into a room and announce: 'Well, ladies and gentlemen, I'm sorry to announce that the company's profits are not as good as expected and as a direct consequence you will all have to take a 5 per cent pay cut.' Do the 'ladies and gentlemen' really care that much about the profit figures? Does their pay go up when times are good, and does it rise as fast as the CEO's, whose reward package is not only grotesquely overvalued but appears to rise irrespective of the health of the company? No, this manager has forgotten that things need to be sold and that they need to be sold in the interests of the consumer not the producer. Might it not be better to start: 'Well, ladies and gentlemen, I'm sorry to announce that the company's profits are not as good as expected, but, despite the threat to all our jobs, we have agreed not to make anyone redundant but to try and save everyone's jobs. This, however, will mean a collective sacrifice: first, the CEO is taking a proportional pay cut and, second, we want to discuss with you ways—including universal pay cuts—we can save enough money to keep the company afloat.' This is not just playing with words and glossing over a devious intent, but reconstructing the problem so that all own the problem and the solution.

Scene 2, take ii: 'Gavin Less Unimpressed goes car buying'

SALES REPRESENTATIVE: Good morning Sir! Can I just say that, although all these cars are extremely good value, this [*pointing at a large executive saloon*] is most definitely the one for you.

GAVIN: Oh yes? Why is that then?

SALES REPRESENTATIVE: Because it has all the features that you need, it's on a special financial deal this weekend, and because we also have a special part-exchange deal operating if you buy this car. Finally, sir, you should know that this car has been voted the most popular car in its range in this year's motoring magazine awards. Indeed, so popular is it that we are giving away a free mobile phone with every purchase.

GAVIN: I might be interested. I'm looking for about £10,000 for a part exchange with mine—it's that one in the workshop.

SALES REPRESENTATIVE: Well sir, the book price for that is around £8,000.

GAVIN: No chance! I'll go and get mine repaired.

Several points are important here. The word 'about' in Gavin's pricing is a give-away on the willingness to come down. This is the equivalent of saying: 'I'm looking for between £9,000 and £10,000' and the sales representative should know that the seller will shift down to the lower price without too much hassle—the question is how far. A rather more sophisticated approach would be to use this 'between' as a double bluff: here, the real price you are looking for is the lower of the two— 'between £11,000 and £10,000'—and the hope is that the buyer thinks he or she will feel good about knocking you down instantly a thousand pounds. Yet this deal does not progress because Gavin's expectations are too high. Having just bought the car, he is under the impression that its value has only slipped slightly, when in fact the first mile out of the forecourt is the most expensive the car will ever do, because its value instantly drops with each ownership, and especially the first. If Gavin were to be offered £9,000 immediately he would probably feel very suspicious that he has not negotiated a good deal—he could have asked for a higher price and got one if the buyer was prepared to snap it up so quickly. But were he to be offered £8,500 after twenty other people have looked at it he would probably think that he had done extremely well to get rid of it at that price. In effect, expectations are crucial to the negotiation.

It is also important to be aware of the flared trouser problem here. Gavin has never before had a mobile phone, but all his colleagues and associates have. Moreover, the deal is too good to be true—the phone is free. So Gavin can be fashionable, and at no cost to himself. Except, of course, for the monthly line rental of £15, the contract cancellation fee of £50, the concern that it might be stolen, and the realization twelve months on that, actually, he's never used it.

We now move back with Gavin to the service manager for a further attempt to resolve the problem.

Scene 3, take i: 'Gavin Nearly goes negotiating'

GAVIN: I tell you what, I can't drive my car to Durham because it probably won't make it. I know you say it probably will, but I can't take that risk, I cannot trust this car, and I am not going to wait until I break down to confirm my distrust. Since you trust it, then perhaps we can make some progress. I'm prepared to take one of your small courtesy cars home today *if* you get one of these larger cars taxed by tomorrow morning for me to use to get to Durham tomorrow.

SERVICE MANAGER: But I don't have a courtesy car today to give you. I told you that before.

GAVIN: Well, I'll ignore the tone of your voice because I need to resolve this problem. What kind of car do you drive?

SERVICE MANAGER: The same as you. Why?

GAVIN: Well, if you loan me your car I'll loan you mine. That way I get to Durham in a decent sized vehicle on time.

SERVICE MANAGER: Oh no, I couldn't do that.

Gavin! You were almost there, and contrary to the government's handling of the mad cow problem discussed in the previous chapter, the risk problem reconstructed as an issue of trust was useful in tipping the balance against that argument. But you just wrapped it up too crudely so that it was all focused upon your own interests. You are forgetting the golden bridge and it now looks as though you have won and the service manager has lost: what will the mechanics say and think? This is meant to be a negotiation not a command situation. Try again, but think about the importance of empathy—what can you do for the service manager?

Scene 3, take ii: 'Gavin Veteran goes negotiating'

GAVIN: I tell you what. I'm prepared to ignore what has happened today and I will not take any further action against you or the company *if* you loan me your car and I'll loan you mine. That way we both drive a car we trust, and I get to Durham in a decent sized vehicle on time, and you get to keep my car so you can fix it at your leisure. Furthermore, if you are prepared to bring my car round to my house when it's finished I'll give you a couple of tickets for the match on Saturday.

SERVICE MANAGER: That seems acceptable, but I'll have to check with my boss first and see whether we have a mechanic available to bring your car round when it's finished. I'm not sure we can manage this.

GAVIN: Look, I can't wait any longer. I wanted the car fixing immediately or a decent sized courtesy car today. You've pushed me back on both counts and driven a really hard bargain here so I'm not feeling good about myself, but is it a deal or shall I walk out now and pursue this issue elsewhere?

SERVICE MANAGER: Well, OK, but we are not liable for any damage to your car for the duration of the swap.

GAVIN: No. I'm sorry, this was not part of the offer and I'm not accepting it. If you want to start negotiating about insurance then we can start all over again, but the other deal will be off the table.

SERVICE MANAGER: OK, OK, it's a deal.

GAVIN: Right, but just let's sit down and write this out so that we both know whose doing what and when.

There are a lot of lessons in this final section, which manages to bring the deal to a close. First, Gavin generates conditional statements that force the service manager to move. Second, he provides a sweetener that embodies two important principles of negotiating: it is conditional upon some reciprocal action; and it is of low cost to the giver and high value to the receiver. Since Gavin cannot go to the match, the tickets are virtually worthless to him, but to the fanatic fans in the garage they are like gold dust! Just because the tickets are of relatively low cost to Gavin does not mean that he cannot sell them for a high value. In fact, there is considerable support for the claim that the symbolic significance of something like match tickets is of much higher value than the equivalent in cash terms. Hence, many companies prefer to distribute rewards for team performance in the form of such tickets or vouchers rather than cash in the bank. Cash in the bank is swallowed up and instantly forgotten; a trip to the game with the rest of the team is something that will probably be remembered for some considerable time. Third, Gavin's summary of the situation is explicitly constructed from the interests of the service manager and not from his own. Fourth, when the service manager begins to prevaricate about the bargain Gavin issues an ultimatum that is not an aggressive threat, but merely a statement that clarifies exactly what will happen if the deal is allowed to fail. Fifth, the service manager tries to sneak the damage waiver in at the end just as Gavin is about to sign up—but he makes it very clear that this is not on and gets the service manager to reconsider. Sixth, Gavin has linked the whole package together and reminds the service manager that it stands or falls as a whole. Finally, Gavin remembers to clarify the deal—otherwise the service manager may 'forget' certain elements of it.

Reader, Gavin got to Durham!

CONCLUSION

There are many very useful book-length guides on negotiating (Fisher and Ury, 1982; Kennedy, 1982; Robinson, 1995), but unless you are blessed with a perfect memory, or want the embarrassment of taking the book in with you to the negotiation, all the useful tips in the world can tend to fall apart under the pressure. In theory, the negotiation can be managed from stage to stage—preparation, goals, opening, argument, signalling, bargaining, close, agreement—as long as you can remember the sequence of those stages, but the implications of virtually all the theories discussed in this book suggest that the world is much fuzzier and more indeterminate than any negotiating guide makes out.

Perhaps the final offering may provide what, after all, is the kind of practical advice that the book intended to generate all along. Not prescriptive commands about how things must be done, but an array of guidelines to help. If it is deemed improper to carry the 'negotiator's bible' into the arena, perhaps the following mnemonic may help: CHEQUEPREPS

Conditional statements are the key to encouraging the other side to negotiate.

High Value/Low Cost is the critical couplet that should drive your trades.

Everything is negotiable—but don't let them know that.

Questions not arguments are the 'strange attractors' to stop the argument.

Unconditional gifts don't work.

Empathy wins—why should they move, and is there a golden bridge to help them?

Preparation is the foundation of successful negotiation.

Relational power, not possessive power, controls organizations.

Expectations are dangerous, handle with care.

Principled not positional bargaining is the first choice.

Signal when you seem to be drowning.

Finally, let me sum up the entire book by reminding readers of my original intent. I began with a paradox summed up in the email message on the first page: either theory is interesting but practically irrelevant, or practice works but no one knows why. I have tried to construct this book so that some of the new (1990s) theories repositioning management in the heads of academics can be reconstructed to provide some practical advice to practising managers. In a reversal of my previous book on management I have made this one more practical as it has gone on, to the extent that the theories become invisible as they become practised. When we first learn to drive, it is obviously impossible to manage the clutch, the steering, the brakes, the other traffic, the map, the rule book, and the instructor simultaneously. After a good deal of practice we can get to work on some mornings wondering what happened to the journey, what happened to the theory?

From Aristotle's binary logic to negotiating is a long journey in space, time, and knowledge, but they are pinned together by a common assumption: the world does actually appear to be fuzzy and it may be that theories which postulate a world of simple decisions (yes/no, right/wrong, etc.) are equally simply inadequate—and this is why we are thrown back to rely upon a practical knowledge base that appears untheoretical or at least atheoretical. Yet it does not have to be like this—there are contemporary theories that offer a way forward when the uncertainty increases and the clarity decreases. The fuzzy logic explored in chapter 1 need not inhibit our freedom of action, but could actually enhance it: if entering that difficult market is not right or wrong, but probably right or possibly right, then perhaps we should negotiate strategies and structures that take account of the fuzzy world rather than pretend it doesn't exist by persuading ourselves that our decisions must be clearly one thing or another. If we are very reflexive about chapter 3 we might want to consider whether fuzzy theories are themselves merely the construction of fashion leaders and therefore we should stick to what is tried and tested. If this is the case, if traditional methods of management do indeed work perfectly respectably, there will be little commitment to any form of novelty—as chapter 4 suggested. However, complacency—or worse, hubris—might be the equivalent of mad cow disease: how can you catch it if you are a sheep? Moreover, the shift from complacency to bankruptcy or redundancy mirrors the speed with which our veritably chaotic butterfly generates a storm; one day you make a bad joke about your goods being crap, or how drugs don't harm anyone, or how eggs are dangerous, or you say 'read my lips'—and the next day, week, month, or year, you are negotiating a redundancy package. Life need not be so precarious. On the contrary, we can acknowledge the indeterminacy of life suggested by chaos theory and construct systems and organizations which operate along rather than against these principles. We can institutionalize forms of deep leadership that form the basis of new model organizations, and we may be able to secure change through such committed organizations—but the evidence remains stubbornly recalcitrant: unless managers themselves are really committed to change, nobody else in the organization will be. For some theories, the inability of managers to manage change successfully merely supports a belief that we are at the mercy of the market, we cannot master it. However, for others such a fatalistic approach replicates the poverty of our belief that we cannot negotiate change. The first part of chapter 5 and the last part of chapter 6, however, suggest that fatalism is as much a consequence of the way our theoretical approach organizes 'reality' as it is to reality organizing us. Indeed, it may well be that, as Procrustes so clearly demonstrated, chopping up the world to fit the theory tends to leave a lasting impression on the world, but not one that is automatically useful. A legless appraisal, courtesy of Procrustes, is neither ideal nor the best we can do in the circumstances. Far from it: if we have the courage to embrace Heisenberg's uncertainty we may secure a radical advancement in knowledge that would render that Procrustean brigand, well, (h)armless. Contemporary theory is not risk-free, and it does not provide the certainty that many traditional theories claim but few have ever been able to justify. But if the kind of risk-free certainties adopted in handling the mad cow problem are anything to go by, then perhaps we should look elsewhere for guidance. To reverse ex-President Bush's claim, the world is probably not like the Waltons in its cosy and controlled family life, it is probably much closer to the Simpsons' version of anarchy and chaos. If this is accurate, if Homer is closer to your boss than Grandma, if Bart and Lisa are closer to your subordinates than Jimbob, then perhaps it's time to change programmes, clear away those clean-cut images, and embrace the new fuzzy world.

References

Abercrombie, N., Hill, S., and Turner, B. S. 1980: *The Dominant Ideology Thesis*, London: Allen and Unwin.

Abrahamson, E. 1996: 'Management Fashion', *Academy of Management Review*, 21, pp. 254–85.

Adams, J. 1996: *Risk*, London: University College Press.

Adams, S. 1996: *The Dilbert Principle*, New York: Harper Business.

Aldrich, H. E. 1979: *Organizations and Environments*, Englewood Cliffs, NJ: Prentice Hall.

Aldridge, A. 1994: 'The Construction of Rational Consumption in *Which?* Magazine: The More Blobs the Better?' *Sociology*, vol. 28, no. 4, pp. 899–912.

Anand, P., and Forshner, C. 1995: 'Of Mad Cows and Marmosets: From Rational Choice to Organizational Behaviour in Crisis Management', *British Journal of Management*, vol. 6, pp. 221–33.

Anderson, B. 1991: *Imagined Communities*, London: Verso.

Anderson, G. 1994: 'Fuzzy Logic: What It Is; What It Does; What It Can Do', *Production*, October, pp. 38–42.

Anthony, P. D. 1977: *The Ideology of Work*, London: Tavistock.

Argyris, C. 1992: 'A Leadership Dilemma: Skilled Incompetence', in Argyris, C., *On Organizational Learning*, Oxford: Blackwell.

Atkins, P., and Brassley, P. 1996: 'Mad Cows and Englishmen', *History Today*, vol. 46, no. 9, pp. 14–17.

Bansal, P. 1995: 'Why do Firms go Green? The Case for Organizational Legitimacy', unpublished D.Phil thesis, Oxford University.

Bansal, P., and Howard, E. (eds) 1997: *Business and the Natural Environment*, Oxford: Butterworth Heinemann.

Barley, S. R., and Kunda, G. 1992: 'Design and Devotion; Surges in Rational and Normative Ideologies of Control in Managerial Discourse', *Administrative Science Quarterly*, vol. 37, pp. 363–99.

Barnard, C. 1946: 'The Nature of Leadership', in Hoslett, D. (ed.), *Human Factors in Management*, New York: McGraw-Hill.

Bass, B. M. 1985: *Leadership and Performance Beyond Expectations*, New York: Free Press.

——1990: *Bass and Stogdill's Handbook of Leadership: Theory, Research and Managerial Applications*, New York: Free Press.

Batstone, E., Boraston, I., and Frenkel, S. 1979: *Shop Stewards in Action*, Oxford: Blackwell.

Beard, H. 1995: *The Complete Latin for All Occasions*, London: BCA.

Beck, U. 1992: *Risk Society*, London: Sage.

Belbin, M. 1981: *Management Teams: Why They Succeed or Fail*, London: Heinemann.

Bijker, W. E., Hughes, T. P., and Pinch, T. J. (eds) 1987: *The Social Construction of Technological Systems*, Cambridge, Mass.: MIT Press.

Blauner, R. E. 1964: *Alienation and Freedom*, Chicago: University of Chicago Press.

Blenkhorn, D. L., and Gaber, B. 1995: 'The Use of "Warm Fuzzies" To Assess Organizational Effectiveness', *Journal of General Management*, vol. 21, no. 2, pp. 40–51.

Blumer, H. 1969: 'Fashion: From Class Differentiation to Collective Selection', *Sociological Quarterly*, 10, pp. 275–91.

Boden, D. 1994: *The Business of Talk: Organizations in Action*, Cambridge: Polity Press.

Bormann, E. G. 1985: *The Force of Fantasy*, Carbondale and Edwardsville: Southern Illinois University Press.

Brinton, M. 1975: *The Bolsheviks and Workers Control*, Montréal: Black Rose Books.

Brown, J. A. C. 1964: *Social Psychology of Industry*, Harmondsworth: Penguin.

Bryman, A. 1992: *Charisma and Leadership of Organizations*, London: Sage.

Buchanan, D., and Storey, D. 1995: 'The Creatively Orchestrated Performance: A Reassessment of Change Management Theory', paper at conference on 'New Perspectives on Technology, Organization and Innovation', Brunel University, 14 September 1995.

Burke, K. 1962: *A Rhetoric of Motives*, Cleveland: World Publishing Company.

Burns, T., and Stalker, G. M. 1961: *The Management of Innovation*, London: Tavistock.

Burr, V. 1995: *An Introduction to Social Constructionism*, London: Routledge.

Calás, M. B., and Smircich, L. 1991: 'Voicing Seduction to Silence Leadership', *Organization Studies*, vol. 12, no. 4, pp. 567–602.

Callon, M. 1991: 'Techno-Economic Networks and Irreversibility', in Law, J. (ed.), *A Sociology of Monsters*, London: Routledge.

——1986: 'Some Elements of a Sociology of Translation: Domestication of the Scallops and the Fishermen of St Brieuc's Bay', in Law, J. (ed.), *Power, Action and Belief: A New Sociology of Knowledge*, London: Routledge.

Caulkin, S. 1995: 'Chaos Inc.', *Across the Board*, July/August, pp. 33–6.

Champy, J. 1995: *Reengineering Management*, London: Nicholas Breaby.

Chandler, A. D. Jr. 1962: *Strategy and Structure*, Cambridge, Mass.: MIT Press.

Chatterjee, P., and Finger, M. 1994: *The Earth Brokers: Power, Politics and World Development*, London: Routledge.

Clark, T., and Salaman, G. 1996: 'Telling Tales: Management Guru's Narratives and the Construction of Managerial Identity', paper presented to Conference on Management Consultancy, Open University, London, 28 September.

Conger, J. A. 1993: 'The Brave New World of Leadership Training', *Organizational Dynamics*, Winter, pp. 46–58.

Coopey, J. 1995: 'Managerial Culture and the Stillbirth of Organizational Commitment', *Human Resource Management Journal*, vol. 5, no. 3, pp. 56–76.

Crosby, A. W. 1986: *Ecological Imperialism: The Biological Expansion of Europe 900–1900*, Cambridge: Cambridge University Press.

Davidow, W., and Malone, M. 1993: *The Virtual Corporation*, New York: Harper.

Dearlove, D. 1993: 'Seeing the Error of your Ways', *The Times*, 19 August.

Dell, E. 1996: *The Chancellors: A History of the Chancellors of the Exchequer 1945–90*, London: HarperCollins.

D'Este, C. 1996: *A Genius for War: A Life of General George S. Patton*, London: HarperCollins.

DiMaggio, P. J., and Powell, W. W. 1991: 'Introduction' in DiMaggio, P. J. and Powell, W. W. (eds), *The New Institutionalism in Organizational Analysis*, Chicago: University of Chicago Press.

Ditto, W., and Munakata, T. 1995: 'Principles and Applications of Chaotic Systems', *Communications of the ACM*, vol. 38, no. 11, pp. 96–102.

Donaldson, L. 1995: *American Anti-Management Theories of Organization*, Cambridge: Cambridge University Press.

Donovan Commission, 1968: *Report of the Royal Commission on Trade Unions and Employer's Associations*, London: HMSO.

Dopson, S., and Stewart, R. 1990: 'What is Happening to Middle Management?' *British Journal of Management*, vol. 1, no. 1, pp. 3–16.

Easterbrook, G. 1996: *A Moment on the Earth*, Harmondsworth: Penguin.

Edwards, R. 1979: *Contested Terrain*, London: Heinemann.

Ellis, J. 1993: *The Social History of the Machine Gun*, London: Pimlico.

Ernest, P. 1994: *Constructing Mathematical Knowledge*, Brighton: Falmer Press.

——1996: 'New Angles on Old Rules', *Times Higher Education Supplement*, 6 September.

Etzioni, A. 1961: *A Comparative Analysis of Complex Organizations*, New York: Free Press.

Evans, J. 1989: 'Decentralization at Everest', unpublished thesis, Middlesex University.

Festinger, L. 1957: *A Theory of Cognitive Dissonance*, Stanford, CA: Stanford University Press.

Fiddes, N. 1991: *Meat: A Natural Symbol*, London: Routledge.

Fiedler, F. E. 1967: *A Theory of Leadership-Effectiveness*, New York: McGraw-Hill.

——1978: 'The Contingency Model and the Dynamics of the Leadership Process', in Berkowitz, L. (ed.), *Advances in Experimental Social Psychology*, New York: Academic Press.

Fiedler, F. E., and Garcia, J. E. 1987: *New Approaches to Effective Leadership: The Leader Match Concept*, New York: Wiley.

Fish, S. 1980: *Is there a Text in this Class?* Baltimore: John Hopkins University Press.

Fisher, R., and Ury, W. 1982: *Getting to Yes*, London: Hutchinson.

Fitzgerald, F. 1972: *Fire in the Lake: The Vietnamese and the Americans in Vietnam*, London: Macmillan.

Flanders, A. 1965: *Industrial Relations: What is Wrong with the System?* London: Faber.

Foucault, M. 1979: *Discipline and Punish*, Harmondsworth: Penguin.

du Gay, P. 1990: 'Enterprise Culture and the Ideology of Excellence', *New Formations*, 13, pp. 45–61.

——1996: *Consumption and Identity at Work*, London: Sage.

du Gay, P., and Salaman, G. 1992: 'The Cult(ure) of the Customer', *Journal of Management Studies*, vol. 29, pp. 615–33.

Gemmill, G., and Oakley, J. 1992: 'Leadership: An Alienating Social Myth?' *Human Relations*, vol. 45, no. 2, pp. 113–129.

Gentles, I. 1991: 'The Impact of the New Model Army', in Morril, J. (ed.), *The Impact of the English Civil War*, London: Collins and Brown.

——1992: *The New Model Army*, Oxford: Blackwell.

Gleick, J. 1987: *Chaos: Making A New Science*, London: Cardinal.

Gombin, R. 1978: *The Radical Tradition*, London: Methuen and Co.

Gordon, C. G. 1991: 'Industry Determinants of Culture', *Academy of Management Review*, 16, pp. 396–415.

Gordon, T., and Greenspan, D. 1994: 'The Management of Chaotic Systems', *Technological Forecasting and Social Change*, no. 47, pp. 49–62.

Gowler, D., and Legge, K. 1983: 'The Meaning of Management and the Management of Meaning', in Earl, M. J. (ed.), *Perspectives on Management: A Multidisciplinary Analysis*, Oxford: Oxford University Press.

Gregersen, H., and Sailer, L. 1993: 'Chaos Theory and Its Implications for Social Science Research', *Human Relations*, vol. 46, no. 7, pp. 777–801.

Grint, K. 1991: *The Sociology of Work*, Cambridge: Polity Press.

——1993a: 'Japanization? Some Early Lessons from the British Post Office', *Journal of Industrial Relations*, vol. 24, no. 1, pp. 14–27.

——1993b: 'What's wrong with Performance Appraisals? A Critique and a Suggestion', *Human Resource Management Journal*, vol. 3, no. 3. pp. 61–77.

——1994: 'Reengineering History: Social Resonances and Business Process Reengineering', *Organization*, vol. 1, no. 1. pp. 179–202.

——1995a: 'Sisyphus and the Social Construction of Computer-User Problems', *Information Systems Journal*, vol. 5, no. 1. pp. 3–18.

——1995b: *Management: A Sociological Introduction*, Cambridge: Polity Press.

——1997: 'Riding Tolstoy's Wave', in Grint, K. (ed.), *Leadership: A Reader*, Oxford: Oxford University Press.

Grint, K., and Case, P. 1996: 'The Reengineering Offensive: Violent and Revolutionary Rhetoric in Managerial Discourse', paper presented to Conference on Management Consultancy, Open University, London, 28 September.

Grint, K., and Kelemen, M. (forthcoming) 'Constructing Identity'.

Grint, K., and Willcocks, L. 1995: 'Business Process Reengineering in Theory and Practice: Business Paradise Regained?' *New Technology, Work and Organization*, vol. 10, no. 2, pp. 99–109.

——1997: 'Reinventing the Organization?' in McLoughlin, I. and Harris, M. (eds) *New Perspectives on Technology, Organization and Innovation*, London: Routledge.

Grint, K., and Woolgar, S. 1995: 'On some Failures of Nerve in Constructivist and Feminist Analyses of Technology', *Science, Technology and Human Values*, vol. 20, no. 2, pp. 286–310.

——1997: *The Machine at Work: Technology, Work and Society*, Cambridge: Polity Press.

Hajer, M. A. 1996: *The Politics of Environmental Discourse: Ecological Modernisation and the Policy Process*, Oxford: Oxford University Press.

Hall, S. 1992: 'The West and the Rest: Discourse and Power', in Hall, S., and Gieben, B. (eds) *Formations of Modernity*, Cambridge: Polity Press.

Hammer, M., and Champy, J. 1993: *Reengineering the Corporation: A Manifesto for Business Revolution*, London: Nicholas Brealey.

Hannan, M. T. and Freeman, J. H. 1977: 'The Population Ecology of Organizations', *American Journal of Sociology*, 82, pp. 929–64.

Heifetz, R. A. 1994: *Leadership Without Easy Answers*, Cambridge, Mass.: Belknap Press.

Held, D. 1987: Models of Democracy, Cambridge: Polity Press.

Hersey, P., and Blanchard, K. H. 1982: *The Management of Organizational Behaviour*, Englewood Cliffs, NJ: Prentice Hall.

Herzberg, F. 1966: *Work and the Nature of Man*, New York: Staples Press.

Hines, R. 1988: 'Financial Accounting: In Communicating Reality, We Construct Reality', *Accounting, Organizations and Society*, vol. 13, no. 3, pp. 251–6.

Hobbes, T. 1968 edition: *Leviathan*, Harmondsworth: Penguin.

Holmes, R. 1987: *The Firing Line*, Harmondsworth: Penguin.

Hosking, D. M. 1997: 'Organizing, Leadership and Skilful Process', in Grint, K. (ed.), *Leadership: Classical, Contemporary and Critical Approaches*, Oxford: Oxford University Press.

Huczynski, A. A. 1993: *Management Gurus: What Makes Them and How to Become One*, London: Routledge.

Jackson, B. 1996: 'The Goose that Laid the Golden Egg?': A Rhetorical Critique of Stephen Covey and the Effectiveness Movement', paper presented to Conference on Management Consultancy, Open University, London, 28 September.

Jeffcutt, P. 1994: 'The Interpretation of Organization: A Contemporary Analysis and Critique', *Journal of Management Studies*, 31, pp. 225–50.

Joynson, S., and Forrester, A. 1995: *Sid's Heroes*, London: BBC Books.

Kamin, L. 1977: *The Science and Politics of IQ*, Harmondsworth: Penguin.

Kaplan, R. E. 1993: '360 Degree Feedback PLUS: Boosting the Power of Co-worker Ratings for Executives', *Human Resource Management Journal*, vol. 32, nos. 2 and 3, pp. 299–314.

Kaplan, R. S. 1994: 'Management Accounting 1984–1994: Development of New Practice and Theory', *Management Accounting Research*, vol. 5, no. 3, pp. 247–60.

Kaplan, R. S., and Norton, D. P. 1992: 'The Balanced Scorecard: Measures that Drive Performance', *Harvard Business Review*, Jan.–Feb., pp. 71–9.

——1996: 'Using the Balanced Scorecard as a Strategic Management System', *Harvard Business Review*, Jan.–Feb., pp. 75–85.

Karier, C. J. 1976a: 'Business Values and the Educational State', in Dale, R. et al. (eds), *Schooling and Capitalism*, London: RKP.

——1976b: 'Testing for Order and Control in the Corporate Liberal State', in Dale, R. et al. (eds), *Schooling and Capitalism*, London: RKP.

Kast, F. E., and Rosenzweig, J. E. 1970: *Organization and Management: A Systems Approach*, New York: McGraw-Hill.

Kastenbaum, R. J. 1991: *Death, Society and Human Experience*, New York: Macmillan.

Keegan, J. 1976: *The Face of Battle*, Harmondsworth: Penguin.

Kelemen, M. 1995: 'The Role of Leadership in Achieving Total Quality Management in the UK Service Sector: A Multi-paradigm Study', unpublished D.Phil thesis, Oxford University.

Kemp, A., and Sibert, J. 1991: 'Cold Water Deaths can be Reversed', *Guardian*, 19 April.

Kennedy, G. 1982: *Everything is Negotiable*, London: Arrow Books.

Kessler, I., and Purcell, J. 1992: 'Performance Related Pay: Objectives and Application', *Human Resource Management Journal*, vol. 2, no. 3, pp. 16–33.

Kessler, I., and Undy, R. 1996: *The Changing Nature of the Employment Relationship*, unpublished mimeo, Templeton College, Oxford.

Kiel, L. D. 1993: 'Nonlinear Dynamical Analysis: Assessing Systems Concepts in a Government Agency', *Public Administration Review*, vol. 53, no. 2, pp. 143–53.

Klein, R. 1996: *Eat Fat*, London: Pimlico.

Kling, R. 1992: 'Audiences, Narratives and Human Values in Social Studies of Technology', *Science, Technology and Human Values*, vol. 17, no. 3, pp. 349–65.

Knights, D., and Willmott, H. 1992: 'Conceptualizing Leadership Processes: A Study of Senior Managers in a Financial Services Company', *Journal of Management Studies*, vol. 29, no. 6, pp. 761–82.

Kondratieff, N. D. 1935: 'The Long Waves in Economic Life', *Review of Economic Statistics*, vol. 17, pp. 105–15.

Kosko, B. 1994: *Fuzzy Thinking*, London: Flamingo.

Kouzes, J. M., and Posner, B. Z. 1987: *The Leadership Challenge*, London: Jossey Bass.

Latour, B. 1986: 'The Powers of Association', in Law, J. (ed.), *Power, Action and Belief*, London: Routledge Kegan Paul.

——1987: *Science in Action: How to Follow Scientists and Engineers Through Society*, Milton Keynes: Open University Press.

——1988: 'The *Prince* for Machines as well as for Machinations, in Elliott, B. (ed.), *Technology and Social Process*, Edinburgh: Edinburgh University Press'.

Law, J. 1988: 'The Anatomy of Socio-Technical Struggle', in Elliott, B. (ed.), *Technology and Social Process*, Edinburgh: Edinburgh University Press.

——(ed.) 1991: *A Sociology of Monsters*, London: Routledge.

Levačić, R. 1983: 'The Bedfordshire Brickworks', in Levačić, R., and Pollard, A. (eds), *Decision Making in a Mixed Economy*, Milton Keynes: Open University Press.

Levi, P. 1993: *If This is a Man*, London: Abacus.

Levin, I. P., and Gaeth, G. J. 1988: 'How Consumers are Affected by the Framing of Attribute Information Before and After Consuming the Product', *Journal of Consumer Research*, vol. 15, no. 3, pp. 374–8.

Levi-Strauss, C. 1966: *The Savage Mind*, London: Weidenfeld and Nicholson.

——1969: *The Elementary Structures of Kinship*, London: Eyre and Spottiswoode.

Levy, D. 1994: 'Chaos Theory and Strategy: Theory, Application, and Managerial Implications', *Strategic Management Journal*, issue 15, pp. 167–78.

Lewin, K., Lippitt, R., and White, R. K. 1939: 'Patterns of Aggressive Behaviour in Experimentally Greated "Social Climates" ', *Journal of Social Psychology*, 10, pp. 271–99.

Lieberson, S., and O'Connor, J. F. 1972: 'Leadership and Organizational Performance', *American Sociological Review*, vol. 37, pp. 117–30.

Likert, R. 1961: *New Patterns of Management*, New York: McGraw-Hill.

Lilley, S. J., and Platt, G. M. 1997: 'Correspondents' Images of Martin Luther King, Jr: An Interpretive Theory of Movement Leadership', in Grint, K. (ed.), *Leadership: A Reader*, Oxford: Oxford University Press.

Lingle, J. H., and Schiemann, W. A. 1996: 'From Balanced Scorecard to Is Measurement', *American Management Association*, March, pp. 56–61.

Lovelock, J. 1987: *Gaia*, Oxford: Oxford University Press.

Luecke, R. 1994: *Scuttle Your Ships Before Advancing*, Oxford: Oxford University Press.

Lyotard, J. F. 1984: *The Postmodern Condition*, Manchester: Manchester University Press.

MacArthur, B. 1992: *The Penguin Book of Twentieth Century Speeches*, London: Penguin.

McGregor, D. 1960: *The Human Side of Enterprise*, New York: McGraw-Hill.

——1978: 'An Uneasy Look at Performance Appraisal', *Harvard Business Review*, May–June, pp. 89–94.

Machiavelli, N. 1981 edition: *The Prince*, Harmondsworth: Penguin.

McKibben, B. 1990: *The End of Nature*, Harmondsworth: Penguin.

MacLeod, D. 1996: 'School Learns Pupil Power', *Guardian*, 1 April.

MacNaghten, P., and Urry, J. 1995: 'Towards a Sociology of Nature', *Sociology*, vol. 29, no. 2, pp. 203–220.

McNeill, D., and Freiberger, P. 1994: 'The Secret Revolution', *Success*, September.

Macrory, R., and Hession, M. 1996: 'High Noon for Mad Cows', *Guardian*, 11 June.

Manz, C. C., and Sims, H. P. 1991: 'Superleadership: Beyond the Myth of Heroic Leadership', *Organization Dynamics*, vol. 19, pp. 18–35.

Marshall, T. H. 1950: *Citizenship and Social Class and Other Essays*, Cambridge: Cambridge University Press.

Maslow, A. H. 1954: *Motivation and Personality*, New York: Harper.

Meyer, J. W. 1983: 'Conclusion: Institutionalization and the Rationality of Formal Organizational Structure', in Meyer, J. W., and Scott, W. R. (eds), *Organizational Environment: Ritual and Rationality*, Beverly Hills, Calif., Sage.

Meyer, J. W., and Rowan, B. 1977: 'Institutional Organizations: Formal Structure as Myth and Ceremony', *American Journal of Sociology*, 83, pp. 340–63.

Meyer, J. W., and Scott, W. R. (eds) 1983: *Organizational Environment: Ritual and Rationality*, Beverly Hills, Calif., Sage.

Michels, R. 1949 edition: *Political Parties*, New York: Free Press.

Mintzberg, H., and Waters, J. 1985: 'Of Strategies, Deliberate and Emergent', *Strategic Management Journal*, vol. 6, no. 3, pp. 257–72.

More, T. 1965 edition: *Utopia*, Harmondsworth: Penguin.

Munakata, T., and Jani, Y. 1994: 'Fuzzy Systems: An Overview', *Communications of the ACM*, vol. 37, no. 3, pp. 69–76.

Nash, R. 1983: *Wilderness and the American Mind*, Yale: Yale University Press.

Norris, W. R., and Vecchio, R. P. 1992: 'Situational Leadership Theory: A Replication', *Group and Organization Management*, vol. 17, no. 3, pp. 331–42.

Open University, 1992: *Professional Judgement and Decision Making*, D300, BBC 2, 20 February.

Overy, R. 1995: *Why the Allies Won the War*, London: Jonathan Cape.

Pascale, R. 1990: *Managing on the Edge*, Harmondsworth: Penguin.

——1994: 'Intentional Breakdowns and Conflict by Design', *Planning Review*, vol. 22, no. 3, pp. 1–7.

Pascale, R. T., and Athos, A. G. 1981: *The Art of Japanese Management*, New York: Simon and Schuster.

Pedler, R. 1996: 'Like Cows to the Slaughter', *The Times*, 18 April.

Peters, T. J., and Waterman, R. H. 1982: *In Search of Excellence: Lessons from America's Best Run Companies*, New York: Harper and Row.

Pick, D. 1993: *War Machine: The Rationalization of Slaughter in the Modern Age*, London: Yale University Press.

Ponting, C. 1994: *Churchill*, London: Sinclair-Stevenson.

Power, M. 1994: *The Audit Explosion*, London: Demos.

Prance, G. 1996: 'Mother Nature: The Classified Story', *Times Higher Education Supplement*, 19 April.

Prather, S. E., and Lazar, E. 1994: 'Giving Birth to the Future', *Healthcare Forum Journal*, Jan./Feb., pp. 53–6.

Pugh, D. S., and Hickson, D. J. 1976: *Organizational Structure in its Context*, Farnborough, Hants: Saxon House.

Pyre, S. 1982: *Fire in America: A History of Wildland and Rural Fire*, Princeton: Princeton University Press.

Roberts, A. 1994: *Eminent Churchillians*, London: Weidenfeld.

Robinson, C. 1995: *Effective Negotiating*, London: Kogan Page.

Rogers, D. S. 1996: 'A Case for Fuzzy Thinking', *Transport and Distribution*, vol. 37, no. 3, pp. 108–10.

Rorty, R. 1982: *The Consequences of Pragmatism*, Brighton: Harvester Wheatsheaf.

Rose, N. 1990: *Governing the Soul*, London: Routledge.

Rosener, J. B. 1995: *America's Competitive Secret: Utilizing Women as a Management Strategy*, Oxford: Oxford University Press.

Rousseau, J. J. 1968 edition: *The Social Contract*, Harmondsworth: Penguin.

Ruddle, K. 1996: 'The Transformational Leader: New Approaches to Management and Measurement', *Templeton Executive Research Briefing*, Oxford University, Oxford.

Rustow, D. A. 1970: 'Transitions to Democracy: Towards a Dynamic Model', *Comparative Politics*, no. 2, 337–63.

Schumpeter, J. A. 1976 edition: *Capitalism, Socialism and Democracy*, London: George Allen and Unwin.

Scott, A. 1992: 'Political Culture and Social Movements', in Allen, J., Braham, P., and Lewis, P. (eds), *Political and Economic Forms of Modernity*, Cambridge: Polity Press.

Scott, W. R., and Meyer, J. W. 1994: *Institutional Environments and Organizations*, London: Sage.

Sears, S. W. 1992: 'The Last Word on the Lost Order', in Cowley, R. (ed.), *The Experience of War*, London: W.W. Norton and Co.

Senge, P. 1990: *The Fifth Discipline*, London: Century Business.

Simmel, G. 1957: 'Fashion', *American Journal of Sociology*, 62, pp. 541–58.

——1978: *The Philosophy of Money*, London: Routledge.

Simonson, I. 1993: 'Get Close to your Customers by Understanding how they make Choices', *California Management Review*, Summer, pp. 68–84.

Simonson, I., and Tversky, A. 1992: 'Choice in Context: Tradeoff Contrast and Extremeness Aversion', *Journal of Marketing Research*, vol. 29, pp. 281–95.

Sims, H. P., and Lorenzi, P. 1992: *The New Leadership Paradigm*, Newbury Park, CA: Sage.

Smith, A. 1974 edition: *The Wealth of Nations*, Harmondsworth: Penguin.

Smithson, M. 1987: *Fuzzy Set Analysis for Behavioural and Social Sciences*, New York: Springer-Verlag.

Spencer, H. 1874: *The Study of Sociology*, New York: D. Appleton and Co.

Stacey, R. 1992: *Managing Chaos*, London: Kogan Page.

—— 1993: 'Strategy as Order Emerging from Chaos', *Long Range Planning*, vol. 26, no. 1, pp. 10–17.

Stewart, R. 1976: *Contrasts in Management*, Maidenhead: McGraw-Hill.

—— 1982: *Choices for the Manager*, Maidenhead: McGraw-Hill.

Stogdill, R. M. 1974: *Handbook of Leadership*, New York: Free Press.

Storr, A. 1996: *Feet of Clay: A Study of Gurus*, London: HarperCollins.

Strauss, A. 1978: *Negotiations: Varieties, Contexts, Processes and Social Order*, San Francisco: Jossey Bass.

Sulloway, F. J. 1996: *Born to Rebel*, New York: Little Brown.

Svyantek, D. J., and DeShon, R. P. 1993: 'Organizational Attractors: A Chaos Theory Explanation of Why Cultural Change Efforts Often Fail', *Public Administration Quarterly*, Fall, pp. 339–55.

Szasz, A. 1994: *Ecopopulism: Toxic Waste and the Movement for Environmental Justice*, Minneapolis, University of Minneapolis Press.

Thiétart, A., and Forgues, B. 1995: 'Chaos Theory and Organization', *Organization Science*, vol. 6, no. 1, pp. 19–31.

Treadwell, W. A. 1995: 'Fuzzy Set Theory Movement in the Social Sciences', *Public Administration Review*, vol. 55, no. 1, pp. 91–8.

Trisoglio, A. 1995: 'Managing Complexity', working paper 1, The Strategy and Complexity Seminar, London: LSE.

Twain, M. 1972 edition: *Life on the Mississippi*, Norwalk, Conn.: The Heritage Press.

Vaughan, D. 1996: *The Challenger Launch Decision: Risky Technology, Culture and Deviance at NASA*, Chicago: Chicago University Press.

Veblen, T. 1953 edition: *The Theory of the Leisure Class*, London: George Allen and Unwin.

Vidal, J. 1996: 'Be very afraid', *Guardian*, 29 May.

Watson, T. J. 1986: *Management, Organization and Employment Strategy*, London: Routledge.

Weber, M. 1978 edition: *Economy and Society*, London: University of California Press.

Williams, R. 1972: 'Ideas of Nature', in Rendell, J. (ed.), *Ecology, the Shaping of Enquiry*, London: Longman.

Woodcock, G. 1962: *Anarchism*, Harmondsworth: Penguin.

Woodward, J. 1965: *Industrial Organization: Theory and Practice*, Oxford: Oxford University Press.

Woolgar, S. 1991: 'Configuring the User: The Case of Usability Trials', in Law, J. (ed.), *A Sociology of Monsters*, London: Routledge.

—— forthcoming: 'Science and Technology Studies and the Renewal of Social Theory', in Turner, S. P. (ed.), *Social Theory at the End of the Century*, Oxford: Blackwell.

Wheatley, M. J. 1992: *Leadership and the New Science*, San Francisco: Berrett-Koehler.

Wright, P. 1996: *Managerial Leadership*, London: Routledge.

Wynn, B. 1996: 'Patronising Joe Public', *Times Higher Education Supplement*, 12 April.

Yearley, S. 1992: 'Environmental Challenges', in Hall, S., Held, D., and Mcgrew, T. (Eds), *Modernity and its Futures*, Cambridge: Polity Press.

—— 1996: *Sociology, Environmentalism, Globalization: Reinventing the Globe*, London: Sage.

Yukl, G. 1989: 'Managerial Leadership: A Review of Theory and Research', *Journal of Management*, vol. 15, no. 2, pp. 251–89.

Zadeh, L. A. 1994: 'Fuzzy Logic, Neural Networks and Soft Computing', *Communications of the ACM*, vol. 37, no. 3, pp. 77–84.

Index

Abercrombie, N. et al. 106–108
Actor–network theory (ANT) 91, 108–13, 181; and generalized symmetry 108–109
Adams, J. 168
adaptive systems 69–70, 72–5
Aldrich, H. E. 134
Aldridge, A. 24
American wilderness 150
Anand, P. and Forshner, C. 171
anarchism 61
appraisals 117–28; and Heisenberg 127–8; and McGregor 125; and Procrustes 124–6; and Spartacus Syndrome 125–6
Argyris, C. 90, 184
Aristotle 4, 10, 13, 16, 22, 23, 182, 186, 192
Aston Studies 130
Atkins, P. and Brassley, P. 156
auditing 118–19
Australian aborigines 16
autistic organizations 86–7
autopsies 18

Bader, D. 120
Bansal, P. and Howard, E. 148
Barley, S. R. and Kunda, G. 48, 51–2
Barnard, C. 116
battle of Agincourt 149
battle of Antietam 77–8
battle of Midway 76–7
battle of Naseby 93, 95
Beck, U. 152–4
Belbin, M. 51
binary logic/opposites 2, 4, 10, 186; and divisions at work 11–12
Blauner, R. E. 129, 130
BMW 25–6
Bormann, E. G. 40
Bradley, General O. 120
Brent Spar oil rig 155
BSE see Mad Cow Disease
Burke, K. 40
Burns, T. and Stalker, G. M. 129

Business Process Reengineering (BPR) 45–7, 89

Calás, M. B. and Smircich, L. 144
Callon, M. 108, 112
Calvinism 102–103
Camelford, 153
Caulkin, S. 65
Champy, J. 44
Chandler, A. D. 130
change management 85–114
chaos theory 5, 59–83; and butterflies 62–3; and causality 63–4; and diversity 64–5; and dominant ideology 106–108; and evolutionary theory 60–75; and fractals 68; modelling of 62; and multiplier effect 67–8; and planning 75–82; and predictability 62–3; and scale-invariant properties 68–9; and self-organization 65–7, 81
charisma and change 38–42
Charles 1 92, 94
Chatterjee, P. and Finger, M. 153
Churchill, W. 40, 132
Clark, T. and Salaman, G. 39, 40
commitment 6, 85–114; and citizenship 98; and clubs 105; and Japanese 97; and NMA 92–5, 97; and NMO 95–100; and small groups 96
configurational systems 69–70, 72–5
constructivism 138–42
contingency theory 131–2
Coopey, J. 106
Corrigan, W. 46
Covey, S. 40
Crassus, M. L. 124–6
creative accounting 13, 25; and chaos theory 70
Creutzfeldt-Jakob disease (CJD) 157–8
Cromwell, O. 92–3, 95
culture 48–9, 50
customer focus 21–4

Dearlove, D. 87, 88
death 16–19; and autopsies 18; definition of 17; and drowning 17–18
deep leadership 140–1, 143
Dell computers 68
Dilbert 138
DiMaggio, P. J. and Powell, W. W. 137
Ditto, W. and Munkata, T. 63
Donaldson, L. 128, 130
Dorrell, S. 171
Durkheim, E. 49

D'Este, C. 120
Earth First 110
Eco-Realists 152
Enlightenment 54
Ernest, P. 14
evolutionary theory 69–75
Exxon Valdez 161

fashion, *see* management fashion
Festinger, L. 105
Fiddes, N. 151
Fiedler, F. E. 131, 133; and Garcia, J. E. 131
fire-fighting 79–82
Fisher, R. and Urry, W. 186
Flanders, A. 48
Ford, H. 50, 69; and Fordism 55
fortune *see* luck
Foucault, M. 179, 186
Friends of the Earth 110, 154
fuzzy logic 5; and binary logic 9–13; chips 14–15; and death 18–19; and the legal system 19–20; and mathematics 13–14; and medicine 15–20; and 'reality' 20–1
fuzzy measurement 24–9

Gaia 150
Gentles, I. 93
Gordon, C. G. 70
Gowland Hopkins Committee 157
Gowler, D. and Legge, K. 39
Greenpeace 110, 154
Grint, K. 4, 55; and Case, P. 44; and Kelemen, M. 139; and Willcocks, L. 90; and Woolgar, S. 4, 17, 112
Groundhog Day 182
Gulliver's Travels 150–1

Hammer, M. and Champy, J. 47
Hannan, M. T. and Freeman, J. H. 134
Hawthorne experiments 96
Hegel, G. W. F. 103
Heifetz, R. A. 141
Held, D. 100
Henry V 41, 149
Henshaw, D. 164
Hersey, P. and Blanchard, K. H. 132
Herzberg, F. 56, 94
Hines, R. 25
Hobbes, T. 49–51
Hogg, D. 158–9
Huczynski, A. A. 39

IBM 86
innovation 28
institutional theory 136–8

Jackson, B. 40
Joynson, S. and Forrester, A. 66, 81

Keegan, J. 68
Kemp, A. and Sibert, J. 17–18
Kessler, I. and Undy, R. 100–102
Kiel, L. D. 61
Klein, R. 154
Kondratieff, N. D. 51
Kosko, B. 13

Lacey, R. 170
Land, E. 88
Latour, B. 111
leadership 115–45; and constructivism 138–42; contingency theory 131–2; as 'deep' leadership 140–1, 143; and institutional theory 136–8; and organizational analysis 128–42; and personality 117–24; and population ecology theory 134–6; and rebellion 117–18; and situational leadership theory 132; and Socrates 115–16; and structural contingency theory 128–34
learning 80, 82; and organization 88
Lee, General R. E. 77–8
Levi, P. 181
Levi-Strauss, C. 48
Levin, I. P. and Gaeth, G. J. 23

Lewin, K. 56
London Brick Company 78
Long Waves of Economic
   Development 51–2
Lovelock, J. 150
luck 59–60
Lyotard, J. F. 37

Maclean, D. 160
McClellan, General G. B. 77–8
MacDonalds 158
McGregor, D. 50, 56, 123, 125
Machiavelli, N. 59, 139, 181
McKibben, B. 151–2
Mad Cow Disease 155–75; and cold
   rendering 157, 161; and
   constructivist approach 169–72;
   and Creutzfeldt-Jakob disease
   (CJD) 157–8; and Gowland
   Hopkins Committee 157; and
   Hogg, D. 158–9; and
   MacDonalds 158; and maternal
   transmission 158–60; and
   Meldrum, K. 160; and Schreuder,
   B. 157; and structural
   approaches 162–5; and
   tuberculosis (TB) 156
Major, J. 159
management and business
   studies 44
management fads and fashions 5,
   31–58, and charismatic approach
   38–42; and distancing approach
   42–7; and institutional
   approach 53–6; and publications
   34; and rational approach 36–7;
   and structural approach, 47
management performance
   26–7
managers: as engineers 60; as
   gardeners 60–1
Mandate of Heaven 95
Marshall, T. H. 98
Marx, K. 151
Maslow, A. H. 56
meat 151
medicine 15–19
Meldrum, K. 160
Meyer, J. W. 137; and Scott, W.
   R. 137
Michels, R. 154–5
Mintzberg, H. and Waters, J. 64
Moore, T. 151

natural laws 151
nature 147–75; end of 151–2; and
   risk society 152–3; and boundary
   destruction 167
negotiation 177–205; and Actor–
   network theory 181; and
   compromise 193; and conditional
   statements 185; cost and value
   210; and facts 186; as farming
   184; as hunting 184; and objective
   value 187; pantomime 190; and
   preparation 186; principled and
   positional 186; and problem
   ownership 196; and
   questioning 194–5; and rational
   argument 189–90; and
   signalling 192; and silence 195;
   and skilled incompetence 184;
   and unpredictability 191
Nelson, Admiral H. 16
Newcastle, Committee of 122
New Model Army (NMA) 91, 92–6,
   97–8, 107, 109–12
New Model Organization
   (NMO) 91, 95–100
normalization of deviance 164

olivarchy, iron law of 155
organizational citizenship 98–9
organizational defence routines
   90
Oxford University 44, 123

Pascale, R. T. 32, 65; and Athos,
   A. G. 106
passive immunity 89
Patton, General G. 41, 119–21
performance/balanced score cards
   27, 118
Peters, T. 39; and Waterman
   79
population ecology theory 134–6
pragmatic paradoxes 9
Pugh, D. S. and Hickson, D. J. 130

risk and avoidance 89–91; and
   action approaches 165–9; and
   Beck, U. 152–3; and BSE 147–75;
   and the Challenger spacecraft
   163–4; and compensation
   hypothesis 168; and constructivist
   approach 169–72; and structural
   approaches 162–5

Rosener, J. 144
Rousseau, J. J. 49–51, 150
Rover 25–6, 43
Rustow, D. A. 99

Science and risk 147–75
Schreuder, B. 157
Shell 155
Simmel, G. 43
Simonson, I. and Tversky, A. 23
situational leadership theory 132
Smith, A. 151
Smith, Captain J. 122
Socrates 115–16
Southwood, R. 155, 170
Spencer, H. 42, 48–9
Stacey, R. 64
Stewart, R. 133, 177
Stogdill, R. M. 117
Storr, A. 141
strategic management 81–2
Strauss, A. 177
structural contingency theory 128–34
Sulloway, F. J. 117–18
Sun Tzu 184

Svyantek, D. J. and DeShon, R. P. 69
sweep-it-under-the-carpet-school of management 87
Systems Theory 65–6

Taylor, F. W. 49, 50, 96; and Taylorism 55
Titanic 94, 109–10
TQM 45, 49; and rational approach 50
tuberculosis (TB) 156
Twain, M. 16

Vaughan, D. 163
Veblen, T. 42
Virgin Group 71
Virginia Company 122

Weber, M. 49, 67, 102, 129
Woodward, J. 130–1
Woolgar, S. 24

Yearley, S. 153
Yukl, G. 116, 133

Zadeh, L. A. and fuzzy sets 13
Zeitgeist 55